a first place

Also by David Malouf

david malouf

a first place

VINTAGE BOOKS
Australia

A Vintage book
Published by Random House Australia Pty Ltd
Level 3, 100 Pacific Highway, North Sydney NSW 2060
www.randomhouse.com.au

First published by Knopf in 2014
This edition published in 2015

Random House Books is part of the Penguin Random House group of companies
whose addresses can be found at global.penguinrandomhouse.com.

National Library of Australia
Cataloguing-in-Publication entry

Malouf, David, author.
A First Place/David Malouf.

ISBN 9780857984043 (paperback)

Malouf, David, 1934
Authors, Australian.
Australian literature.

820.80994

'Made in England' reprinted with thanks to Black Inc.

Cover design by Christabella Designs
Typeset in 11/18 pt Sabon by Post Pre-press Group, Brisbane
Printed in Australia by Griffin Press, an accredited ISO AS/NZS 14001:2004
Environmental Management System printer

Random House Australia uses papers that are natural, renewable and recyclable
products and made from wood grown in sustainable forests. The logging
and manufacturing processes are expected to conform to the environmental
regulations of the country of origin.

To Carmen Callil

CONTENTS

AUTHOR'S NOTE

Poems, novels, short stories, as works of the imagination, are written out of inner necessity; they come to us out of who-knows-where, choosing their own time and having no existence until they are there on the page. They are entirely personal. Till we give them over to their public life in the hands of readers they are of no concern to anyone but ourselves, have nothing to do with the world of opinion, including our own, and if they have a message or purpose it is one over which we, as writers, have no control.

The pieces in this collection are of another kind altogether and have a different source. They were from the beginning someone else's idea; I wrote them on invitation, or at someone else's suggestion. 'A First Place' as the Blakelock Lecture at Sydney University in 1984, 'As Happy As This' at the invitation of a fellow writer, Beth Yahp, for an anthology on family, 'My

Multicultural Life' for a conference on Australian literature in Milan, 'The House of the Dead' for the *New York Review of Books*, etc.

These pieces of writing are personal in that they have their basis in personal experience and represent personal opinions, but their purpose was from the beginning public; they belong to that part of my life that is conscious and considered rather than dreamily obscure till it demands to be expressed; to the world, that is, of analysis, and open opinion and discourse.

What the two kinds of writing, different as they may be, have in common – or ought to have – is that they are shaped by the same temperament and come to the reader in something like the same voice.

My thanks to the editors and academics who invited me to dip into my experience and write these pieces, and to Meredith Curnow and Patrick Mangan, at Random House Australia, for their expert care in re-enlivening them, in giving them, scattered as they were across three decades, this single life as a collection.

Sydney 2014

THE TRAVELLER'S TALE

ONE OF THE OLDEST STORIES we tell is the story about leaving home. It is the story which, in reproducing one of the hardest facts of our existence, prepares us for the inevitable business of moving on from what is known to what is as yet unknown: from childhood to adulthood, from our father's house to the house we ourselves must build, from living to whatever lies beyond. The story moves us so deeply because it touches our lives at the two extremes of our experience, the moment when we leave our mother's body and the moment when we must leave our own, but it speaks as well for the daily business of going out into the world – to hunt or on a war party or simply to see what is there – and then the return to the homeland or hearth. It speaks, that is, for both a personal and a tribal history.

But there are really three versions of the story.

The first is essentially comic: the folk hero sets out, has adventures, answers riddles, undergoes tests and gets lost for a time, but in the end reaches home, always richer than when he left, if only in experience. This is the story of Odysseus but also of Jacob and Joseph in the Bible, and any number of seventh sons and soldiers and other clever young fellows in folk and fairy tales.

The second version is tragic: the hero never gets home. Either because of some crime he has committed or because by nature he is an outcast doomed to perpetual movement and exile. He is the Wanderer of northern mythology, and in legend the Flying Dutchman or the Wandering Jew.

But there is a third version of all this, neither comic nor tragic but with elements of both. In this version too the hero never gets home; he finds a new home elsewhere, as Aeneas does in *The Iliad*, and founds a new world on the 'other shore'. It is a story of hardship and loss, but the end is open and therefore hopeful.

The vast number of such stories, and their variety in all three versions and across many cultures, suggests how necessary they may be as models for what, as humans, we are and what we must learn to bear. To hear them is healing to us. They give shape to everyday living, but suggest as well a shape for those larger ventures – war, exploration, painful but necessary migration – that make up so much of what we call history, including the history we are living now. In no other age, perhaps, have so many men and women been forced to leave the place they were born in to make a new life elsewhere.

It is worth exploring a little what it means, this leaving the place where your ancestors' bones lie in the local churchyard, the streets where you first played games of hopscotch or taws, the field you first ploughed, the food that seemed, once, to be the only food a man might have a table for since it was what the land produced, and what your mother and grand-mother knew how to cook; most of all, to let go of language, the words through which the world of the senses – all you saw and heard and touched – was alive on your tongue; to leave what was familiar, what belonged to a first place and to family, for a place where all that is most immediate to your nature would be forever not just different but second-hand and questionable; where the life you live, whatever success you may have there, will always to a degree be ghostly, since it is a *second* life, and your first life – the one you had begun to grow up in, at least in the part of you that belongs to memory and to dreams – is still with you. No man or woman really migrates. They bring their first life with them, and that too goes on in the new land, and peoples it with shadow lives as well as real ones.

In places like Australia, or Canada, or South

America or the United States, we are all voyagers of this sort, settlers; in having experienced in our bones (that is, in the lives of our fathers and grandfathers, parents and grandparents) the painful business of leaving a first place and remaking ourselves in a new one. Which is why all stories about those who leave home and do not get back, and must start again on another shore, seem like our own story, the one that belongs to history, but also has the shape of what is oldest and deepest in us.

Of course every man or woman who gives voice to it will have a different story to tell – different in its particulars – and those who have the gift for it, for telling and showing and bearing witness, speak for all of us the *shape* of the thing, but in the particulars speak only for themselves. It is through these particulars, unique individual details, that we enter their story and experience it as our own.

Introduction to The Journeyman, *a series of woodcuts by Salvatore Zofrea, text by Sally McInerney, Picador 1992*

A FIRST PLACE

To BEGIN WITH TOPOGRAPHY.

The first thing you notice about this city is the unevenness of the ground. Brisbane is hilly. Walk two hundred metres in almost any direction outside the central city (which has been levelled) and you get a *view*, a new view. It is all gullies and sudden vistas, not long views to the horizon – and I am thinking now of cities like Melbourne and Adelaide, or Manchester or Milan, those great flat cities where you look away down endless vistas and the mind is drawn to distance. Wherever the eye turns here it learns restlessness, and variety and possibility, as the body learns effort. Brisbane is a city that tires the legs and demands a certain sort of breath. It is not a city, I would want to say, that provokes contemplation, in which the mind moves out and loses itself in space. What it might provoke is drama and a kind of intellectual play, a delight in new and shifting views, and this because each new vista as it presents itself here is so intensely colourful.

The key colour is green, and of a particular density: the green of mangroves along the riverbanks, of Moreton Bay figs, of the big trees that are natives of this corner of Queensland, the shapely hoop-pines and bunyas that still dominate the skyline along every ridge. The Australian landscape here is not blue-grey, or grey-green, or buff as in so much of southern Australia; and the light isn't blond or even blue. It is a rich golden pink, and in the late afternoon the western hills and the great flat expanse of water that is the Bay create an effect I have seen in other places only before or after a storm. Everything glows from within. The greens become darkly luminous. The sky produces effects of light and cloud that are, to more sober eyes, almost vulgarly picturesque. But then, these are the subtropics. You are soon made aware here of a kind of moisture in the air that makes nature a force that isn't easily domesticated – everything grows too fast, too tall, it gets quickly out of control. Vegetation doesn't complement the man-made, it fiercely competes with it. Gardens are always on the point of turning themselves into wilderness, hauling down fences, pushing sheds and outhouses over, making things look ramshackle and halfway to ruin. The weather, harsh sunlight, hard rain, adds to the process, stripping houses of their paint, rotting timber, making the dwellings altogether less solid and substantial, on their high stumps, than the great native trees that surround them.

I'll come back to those houses in a moment. It is no accident that they should have invaded a paragraph that is devoted to nature, since they are, in this place, so utterly of it, both in form and substance. Open wooden affairs, they seem often like elaborated tree-houses, great grown-up cubby-houses hanging precariously above ground.

Now what you abstract from such a landscape, from its greenness, its fierce and damply sinister growth, its power compared with the flimsiness of the domestic architecture, its grandeur of colour and effect, its openness upwards to the sky – another consequence of all those hills – is something other, I would suggest, than what is abstracted from the wide, dry landscapes of southern Australia that we sometimes think of as 'typical'. It offers a different notion of what the land might be, and relates it to all the daily business of life in a quite different way. It shapes in those who grow up there a different sensibility, a different cast of mind, creates a different sort of Australian.

So much then for the lay of the land; now for that other distinctive feature of the city, its river. Winding back and forth across Brisbane in a classic meander, making pockets and elbows with high cliffs on one side and mud-flats on the other, the river is inescapable. It cuts in and out of every suburb, can be seen from every hill. It also keeps the Bay in mind, since that, clearly, is where all its windings, its odd turns and evasions, lead. But this river does not have the same uses for the citizen as the rivers that flow through other towns.

We think of the Thames, or the Seine or the Tiber or the Arno, and it is clear how they are related to the cities that have grown up on their banks. They divide them, north and south. They offer themselves as a means of orientation. But the river in Brisbane is a disorienting factor. Impossible to know which side of it you are on, north or south, or to use it for settling in your mind how any place or suburb is related to any other.

So the topography of Brisbane, broken up as it is by hills and by the endless switching back and forth upon itself of the river, offers no clear map for the mind to move in, and this really is unusual – I know of no other city like it. Only one thing saves you here from being completely mapless, and that is the net – the purely conceptual net – that was laid down over the city with the tramline system.

Ideally it is a great wheel, with the business centre as the hub and a set of radial spokes that push out into the suburbs. The city is conceived of in the minds of its citizens in terms of radial opposites that allow them to establish limits, and these are the old tram termini: Ascot/Balmoral, Clayfield/Salisbury, Toowong/Grange,

West End/New Farm Park, to mention only a few; and this sense of radial opposites has persisted, and continues to be worked with, though the actual tramlines have long since been replaced with 'invisible' (as it were) bus routes. The old tramline system is now the invisible principle that holds the city together and gives it a shape in people's minds.

But that wheel shape, as I said at the beginning, was ideal, not actual. I lived at Ascot. I have always thought of Balmoral as being at the other end of the city geographically – say, an hour's tram journey or twelve to fifteen miles away. But when I looked at a map recently I discovered that it is, in fact, only half a mile away on the other side of the river.

Space, in this city, is unreadable. Geography and its features offer no help in the making of a mental map. What you have to do here is create a conceptual one. I ask myself again what habits of mind such a city may encourage in its citizens, and how, though taken for granted in this place, they may differ from the habits of places where geography declares itself at every point as helpful, reliable, being itself a map.

I have already referred briefly to the Brisbane house, setting its insubstantiality for a moment against the solidity of the big local trees, and evoking the oddness with which it places itself, reared high on tree-stumps on the side of a hill.

The houses are of timber, that is the essence of the

thing, and to live with timber is to live with a material that yields at every step. The house is a living presence as a stone house never can be, responding to temperature in all its joists and floorboards, creaking, allowing you to follow every step sometimes, in every room. Imagine an old staircase and magnify its physical presence till it becomes a whole dwelling.

Children discover, among their first sensual experiences in the world of touch, the feel of tongue-and-groove boards: the soft places where they have rotted, the way paint flakes and the wood underneath will release sometimes, if you press it, a trickle of spicy reddish dust. In earlier days they often made themselves sick by licking those walls and poisoning themselves with lead.

You learn in such houses to listen. You build up a map of the house in sound that allows you to know exactly where everyone is and to predict approaches. You also learn what not to hear, what is not-to-be-heard; because it is a condition of such houses that everything *can* be heard. Strict conventions exist about what should be listened to and these soon become habits of not-listening, not-hearing. So too, habits grow up of not-seeing.

Wooden houses in Brisbane are open. That is, they often have no doors, and one of the conventions of the place (how it came about might be a study in itself) is that doors, for the most part, are not closed. Maybe it is a result of the weather. Maybe it has something to do with the insistence that life as it is lived up here has no secrets – or should have none. Though it does of course.

Whatever the reason, bedroom doors in a Brisbane house are kept open – you get used to that. Even bathroom doors have no locks and are seldom closed. The proximities are dealt with, and privacy maintained, by just those subtle habits of not-seeing, not-hearing that growing up in such a house creates in you as a kind of second nature. How different from life as it is lived in brick houses, with solid walls and solid doors and the need to keep them sealed against the air. Brisbane houses are unsealable. Openness to the air, to the elements, is one of the conditions of their being – and you get used to that too.

So there it is, this odd timber structure, often decorated with wooden fretwork and scrolls of great fantasy, raised on tree-stumps to leaf level and still having about it some quality of the tree – a kind of tree-house expanded. At the centre a nest of rooms, all opening on to a hallway that as often as not runs straight through from front to back, so that you can see right through it to trees or sky. Around the nest of rooms, verandahs, mostly with crossed openwork below and lattice or rolled venetians above; an intermediary space between the house proper, which is itself only half closed in, and the world outside – garden, street, weather.

Verandahs have their own life, their own conventions, but serve for the most part to make the too-open interior seem closed, therefore safe and protected. Weather beats in on the verandah and the house stays dry. Hawkers and other callers may be allowed up the front steps on to the verandah, but the house, utterly visible and open right through, remains inviolate. There are conventions about this too. You develop a keen sense, from early on, if you grow up in such a house, of what is inside and safe and what is out there at the edge, a boundary area, domestic but exposed.

Inside and out – that is one aspect of the thing: the nest of rooms at the centre and the open verandah. But there is also upstairs and down, and this doesn't mean the same thing here as in the two-storeyed terrace, where upstairs means sleeping and downstairs is public life. Upstairs in the Brisbane house is everything: the division between night and day might at the very least be established as one side or the other of a hall. Downstairs here means under-the-house and that is in many ways the most interesting place of all.

It comes into existence as a space because of the need to get those houses up on stumps; to get them level on the hills it might be, or to keep them cool by providing a buffer of air underneath. There are several explanations, no one of them definitive.

So the space down there may be a cube, but is more often a wedge of deepening dark as the high house-stumps at the back diminish till they are as little at the front as a metre or half-a-metre high.

The stumps are capped with tin and painted with creosote against termites. The space they form is closed in with lattice, sometimes all the way to the ground, sometimes to form a fringe of a half-metre or so below floor level. The earth is bare, but flooring boards being what they are, a good deal of detritus falls down there from the house above: rusty pins and needles, nails, tacks, occasionally a peach stone or some other rubbish where a child has found a crack big enough to push it through. And a good deal of what the house rejects in other ways also finds its way down there: old sinks or cisterns or bits of plumbing, bed-frames, broken chairs, a superannuated ice-box or meat safe, old toys.

It's a kind of archaeological site down there, and does in fact develop a time dimension of its own that makes the process of falling below, or sending below, or storing below, a passage out of the present into limbo, where things go on visibly existing as a past that can be re-entered, a time-capsule underworld. Visiting it is a way of leaving the house, and the present, and daylight, and getting back to the underside of things.

It's a sinister place and dangerous but you are also liberated down there from the conventions. It's where children go to sulk. It's where cats have their kittens and sick dogs go. It's a place to hide things. It is also, as children discover, a place to explore; either by climbing up, usually on a dare, to the dark place under the front steps – exploring the dimensions of your own courage, this is, or your own fear – or by exploring, in the freedom down there, your own and other people's bodies. There can be few Brisbane children who do not associate under-the-house, guiltily or as a great break-out of themselves, with their first touch or taste of sex.

A landscape and its houses, also a way of life; but more deeply, a way of experiencing and mapping the world. One of our intellectual habits, it seems to me, is the visualising, in terms drawn from the life about us, of what is not visible but which we may need to see. One such entity is what we call mind or psyche. One observes in Freud's description of how the mind works how essential architectural features are, trapdoors, cellars, attics, etc. What I wonder is how far growing up in the kind of house I have been describing may determine, in a very particular way, not only habits of life or habits of mind but the very shape of the psyche as Brisbane people conceive it; that is, how they visualise and embody such concepts as consciousness and the unconscious, public and private areas of experience, controlled areas and those that are pressingly uncontrollable or just within control – and to speak now of my own particular interest, how far these precise and local actualisations may be available to the writer in dealing with the inner lives of people. What I mean to suggest, at least problematically, is ways in which thinking and feeling may be intensely local – though that does not necessarily make them incomprehensible to outsiders, and it is the writer's job, of course, so long as we are in the world of his fiction, to make insiders of all of us.

We have tended, when thinking as 'Australians', to turn away from difference, even to assume that difference does not exist, and fix our attention on what is common to us; to assume that some general quality of Australianness exists, a national identity that derives from our history in the place and from the place itself. But Australians have had different histories. The states have produced very different social forms, different political forms as well, and so far as landscape and climate are concerned, Australia is not one place. It might be time to forget likeness and look closely at the many varieties of difference we now exhibit; to let notions of what is typically Australian lapse for a time while we investigate the different sorts of landscape the country presents us with, the different styles – social, political, educational – of the states, the different styles of our cities, and even of suburbs within cities, and for those of us who are concerned with literature, for example, to ask ourselves how many different sorts of Australian writing there may be and how much the differences between them may be determined by the particular social habits and physical features of place. Is there, to come back to the present occasion, a Brisbane way of experiencing things that we could isolate in the works of writers who, even if they have not spent their writing life in the city, grew up there, and were in their first experience of the world shaped by it? Is there something in the style of mind of these writers, even in their use of language – a restlessness, a delight in variety and colour and baroque effects, in what I called earlier 'drama' and 'shifting views' – that we might trace back to the topography of the place and the physical conditions it imposes on the body; to ways of seeing it imposes on the eye, and, at some less conscious level, to embodiments of mind and psyche that belong to the first experience, and first mapping, of a house?

1984 Blakelock Lecture

MY MULTICULTURAL LIFE

AUSTRALIA BEGAN AS A MYTH, an idea in the mind of Europe, and when something approximating to the shape and bulk of it was discovered by European navigators in the seventeenth century, it continued to occupy a largely fabulous place in the minds of those who were transported or migrated there and had to live with its unpredictable and sometimes harsh reality. It has taken us a long time to accept the place as where it is and what it is; to link up its settled parts and see it, and ourselves, as whole. Perhaps it was to avoid the problem that we accepted for so long the myth of its uniformity. It was a way of not having to face how different the place is from city to city and state to state. It afforded us the comfortable illusion that there was a general Australian type as well. The question of Australian identity has arisen, in its present form, precisely because we are so aware these days of Australian diversity.

In fact the diversity was always there. The difference is that we can see it now because the evidence, on TV, on talk-back radio shows, in the newspapers, is so clear. Evidence of what we are. Not as a newly multiracial people – this is a surface thing – but as people. The truth is that diversity, a kind of multiculturalism if we want to call it that, is the norm in any society. We only see societies as uniform when the power of the word is in the hands of a single group.

Women and men who live together and share their lives also, to some extent, inhabit separate cultures; that is, have different aims, different interests, codes, icons, and when speaking among themselves, a different language. Children, for a time, live in a different culture again, and so, to take just a few examples, do Catholics as opposed to Protestants, people who go to private schools and those who go to state schools, readers of *The Herald Sun* and *The Age*, supporters of Rugby League and Rugby Union or soccer or Australian Rules. Most of us belong to several of these groups, sometimes in surprising combinations, or we shift from one to another in the course of a lifetime. Our individual encounter with the culture, the strands we choose to take up out of the mix, is just that, an individual mixture, an adherence to some of the many moralities the society offers – one or two of them, of course, widely shared – its many interests and allegiances, and the various dialects that compose its speech. This is already a 'multicultural' situation, before we add in what might come with our being, say, both Australian and Welsh, or Irish, or – these days – Greek, or Chinese, or Chilean, or Vietnamese, or an urban black, or a ghettoised gay male, lesbian separatist, Pentecostal Christian, Moslem, or any other of the newly visible and vocal minorities.

There is only one way to challenge the generalising tendency that comes from the domination of one voice, and that is by being specific. The experience of each Australian is essential as evidence of a complex and paradoxical whole. It is in this spirit that I mean to talk specifically about the strands that went to the making of this particular Australian, and it is the variousness of the strands I want to keep in sight. The individual at the centre is there only to make them appear. I offer myself as a specific example but a general case.

*

The fact that I am a writer means that much of what I have to say has already appeared elsewhere but in a disguised and transmuted form. A good deal of Australian writing, I think, is an attempt not only to render actual experience but to discover what this actual might be, to make it stand, in all its specific detail, against a stereotype that is generalised and needs to be challenged because from the individual writer's experience it does not fit. This in fact is one of the great subjects of all writing, but Australians have had a harder time than some others in grasping what is authentic in their experience. For one thing, they had to throw off the purely English stereotype – the job of early Australian writing, and living too, was to disentangle what was local from what was trans-ported English. But this 'local' keeps changing and it has been the job of succeeding generations to revise, in terms of their own experience, that later stereotype as well.

But there was, from the beginning, a complication here: the influence of reading, and especially of fiction.

Australians are, and have always been at every level of society, readers, among the most literary, if not the most literate people in the world. Now what fiction presents is not life as it *is* but life intensified, drawn to a pitch and given significance. To assume, in a naïve way, that the world you get in a novel is the way life actually is, and then require ordinary, everyday existence to live up to it, can make your life seem impoverished, make you believe that real life can be experienced only in Moscow or Paris or on the Yorkshire Moors. This is in itself one of the greatest subjects for fiction. I touched on it, lightly, in *Johnno*, which takes up both of these themes, the difficulty of establishing your own problematical and perhaps uncharacteristic nature against the local stereotype, but also the gap between fiction and living; and the irony to be got, and the tragedy created, from the failure to discriminate between them. I wanted to turn life as I actually knew it into fiction of my own, resisting the nostalgia for a life lived more fully elsewhere, giving fictional life, against all expectation, including that of my narrator, to what had always seemed to me, in my literary way, to be the most unliterary place in the universe, the Brisbane I had grown up in.

So let me home in on a particular moment, a Saturday night in 1943 in the very middle of the war.

I am nine and I am sitting at the end of my grandfather's bed in the living quarters above my grandmother's shop, at the corner of Melbourne and Edmondstone Streets, South Brisbane, a corner shop, a large, well-appointed one that sells groceries and fruit but also malted milks and creaming sodas from a real American-style bar. Behind the shop is a courtyard with a scrubbed wooden table where they eat; behind that a garden with a grapevine, and a shed where ropes of garlic hang over sacks of rice and cracked wheat. All this back part of the shop is very odd and foreign. There is nothing like it in our own house, or in the houses of our friends when we go and visit. My sister and I are embarrassed by it, and especially doubtful about *eating* at our grandmother's; there is something shameful, surely, about eating in the backyard from a table with no cloth. They eat cabbage-rolls and yoghurt with cucumber and mint, and chopped-up salad with oil on it. At home we have proper meals: stew or cutlets with mashed potatoes and peas, all hot, and a nice boiled pudding with custard. Salad, which we eat only at lunchtime, is a lettuce leaf and half a tomato, with two or three slices of beetroot and a dob of bottled mayonnaise.

My grandfather is dying. I sit on his bed to keep him company. I am reading *Lamb's Tales from Shakespeare*, a funny title: *Cymbeline*. (The better-known tales I have already read.) Every now and then my grandfather asks for something and I get up and get it for him, though he speaks no English and I understand no Arabic.

There is an altar in the room with pictures of saints, a plaster Virgin, and several vases filled with wax roses and lilies. I am a Catholic but I disapprove of such garish paraphernalia because my mother does. She is not a Catholic. In fact she is *anti*, and regards my grandmother and my father's sisters, all three of them at this time still unmarried, as bigots: they serve Protestants in the shop but do not let them into the house. My mother is anti-Catholic because, as she has told us many times, she was made to 'sign us over' before we were born, though she did a deal with my father at the same time that we would never go to Catholic schools. Being anti-Catholic she is also anti-Irish and anti-Labor, since Queensland politics is dominated by the Labor Party, Labor politicians are mostly Irish, and the priests tell you at mass how to vote. Still, she does send us to mass.

I am a Catholic like my father, who is very simply pious (my mother insists he is a saint), but I am also anti-Catholic out of loyalty to her.

Because we are Catholics but do not go to Catholic schools, in a city where everything – schools, clubs, department stores, even dancing-classes – is either Catholic or Protestant, we are neither one thing nor the other. In fact my mother is Jewish, but she cut herself off from her family when she married, so at this point I am only dimly aware of that.

My parents, tonight, are at the pictures, in the seats that are held in their name, each Saturday night, at the Regent. Normally, we too would be there, but children have been barred from the city theatres in case of air-raids. We have, however, been to the matinee at West End: an episode of *The Spider*, a Hopalong Cassidy, then the Big Picture – all American. Half of my life is spent in an American dream made up of Judy Garland and Mickey Rooney musicals, Flash Gordon, Dagwood, the Katzenjammer Kids, the *Reader's Digest, Life* magazine, rounders, American pop songs (even if I do learn the words from the *Boomerang Songbook*), Wrigley's chewing-gum, and Nigger and Cowboy chews. I live in one-storeyed, wooden, subtropical Brisbane but also in the dream of a twentieth century that has, as yet, reached us only in brilliant reflection on the screen, and is, as I see it, in every respect American, since 'America' means up-to-date and modern – though I am also in love with 'the olden days', which are English. Just at the moment I have got as far back as Ancient Britain with Cymbeline, unless my grandfather wants something in Arabic, in which case I step back into the present and fetch it for him.

At home, just two doors from my grandmother's, I am enjoying, in this fourth year of the Second World War, an almost perfect Edwardian childhood, recreated in reach-me-down Australian terms by my mother, in imitation of her own growing-up in London before the First World War.

Everything in our house, except for us, is English. We eat heavy English meals, quite irrespective of the heat, off English china. We listen to the BBC news. In the afternoon, my mother and our 'girl', Cassie, take turns at reading while they shell peas or darn socks: *The Channings*, *Lord Oakburn's Daughters*, *John Halifax, Gentleman*, *The Lamplighter* – the books my mother read as a girl. The front of the house is sand-bagged; we have a slit trench in the yard; and I am living a barefoot version of the long Edwardian summer, broken only by coconut ice-blocks, the occasional tropical storm, and at six-fifteen each weeknight another episode of *The Search for the Golden Boomerang*, which is brought to us by the makers of Hoadley's Violet Crumble bars. We are very much concerned about the Heart of the Empire. My mother calls it 'Home'. My father, rather confusingly since he was born in Australia, calls it 'the Old Country'. But when my grandmother refers to 'the Old Country' she means Lebanon.

On summer weekends we go to Scarborough, down the Bay, and live another life altogether. In the early days we had a tent. Now we have a caravan built by my father in our backyard.

At Scarborough we play rough games on the sands, have gang wars, and our parents at night play cards, even Black Jack, which my mother would never tolerate at home – even she becomes more 'Australian' down here.

The campers are an easy-going lot and my father knows every family, as we kids do. We go to Methodist Sunday School on the beach and on lantern processions where we sing hymns like 'Jesus Died for All the Children' and 'Build on the Rock' – not very Catholic of course but this is the beach.

This Australia, 'down the Bay', is older than 1943 and is just about to disappear. It is an English/Australian watering place with amusement arcades and a pier. In just a few years, like everyone else, we will desert it for Surfers Paradise and the more glamorous, up-to-date, Californian world of the surf.

I would pause here, just for a moment, to ask what class I belong to in all this, and the question, in a very Australian way, is hard to answer. When I look back at the Australia of my childhood it seems to me to have been uniformly working class, whereas today, wherever you go, it is one or another version of middle class.

As the eldest son of poor immigrants my father left school at twelve, worked for a while for a grocer, then got a horse and cart of his own and made deliveries. At the time I am now evoking, 1943–44, he owns three trucks, three houses and a block of flats, but still drives one of the trucks himself, leaving at six each morning for the Markets, in shorts and leather apron, and coming back at five in the afternoon. He would certainly call himself a working-man.

My mother, on the other hand, would define herself in terms of the life her parents lived in London before the bank crash that brought them to the other end of the world: a big five-storeyed house at New Cross, with a cook, chambermaids, a nurse, and her parents, as in the portraits we have of them, in flash evening-dress. We have a 'girl' ourselves – Cassie. It isn't a very grand thing for the time, but it does suggest a certain degree of 'comfortableness'. On the other hand, I go to one of the roughest schools in Brisbane, West

26

End State, where there are many Greeks (all of South Brisbane is migrant territory) and few of the seventh-graders will go on to secondary school.

Like each of the states, Queensland had its own, quite peculiar education system.

Before it became the most backward place in Australia, Queensland was, for a time, the most progressive. In the last years of the nineteenth century a scholarship system was set up. Somewhere between twelve and fourteen every child in Queensland did an exam called the Scholarship. If you passed, the government paid half your secondary-school fees. The catch was that having offered half payment of fees the government felt it could leave the establishment of the schools themselves to some other authority. Most secondary schools in Queensland were private, the majority of them run by a church. (Brisbane, for example, had only one state high school, plus a commercial and industrial college, till 1957 – and this for a city of half a million.) The result was that only about 7 per cent of Queensland children were educated beyond primary level. The rest, among them some of the brightest, went straight to work, and, self-educated and aggressively proud of it, became some of the top men in industry, the public service and even ministers in the government.

Some of my contemporaries have asserted that the education they got contained nothing 'distinctively

Australian'. This may be true of other parts of Australia, but was not our case.

The intention, clearly, of what appeared in the Queensland School Readers, for example, was to introduce young people whose formal education might go no further to as much of their cultural inheritance as could be crammed into seven short volumes, and it was taken for granted that a good proportion of that shared culture would be local. So short stories and poems by Lawson, Kendall, Adam Lindsay Gordon, Mary Hannay Foott, Roderick Quinn, Victor Daley and Dorothea Mackellar (to mention only those whose names are still known) appear in these readers alongside the Greek myths, Aesop's fables, tales from *The Arabian Nights* and later tales by Perrault and Hans Andersen, excerpts from twenty or more novelists from Bunyan and Defoe to Robert Louis Stevenson, and the whole range of English poetry, including a dozen or more excerpts from Shakespeare, several poems from *Childe Harold*, the whole of 'The Ancient Mariner', and rather more than one might have wished of Longfellow. Some of the material was European rather than British – French, German, Scandinavian, Russian (there were short pieces by both Tolstoy and Turgenev) – and some of it was American, including Emerson's essay on Lincoln. There were also inspirational essays on artists (Dante, Beethoven, Millet and the Renaissance potter, Bernard Palissy) and another set on scientists (Newton, Jenner, Pasteur and the Curies).

As for the Australian material, the tone of that was aggressively national, full of the spirit of achievement, of Australian independence and mateship and triumph over the odds.

Life in Australia, we were told, was grim – I am thinking now of pieces like 'Out Where the Dead Men Lie' and George Essex Evans' 'The Women of the West', which might account for the insistence, throughout the readers, on hard work, obedience, moral forti-tude and mutual dependence; but some of the poems, notably Kendall's 'The Bellbirds', do respond to the beauty of the place, and there is at least one sugges-.tion, in Kendall's 'The Last of His Tribe', that not all suffering in Australia was white. There was, especially in later books, a good deal about social justice, and some recognition that the love of freedom was not exclusively British (Mazeppa appears as a prototype national hero, along with Boadicea and Hereward the Wake) and the seventh-grade reader, put together in 1927, is strongly internationalist and anti-war.

The set novel in my Scholarship year, 1946, was also Australian, *We of the Never Never,* a book, for all its being a local classic, that was as remote from my experience then as *The Hunchback of Notre Dame* or *Wuthering Heights* or *Barnaby Rudge,* except that these novels, which I read at much the same time, told me something I wanted to know about, which was how passionate and cruel and irrational life could be, and what it was, behind all their concern for cleanliness and godliness, that the adults of my world might actually be up to. These non-Australian works went deeper into my imagination, into my nature too, than anything Mrs Aeneas Gunn had to tell. Like most youthful readers I wanted something that would feed my sense of possibilities, show me how rich and excessive life could be, how dangerous, how glorious too. With *Wuthering Heights*, *Barnaby Rudge*, *The Hunchback of Notre Dame* I was embarking on those dangerous seas of 'fiction'. There would be time later to come to the mature conclusion that it was not to be confused with 'life', and then to see that it *was* life too, just as our lives could be the matter of fiction.

What I mean to illustrate in all this is the different periods and places a little mind may be simultaneously at large in; without stress and without feeling it as anything other than normal. It is of the essence of minds that they are capable of existing in contrary states. The process that made me is a typical one and a typically Australian one. How typical an Australian it made me is another matter.

The migrant background – the double one, Lebanese and English – gave me, I think, a particular sense of how accidental, how contingent the facts of a life may be. For many migrants who came to

Australia, as my mother did, in late childhood, when their lives had already begun to assume an expected shape, translation to the new place was never quite complete; the old one continued in a ghostly way as an alternative life unlived, a promise broken.

For all its being daily and real, life in the new place had an accidental or provisional quality. I sensed this quite strongly in my mother and felt it again later in others. Closely related to this was the accidental quality of what I felt *I* was.

All children are fascinated by the long-shots and chances that made them what they are, the fatality, for example, that brought their parents together. There is a moving poem of Thomas Hardy, 'A Church Romance (Mellstock: circa 1835)', in which he reaches back to his own moment of beginning, when his mother

> Turned in the high pew, until her sight
> Swept the west gallery, and caught its row
> Of music-men with viol, book, and bow

And recorded

> A message from his string to her below,
> Which said: 'I claim thee as my own forthright!'

Hardy is recognising how he came to be from the meeting of two glances in a small community in Dorset.

But the space my parents had to cross, the unlikeliness of their having come together at all, was extraordinary. It too was an especially Australian eventuality. I have always been impressed by the degree to which accident may be fate.

Australia is often seen as a special case because we are trying to make a life of the mind, as well as a daily life, in a place that was not originally ours. This may be of special interest to Australians but it is not unique. Human history everywhere is about the movement of people, about migration and settlement. The classical world knows this well enough to make it the subject of all foundational myths. To occupy new land – to take its flora and fauna into your consciousness and spiritualise it and make it your own – is an activity that is essentially human, part of the great work of culture. It takes time.

In Australia that has already been done once, in their own way and over forty thousand years, by the Aborigines. We are doing it again, in ours. But the English, to take just one example – I could take the Hungarians, the Turks, the French – are not the aboriginal inhabitants of their land either. They too were settlers, latecomers. We just happen to be two, rather than fifteen, hundred years along the way.

As for how you do this, we are sometimes told that a real culture can only be made in specifically local terms and with local means; that there is something inauthentic about living through what is taken up from elsewhere; and it is true that some great literatures *have* been made in this purely native way, or some parts of them. But what are we to say of how the Elizabethans used Renaissance Italy, appropriating Italian forms, and tropes and ideas, and a vocabulary too that was in no way native, to discover a richer sense of what it was to be English? Or the way German writers of Lessing and Goethe's generation discovered the fullness of their Germanness in the Classical world.

What these examples speak of is the imaginative possibilities of living in and through other cultures to find your own, misreading sometimes, and misadapting as you translate into your own terms, but getting it wrong in the right – that is, the most useful – way. Such local adaption is not just translation or appropriation but a critical dialogue with what it takes up that is itself a work of culture.

The truth is that nations, like individuals, can live simultaneously in different places in the same place, and are no less complex and resourceful than minds are in using diverse, paradoxical and sometimes contrary influences to make something that will be entirely their own.

Campagnatico 1984 – address to Australian Literature Conference, Milan, November 1984

33

AS HAPPY AS THIS

1

I GREW UP WITH ONLY one set of grandparents. My mother's mother died in 1929 and for four years afterwards my mother, the youngest of her family, kept house for her father in rooms full of ceiling-high Edwardian wardrobes above a shop in the Valley. She and my father had been 'going together' since she was a girl of eighteen. They were held back from marriage by a difference in religion that in those days was very nearly insuperable, but also, after my grandmother died, by her attachment to her father. After fourteen years they must have decided to force the issue. They married in October 1933 and I was born in the following March. My grandfather died three months later.

So I knew my mother's parents only through the stories she told, but she told them so often, and with so many vivid appeals to what she knew would impress and excite us, that these middle-class English grand-parents, who had left a five-storeyed house in New Cross with servants' bells in every room for a tent on the goldfields at Mount Morgan, though I had never seen them in the flesh, were more real to me than my father's people, who lived two doors away and whom I saw every day of the week. More real because – unen-cumbered by the actualities of sweat-circles under the arms, a torn buttonhole – they came with the clarity and far-off glow of figures I knew only through my mother's anxious devotion to them, and my own eagerness as a child to be caught up and enveloped in what she felt.

My mother, the youngest of seven, had left England when she was ten. One of the things she kept all her life was a coloured postcard of the ship they came out on, the *Orsova*, thirteen thousand tons, and the year 1913 – a whole string of unlucky numbers. Another was a pair of miniatures out of a locket: my grandfather in his thirties, looking princely in a stiff shirt-front, waxed moustaches, a Van Dyck beard; my grandmother, round-chinned and pampered, in satin leg-o'-mutton sleeves. How could my father's people compete?

Our grandmother kept a corner shop. Though fine boned and doll like, she had worked hard all her life and when I knew her wore always the same floral apron over a frock of some dark, silky material. Her stockings were rolled above the knee, and sometimes, when she came in tired from the shop and sat to rest her feet, or lifted her skirt very delicately between thumb and forefinger and shook it to make a breeze, you saw the shocking white of her thighs above the rolled wad. My grandfather, fuzzy with stubble, was most often in the saggy pants and collarless striped shirt in which he gardened at the bottom of our yard. As for servants, all they had was Della, a big slummocky girl of forty with thinning hair who was always half asleep on her feet.

My father's parents were foreign. They ate outside, at a pinewood table in a courtyard behind the shop, with forms instead of chairs and no cloth; they smelled of garlic. But they were not exotic like my English grandparents. If we asked no questions about them it was because none occurred to us – they were there and visible – but also because we knew the sort of answers we would get. Our father was silent by temperament, but also, I think, because, unlike our mother, words did not suit him, he was uneasy with them. Perhaps this came from a sense he had of their treacherous power. As a child he had been his parents' interpreter and had seen them shamefully stripped of their authority while he stepped in, very bright and winning as he must have been, to deal between them and a baffling and sometimes hostile world.

Like all his brothers and sisters he was born in

Australia and spoke only English. If he still had some understanding of Arabic by the time I knew him, he gave no indication of it. And the truth is that however painful it must have been to my grandmother to lose contact with her children in this way, she herself had set them on the path. Since there was no Melkite church in the place, she had insisted on their going to mass each day at St Mary's, Boundary Street, where the form of Catholicism they got and the values and culture they took on were Irish. After a time, they might just as well, for all the difference it made, have been O'Dwyers or Flynns. My father especially, who was the most outgoing of his family, as well as the eldest, was soon as unambiguously Australian as any other member of the rough Rugby pushes that in the years before the Great War made up the mixed and lively world of South Brisbane. When the time came there can have been no question of his pleasing his parents by choosing some nice girl out of the ten or twelve families of their close-knit, islanded community. He acted like a local and chose for himself.

2

They met in 1920. It was my mother's father who introduced them.

37

A descendant of Daniel Mendoza, the creator of modern boxing, and himself a keen follower of the game, he had taken a fancy to my father, who was in those days a promising featherweight, and had brought him home, perhaps out of a wish to help this attractive young working man in his more ordinary career as a carter – one of my mother's brothers, Bert, who also lived at home, owned a section at the Markets. My father, who had left school at twelve to become a postboy with Cobb and Co., then a storeman and delivery boy for a local grocer, was in business for himself by the time my grandfather met him, with his own horse and cart. He was twenty-three and my mother eighteen.

That she was immediately interested is proved by the box of newspaper cuttings she kept, the earliest of which dates from the same year: 'George Malouf's brilliant victory over Soldier Ernie Andrews has started the popular Railway League footballer on a campaign for the highest in the game . . . Malouf has got the punch and the fighting temperament to carry him far, and as he is an exemplary liver, nothing should be beyond him.'

My grandfather, no doubt, in his role as patron, found these qualities entirely admirable, but he can hardly have seen this clean-living young footballer, for all the talent he showed in the ring, as a prospective son-in-law. My mother did, and must have been determined, well beyond her experience and her years, that this gentle, fine-looking fellow, even if he was the wrong religion, was to be her addition to the family, not her father's. Quite soon they were seeing each other virtually every day. He would call in at the Valley shop on his rounds. On Friday nights they went to the pictures, at the weekend on picnics down the Bay to Cribb Island or Amity. At Christmas they exchanged cards. When my mother went to Coolangatta for a week – but this was five years later, in 1925 – they corresponded, he rushing home from work each day to write his three or four pages to catch the post. These letters my mother also kept.

He had little education. The phrases he falls back on are often conventional. But there are moments when, under the pressure of emotion, he manages an old-fashioned gracefulness of expression that is all his own. 'Dear,' he writes, 'I was not far away when you left this morning but could not come close enough to let you see me or I would of broken up. As a matter of fact I did when I was on my own . . . Fancy having to wait another six days to see you!' They were to be separated only twice more in the following forty years. Once married, they never again spent a night apart.

In January 1927, my mother and brother Bert took my grandmother, who was already ailing, to Stanthorpe, where he had friends among the apple and pear growers. Perhaps they were getting their mother away from Brisbane's fierce summer heat. Once again, my parents wrote daily and each night she rang him.

(I see him seated in the shop in the swelter of a January night. Flying ants are wreathing the lights under the high ceiling, which is of beaten tin with a fleur-de-lys pattern, painted cream. A ceiling fan clicks and stirs the soupy air. The refrigerator hums and shudders. He is figuring in his near hand the area of various rooms in the block of flats he is planning for the site of some dirty tumbledown shops in Melbourne Street, and which he will build nine years later after a fire. When a child comes in for a pound of sugar or two slices of Windsor sausage, he gets up to spare his mother, keeping the figures, and the rooms, in his head, while the child, all eyes for the black jelly-beans in a lolly jar, waits on one foot for his note to be deciphered. At last the phone rings. He lifts the receiver down from its hook, leans in to the flower-like black trumpet, torn between his wish to talk up and bring himself close to her and the need to be low and intimate.)

While she was away he kept himself busy building what he calls a 'humpy' – presumably the little half-open shed in his parents' yard where my grandfather kept sacks of rice for cabbage rolls, wheat for *kibbeh*, his rake, shovel, wheelbarrow and the sieve with which, in my clearest memory of him, he is standing out in the sunny expanse of the yard winnowing grain.

'Dear,' my father writes, 'what's the use of going out. I could not enjoy it myself. I am quite contented, or at least, I have made myself contented, doing that little work on the humpy. By the time you come home it will be nearly finished, or at least, I hope so.' He asks after her mother, envies them the cool nights and mornings up there, is glad she has put on a few pounds, and hopes her brother will do the same.

She and my uncle must have been rabbit shooting. 'Shooting,' he writes. 'Just fancy you out at five, shooting!' He also enquires: 'Did you like the little cards? I thought they would make you laugh.'

In each of his letters, this time, he has enclosed a funny postcard. They suggest a larkier side of him, cruder, more down to earth, than one might guess from the letters, which are always very formal and high-minded, as if writing, with its many constraints, were for setting down only what belongs to the realm of sentiment, high feeling. The postcards, precisely because they are humorous, allow subjects to be broached between them that are too painful, too dangerous perhaps, for more open discussion.

The first shows a young, not-so-young couple in the parlour. *So*, the young man is saying, *your father says I mustn't see you any more. Righto! I'll turn out the light!* He writes on the back: 'This is how they met?'

Another shows a drunk, in a suit and hat but with his tie loose, creeping through the front door. Half

41

hidden round the corner is his Missus armed with a hairbrush. The caption: *Where-eee-e's my sweetie hiding?* My father writes: 'Oh, wouldn't it be joy waiting for the brush?'

In a third a policeman and a crowd of neighbours are about to break up a domestic dispute. *If you don't stop fighting I'll run you both in*, he threatens. *Oh don't do that, officer – we've just started our 'oney-moon.* 'Dear,' my father comments, 'wouldn't you like to be as happy as this?'

They had now been promised to each other for a biblical seven years. What they could not know was they had another five to wait.

They were so dutiful, both; so much children of parents they loved and respected and were unwilling to hurt; children too of a time when duty, not only to others but even more to yourself, was as strong as any of those more imperative passions we think of now as sweeping all before them. Duty was itself a passion. That they waited so stoically and for so long was a sign not of timidity but of a terrible strength. Still, when they are parted again, for a slightly longer period, in 1932, something has changed. My mother's mother has been dead for three years. She is her father's housekeeper but has gone off to Maryborough, in the company of an older sister. Rose, who is married with a child and has offered herself, I suppose, as my mother's chaperone; but she is the wildest of the bunch, this Aunt Rose, a 'bolter', and no doubt has her own reasons for getting away for a bit from a husband who is difficult and a domestic life that does not suit her. They are gold buying.

It is one of the worst years of the Depression. All up and down the country poor people, to get a little cash, are selling gold chains and other trinkets. At the table in farmhouse kitchens, gold buyers, mostly amateurs with no other form of occupation, are unfolding little sets of scales, taking the stoppers off bottles of *aqua fortis*, totting up figures, making offers. My mother and Aunt Rose have set up like real commercial travellers in a room at a hotel, where they wait each day for respondents to the ads they have placed in the local paper. But they have no luck.

'It certainly looks,' my father writes, disguising perhaps a quiet satisfaction, 'as if the gold is finished. You should be the best judge.'

They refused to give up, but after a couple of weeks Aunt Rose, whom my father always refers to very respectfully as 'Mrs Diamond' (my guess is that he cared less for her than for the rest of my mother's family; found her too flighty, or perhaps he thought her a bad influence, or was simply jealous of their closeness), came back; my mother went on alone. That she did so says a good deal for her courage and strength of will, or for her determination to establish a little independence for herself.

Was that the reason for the trip? To get a little money of her own – but even more perhaps to make plain that she did not intend for another three years to be her father's keeper. My father was by nature patient. She was not. For all the longing his letters express, the waiting may have been harder for her; not because she felt more than he did but because she had a different attitude to the world. She was still waiting, at thirty, for her life to begin.

And his letters of 1932?

They are the letters now of a man, not a boy, but the real change is the image of *her* that comes through them. He no longer fusses over her health or presents himself as her protector; the implication is that she does not need one. He no longer fishes for assurances (that she misses him). All that now is 'understood'. He knows now, and absolutely, the role she is to play in his life and he is awed by it. Not intimidated, because he has seen that if her strength is to come to anything, if what he has seen in her is to become real, it can only be through him. Meanwhile, he takes occasion to point out the little services he can do her along the way. 'It certainly was lucky,' he writes, 'to get you on that late train. The boys in the Railway are very good to me, I must say.' She had run into someone on the train who knew him. 'Did Mr Potter help you in any way on the trip?' he asks. 'Fancy him thinking we were married. Fancy him talking well of me. Do you know, he and I had many a punch at one another during our football careers.'

He also affords two glimpses of a side of himself that we knew well as children and which must have given her his measure, if she didn't know it already. 'Pleased to see,' he writes, 'that you are getting another skirt, and pleased to hear, dear, that you are giving a few shillings to one who needs it – she seems very reasonable in her charges.' And a few days later: 'Mr Taylor came to the markets today, with a pitiful tale, so I asked him to come home. I am expecting him any minute now. He will be staying till Saturday. I will explain everything when I see you.'

It was the last of their partings. Just over a year later they married and moved into a house of their own at 12 Edmondstone Street, two doors from his mother's.

3

We had in the house when I was a child three framed and tinted photographs of the wedding: one of the bride and groom, one of my mother with her bridesmaids (my father's sisters, Ruby and Marion), and one of the whole party – my mother and father, the bridesmaids and my father's groomsmen, his brothers Mick

45

and Joe: the men in white tie and stiff shirt-fronts, the bridesmaids with tiered skirts falling to just above the ankle in dusky pink, and large-brimmed floppy hats. It did not occur to me to ask why none of my mother's family was present or to see her on this day as both isolated and hemmed in, though I knew it had not for her been an entirely happy one. She must have told us a thousand times when we were children how she had been married 'at the side of the altar', and how, before the ceremony, she had had to 'sign us over', still unborn as we were, to the Church. In fact any unhappiness she might have felt that happy day derived from another quarter altogether, but I was to discover that only forty years later, when both my parents were dead. It struck me then that for all the stories she had regaled us with, that made her family and all the facts of her early life so real to us, she had kept back more than she told.

Like many families, but more I think than most, hers was a nest of secrets, kept guarded by a severe sense of propriety and a code of loyalty rigorously imposed. By the time I became aware of the gaps in what she had told it was too late to ask the questions that might have filled them. Or almost.

One day, two or three years after my mother's death, my sister and I were visiting our Aunt Rose, the Mrs Diamond who had gone gold buying with our mother and had been in those days her closest friend.

Seven years older than my mother, but always younger in spirit, she was the liveliest member of the family and had to a high degree a quality of boldness, of eccentricity, that was unequally shared among them. (It was a quality my mother was always very eager to distance herself from, which might in itself have made me suspicious.)

As a girl Aunt Rose had been stagestruck, her father disapproved, and though she married early and 'settled', she continued to perform under a stage name in concert parties and at charity functions for the next forty years. Her big break came with the war, when she could pass off as patriotic enthusiasm the moment at the end of her act when, after belting out a Sophie Tucker number of doubtful taste, she hoisted her skirts, kicked her heels up and showed a pair of red, white and blue bloomers. (Only after her death did we discover that her yearly shopping expeditions to Sydney had been a cover for something quite different, a week-long engagement at Chequers, the nightclub.)

It surprised my sister and me that Aunt Rose and our mother had once been close. When she spoke of her now our mother was lightly, affectionately dismissive. Perhaps she wanted to confirm herself in our father's eyes as belonging to the serious side of the family; or was it my sister and me she had in mind? Warning us, at the expense of a small disloyalty, against a dangerous because alluring model. If so, she did not succeed.

We thought Aunt Rose, with her violet eyelids and the little beauty spot at the corner of her mouth – not to speak of those flashes of red, white and blue – as the most dramatic figure our parents ever presented us with, and the only one of our relations with a style we might some day be tempted to explore.

Then, as often happens, in the last years of her life my mother turned back to this much-loved sister and audacious companion of her youth. Though still critical (a surviving gesture to our father's memory) of her 'extravagance', her 'silliness' – the silver Daimler, for example, that she drove at a murderous fifteen miles an hour – she found in Aunt Rose's company, after our father was gone, a security and simple enjoyment that none of the rest of us could provide. She had gone back to the family: most of all, to what they shared, these sisters, of the family story and its many secrets.

It was one of these that Aunt Rose was eager to disburden herself of when my sister and I went to pay what was to be a last visit. She was disposing of her many possessions, and began by asking my sister if she would like a portrait of the family – a big group picture taken in the nineties, before either she or my mother was born. I knew it from my Aunt Franie's house, where it had hung above the upright piano in her cramped little front room, and was associated, in my mind, with the tunes she played me when I went to be minded while my mother was shopping in the Valley, long-forgotten numbers from *Florodora* and *The Quaker Girl*.

'Your mother's not there,' she told us now. 'Neither am I.' The idea appeared to amuse her. 'It's the others – Mark, Bert, Queenie, Frances, Sam, Joe . . .' Was it the sense of being the wrong side of things, the only survivor, that made her look suddenly alarmed? 'Years ago. Before they left Home. Before they came to . . . Australia.'

There was a pause in which she frowned, ground her teeth a little. Taking advantage of the moment, I leapt in with a question: Why did they? Why did they come to Australia? I was trying to fit together two bits of my mother's storytelling that no longer made sense to me – the grand house at New Cross and then the voyage, third-class to Australia, and the tents at Mount Morgan – enquiring into what had been the great rift in my mother's life.

She looked startled, then puzzled.

'Grandma and Grandpa,' I prompted. 'Why did they come to Australia?'

Casting a glance behind her into the corners of the room where her ghosts were, she brought a hand to the beauty-spot, then to her hair. She was about to open one of the sealed books of her parents' life and of a whole world back there whose forms of pride, and dread, and shame, we would never understand.

'Because,' she said boldly, 'they lost all their money. In a bank crash in 1912.'

She gave an odd little laugh at the enormity, the amazing finality and fatefulness of it. My sister and I sat silent. Our lives too had been part of it. But the relief she felt at having got rid of one secret led her swiftly to another.

'You know,' she said, 'I did something terrible once to your poor mother. Terrible!' She began to pluck at the wool of her bedjacket. 'We were out shopping. In the Valley. "What are you going to wear to the wedding?" she asked. And I had to tell her. I wasn't going. None of us were. Papa had forbidden it.'

Under other circumstances the old-fashioned formulation would have struck me as comic, but there was nothing comic in it. She had been a woman ten years married with a child of her own, but her father had spoken and she had obeyed. So did the others, every one. That bluff man of the world, large-hearted, debonair, had in the end turned against them, against my father – my mother too. Why? Not surely because she was marrying out – two of his other children had already done that. Was it because she was pregnant? Did he think of my father, after all those years, as having betrayed his trust? Was it wounded pride? An old man's petulance? An old man's terror at being left? I do not even know whether, in the nine months before he died, he relented and was reconciled. My mother could not speak of reconciliation because in the story as she told it, there had been no rupture.

Every night, so long as we lived at Edmondstone Street, she lit a little oil lamp beside her bed (I loved this lamp with its bronze base and milky globe; I could see the glow of it from the verandah where I slept) and I knew she did it, religiously, in memory of her parents. What I did not know was that it was a Jewish custom, the only one she kept. I took it as part of a personal religion: our mother worshipped her parents, who were ever-present ghosts, so that the little lamp on the night table had the same status in the room as our oil painting of the Sacred Heart of Jesus, with its own painted lamp throwing beams out of the Saviour's breast, that looked down from the wall above their bed. Of our mother's Jewishness I heard nothing, or understood nothing, till I was eight or nine years old, when my father's father died and we began visiting his grave at Toowong Cemetery on Sunday afternoons and would stroll downhill afterwards, through uncut grass and leaning headstones, to where my mother's parents were buried in the Jewish section, on the other side of the drive. (Years later, my mother would be buried close to them, in a plot at the very edge of the gravel pathway, and with my father just feet away on the other side, at a point, near a half-latticed hut with a tap for water, where the two sections very nearly touched.)

4

So they moved into the big, old-fashioned weather-board, new lino on the floors, fresh paint on the walls, a dining-room suite and bedroom suite designed by one of Brisbane's most stylish furniture makers, waxed paper in gay geometrical designs in the glass panels of the doors, an ice-chest, meatsafe, wringer for the tubs, a housekeeper called Mrs Hall, and my father's people just two doors away.

She must have been delighted to have a life of her own at last, a house to fill with visitors, my father home each night at five. She must also have discovered, and on the very first day, that for all the objects with which they had surrounded themselves that were shining new, with as yet not a mark or scratch upon them – the sign of fresh beginnings – there were other things that were not to change.

Stepping out to her new front door to greet the postman, she collects a little bundle of envelopes, all addressed to herself, and is informed by the postie, Mr Schultz, that there are two letters as well for her husband. He has left them, as usual, down at the shop. Why? Because that is what he has been told to do. He is to go on delivering our father's mail 'down home'.

I do not know what explanation my father gave, but Mr Schultz was to go on delivering our father's mail 'down home' for as long as we lived in Edmondstone

Street. Alighting at tramstop 4 on her way back from town, my mother would be hailed by one of her sisters-in-law who had come out especially to catch her. 'There's a letter for Georgie,' she would announce.

My mother believed they were afraid she would open his mail – because that, she was convinced, was what they did. But the real reason, I think, was simpler. It was to ensure that each evening, when he had washed after work and before our six o'clock tea, my father would have to go down and listen for half an hour, as he had always done, to his mother's troubles; read through official letters and explain what they wanted of her, look at a fuse that needed mending, give my Uncle Johnny, who was a wild man, a bit of a talking to (or ring someone up and get him out of a scrape); deal, as he had been doing since he left school at twelve and became the effective head of the family, with the innumerable crosses and crises of his mother's life.

She relies on him and has no intention of letting him go. Her hold on his affection, the appeal she makes to his manliness, goes back too far to be broken now. By insisting that he come each day to collect his mail she is confirming not her own dependency but his. She knows him through and through. For all the ease with which he moves in the world of men, he isn't really a man's man; it is women he is tied to. My mother must have known it too, and known that if he was tied so closely now to her, it was because he had been tied first to his mother. She was the woman who had revealed to him what he was.

A crisis occurred almost immediately, over my mother's housekeeper, Mrs Hall. A sensible woman in her fifties, but a Protestant, she had from the beginning been a source of concern to my aunts. Could she be trusted, on Fridays, to use oil rather than fat to cook the fish? They began dropping in unannounced to check up on her, and once there, ran their fingers along shelves, peeped under lids of pots, offered advice on what my father would and would not eat – there was no point, they insisted, on my mother's trying to change his habits: no roast potatoes, only mashed or chips, no green vegetables but peas. Mrs Hall couldn't stand it. She told them what she thought of them, apologised to my mother, and took off. My mother solved the problem by engaging a farm girl from Harrisville called Cassie, who was Catholic, but more importantly could stand up for herself and had no time for snoopers.

My mother in these early days had a poor opinion of my father's sisters. A voracious reader, very quick and curious, she despised their easy-going ignorance. They were simple women and I think now that she misjudged them: if she had asked for their affection they would have given it. But her own complex nature got in the way. She was prickly, defensive, afraid always that they were making mischief behind her back, and they, wounded that their good intentions should be suspected, withdrew. And of course in the conflict between my mother and my grandmother they were bound, as we were later, to take their mother's part. Between the two households a determined coolness prevailed.

There was also my grandfather. He came each day to garden at the bottom of our yard, and though he never ventured into the house, liked to stop and chat with my mother at the bottom of the back steps. He was, in his shy way, fond of her, but afraid of showing it in front of my grandmother, who was powerfully jealous. For some reason, among the bits and pieces of darning my mother and Cassie got through on Wednesday afternoons there was often an old shirt of Grandpa's or a pair of his trousers that needed a new fly button (I don't know why it was my mother rather than one of the aunts who did this), and later, when he was dying in the front bedroom upstairs at the shop, on a high brass bed beside a dressing table decked out like an altar with statues, holy pictures, wax flowers, she often went to sit with him for an hour or two, and when she couldn't, sent me to climb up on to the end of his bed and read while he dozed and mumbled, and to call someone quick if he needed the bedpan or began to choke.

We liked going down to Grandma's, a small but obvious betrayal.

There was the shop itself, with its busy traffic, and the big old-fashioned kitchen behind with a real wood stove in an alcove and a smell quite different from our kitchen at home, a little sour from the cheese bag dripping its whey into the sink and the sharpness of chopped mint. I liked looking into their downstairs lavatory, which was outside, and had walls of white-washed stone, though I preferred not to use it. I liked looking into the bedrooms upstairs, whose tongue-and-groove walls were painted sky blue, lime green, rose, and in one of which our father had once slept. I liked stepping out past the blown muslin curtains of Grandpa's room to the cast-iron balcony that hung over the street. Leaning far out over the rails you could see all the way down the tramlines, past Kyogle Station and the Trocadero, to the Blue Moon Skating Rink and the Bridge.

What made my mother uneasy about these visits was, I think, precisely what attracted me – the company that gathered at my grandmother's court-yard table. Housewives in worn-down slippers who *smoked*, and ought, at four in the afternoon, to have been at home getting their husband's tea but would not leave for fear of 'missing something'. Nuns from St Mary's, who quizzed me on the Catechism and asked what prayers we said – and no doubt reported our answers to the Dean. After the Japanese war began, Yanks, including a loud-mouthed top-sergeant called

Duke, who was a fixture there at one stage and was supposed to be sweet on their girl Della, though I think this was a teasing invention of my aunts. And sometimes a lady friend of Uncle Johnny's called Addie, who would wait, attended on by one or other of the aunts, in the half-dark of the kitchen while he was out walking his greyhounds round Musgrave Park. A dumpy person with jet-black ringlets and too much rouge on her cheeks, she worked in a 'house' in Margaret Street – did my aunts know this? They treated her, according to my mother, like the Queen of Sheba, whom she resembled I thought in the beaded finery of her get-up, which might have been just what was expected in Margaret Street, at half-past midnight, but was extraordinary in the heat of my grandmother's kitchen at four in the afternoon.

'Was that Addie there?' my mother would enquire when we got back from a message.

What got her goat was that 'a woman of that sort' should be made so much of, whereas all she got out of them was a strained politeness.

Under Cassie's Spartan regime we were forbidden to accept anything on these visits, on the grounds that children ought not to be encouraged to wheedle for sweets and that Have-a-Hearts and sherbets would ruin our teeth. But my grandmother was eager to spoil us, and since I was especially attracted to Conversations – little pastel-coloured hearts and lozenge-shapes with the corners nipped off that had words, love-messages, on them that could be read then licked off (the combination of words, the scent of patchouli, and their apricot, mauve and yellow colours, was irresistible to me), I frequently fell and was given away, when I got home, by the musk on my breath.

Exacerbated by sensitivities of a kind neither thought possible in the other, jealousies, misunderstandings, and the hundred little niggling resentments with which my mother especially, who was all nerve, fed her lively indignation, the two households were often at crisis point, but the crisis never came.

My grandmother's complaint against my mother – the one, anyway, that she made public – was that she had compromised our father, who had always been so scrupulous in his faith, and us children too, by a marriage which, no matter what sort of strings Dean Cashman had pulled, was no more than a got-up *legal* affair.

What my mother on the other hand could not forgive was that my grandmother, for purely selfish purposes, had deprived our father of an education, made him a slave to her needs and kept him, until *she* came along to open his mind and free him, as tied to narrow old-country superstitions as the most ignorant of his sisters.

Some of my grandmother's ways she found merely ludicrous, others barbaric. In the first category was her custom of going to bed when she had a fever with a hot brick wrapped round with hessian – and this in the days of cheap hot-water bottles! In the second (a sight that made my sister and me squirm with delighted horror) was her trick of forcing open the beak of a fowl she had just throttled to pour a cup of vinegar down its gullet, which made the dead bird twitch and flap its wings in demonic resurrection.

Which of our mother's ways our grandmother found similarly objectionable we never knew. No doubt they formed one of the subjects of those secret communings between mother and son that my mother resented and stewed over and of which my father reported, I'm sure, not a single word.

Then quite suddenly, almost overnight it seemed, everything changed. Two of my aunts got married, one at forty, the other at thirty-seven, just when they appeared, as my mother put it, to have missed the bus. (But by then we were in the middle of the war. Anything was possible.) One day in 1944, while he was supervising the unloading of a truck down at the docks, my father missed his footing on an upturned fruitcase and fell, bruising his back. It was a minor occurrence and did not, among the huge events that in those days shook our world, seem likely to change our lives. But the pain persisted, and after several months of seeing one specialist, then another, he had to admit that the injury was permanent and the sort of work he was used to, and had done all his life, was beyond him. He sold his trucks and for some time, I think, he and my mother must have wondered how they would survive. They were saved by a second accident.

At an auction she was attending my mother made a bid on a lot of cheesecloth curtaining – fifty yards, she thought, at so much a yard: it turned out to be fifty bolts. She panicked at first, then considered a little and put an ad in the *Courier-Mail.* All day long women hungry for uncouponed material kept ringing at our door. She thought that she might dispose in the same way of one or two other things she had no use for – an Aynsley tea set, a red fox fur – and when the same thing happened it struck her that there was a trade to be done in commodities that because of the war could no longer be imported and were in short supply. She advertised again, this time to *buy*: dinner sets, tea sets, crystal, canteens of cutlery. Quite soon our front room, and the trestle tables she had set up on the side verandah, could no longer accommodate the stock she had acquired. She took a shop.

No more shopping expeditions to the Valley with tea at McWhirters. No more long afternoon rests when we joined her on a bed on the cool side of the house. All the weights and balances of her life had shifted. Of her personality too. Though humorous and down-to-earth, she had also in the past been high-strung, wilful, inclined to sulk. We had learned as children to deal with her moods, which for whole days sometimes would hang like a cloud over every room in the house, though it had taken me a long time to realise that not all her 'states' had to do with me. This was because the real offender, my father, simply ignored these displays of atmospherics (the unbroken storms that occasionally rolled about them were a darker aspect, though I saw this only later, of the high charge between them that for the most part gave our household its luminous calm) till, by some act of wizardry that was invisible to us children, and therefore miraculous, his spirit triumphed and the house was itself again.

I had thought of her in those days as a more conventional character than some of her friends; her favourite bridge partner for example, Maisie Panos, who had been a dancer in vaudeville, and wore neat little suits with white piping on the lapels, and was hard-boiled, risqué, and smoked. Now, with all her energies taken up, she was so clearly superior to the women she had moved among, and whose easy attractions she had allowed to shine out and dazzle us, that I was amazed at my own blindness. I could only assume that for most of the time I had known her she had been in disguise, playing a role as suburban wife, contented mother, that had nothing to do with what she was.

One of her first decisions, now that the war was ending, was that we should move: away from South Brisbane, out of the shadow of my father's family. My father, poring over sheets of draughtsman's paper, began to design us a new house. Of brick, not timber and two storeyed, with a tiled bathroom and all-electric kitchen. Up to date, almost American, it would establish us in a new era, After-the-War, but was also, for him, the entry into a sphere of interest in which, to my mother's delight, all his talents would at last be at full play.

Caught up in the excitement of a time when Australia, or our part of it anyway, was about to wake up, catch its second breath, we assumed that all these changes in our lives were a product of the times. I see now that their only originator was my mother.

I don't know how she managed it, but objects that had been central to the world of Edmondstone Street, and from which powerful emanations had moved out through every room to hold and define us, the painting of the Sacred Heart for example that had been my grandmother's wedding present, and through all the nights of their marriage had looked down on their bed, did not make the transition to Hamilton. Neither did its counterpart, the little lamp. Perhaps in her new and more assured self my mother had no need of ghosts.

I found some of these changes in her disturbing because unexpected. I see now that I would have been better prepared if I had paid closer attention to the books she read me, old romances full of unlikely transformations. If I had looked there, I mean, for what she might have seen in them rather than what appealed to me.

She had launched herself on one of those late changes of character, those apprehensions of the openness and infinite possibility of things, by which characters in fiction break free of the mechanics of mere plot to find happy endings.

What surprises me now is not that she did it, or how, but that I should have been surprised when my father clearly was not. He had never read a book in his life, knew nothing of what fiction tells us of how characters develop and stories unfold. What he knew was her.

Looking back now at his letters, I see, beyond the set phrases, that what holds him, awed and a little fearful, is all he has seen that is still to come – but only if he can convince her that what he has perceived in her is what she must become, and that it can happen only through him. More than his own life is dependent on this.

Pen in hand, only the most ordinary words in his head, these sheets still empty before him, he feels weak before all he must get down. But he has one great advantage: patience. He knows that what he has seen will take time – and it does, long years of waiting on the moment, and all of it in the midst of events, larger, more violent, that take other lives and blow them about like bits of rubbish, mere chaff, ash, beyond the reach of happy endings. But patience is in his nature, an aspect, entirely active and physical as he is, of his strong passivity, his willingness to subject their lives to time itself, as if all the time in the world has been granted them, or at least all the time they will need: the forty-four years that, as he begins to write, are already there to be entered and filled, and have been from the first moment he laid eyes on her.

My grandmother died in 1951, my father in 1964. My mother, who had learned by the end a little of his patience, waited another eight years.

Beth Yahp (ed.), Family Pictures, *1994*

THE NORTH:
THE EXOTIC AT HOME

EARLY IN 1982 WHEN I had just finished Fly Away
Peter and was writing back and forth to my publisher
at Chatto about how it was to be published, I wrote
an afterword to the book. It was an account of my
experience with the world of birds and of my early
discovery of flying.

At twenty-one, I had spent five days on a hunting
trip to the Valley of Lagoons in Far North Queensland,
a vast waterland swarming with game birds of every
description. Earlier I had discovered something of
the wonder of flight. On my seventeenth birthday,
in 1951, I had joined the University Air Squadron,
was taken up in a Tiger Moth and, on our first camp
at Amberley Air Base, outside Ipswich, had spent
a good deal of my free time, when I could inveigle
one of the officers in the mess into taking me, on one
of the flights that in those early days after the war

were still being made in the station's surviving fleet
of Liberators. These flights covered most of southern
and Central Queensland and I got used to seeing, laid
out in a map below me, a world I already knew at
ground level. I took it in turns with the other 'baby'
of the squadron, GS, to hunch in solitude in the rear
gun turret under the tail, where there was nothing
between me and the landscape below but a thin wall
of Perspex and empty air.

In the event, the afterword never made it into print.
Here, twenty-five years later, are its opening pages,
which themselves refer to a period twenty-five years
before that when I first went north; a vision of the Far
North as I first imagined then saw it, in August 1955.

In the far-off 1950s, when I was just out of university and knew nothing of the world beyond books, I
set off alone and for the first time to the Far North.
I took the train from Brisbane to Cairns. Not the
new, air-conditioned Sunlander, but the second division Pullman that left Brisbane at nine o'clock on
Thursday night, made its first stop for late supper
at Landsborough under the Glass House Mountains,
and all being well, and the Burdekin and other
streams permitting, would arrive at Cairns about two
o'clock on Saturday afternoon.

I had chosen the Pullman because it appealed to the romantic side of me. It looked like the old trains in Western movies. With its brocaded curtains and upholstery thick with decades of dust, ironwork, luggage racks, and all its loops and scrolls and filigree, pressed-metal ceilings and cedar panelling, it belonged to a century when the railways were still new. Equally reminiscent of those days was the speed at which it travelled. The Queensland Railways, with its narrow gauge lines, had a theme song: I walk beside you.

One of the advantages of travelling on the old Pullman was that you had time to get used to travelling. You could watch the country change, feel the temperature rise, the air dampen, and tell yourself as you counted off the hours that the journey you were making was the equivalent of Paris to Moscow. That, somehow, in those days, made the distance real. Brisbane to Cairns had no such currency, and might, if you were to justify the time spent and the conditions endured, have put more pressure on the landscape, and on your fellow travellers, than either would bear in the way of variety or interest. There were no borders to cross, no bearded and uniformed officials, no changes of coinage or tongue, no colourful peasants to clamber aboard at windswept junctions, no little mujiks to tap away under the wheels.

That was a long time ago – I would feel differently now – but the things glimpsed from the Pullman window, and even some of my fellow passengers, have stuck in my head longer than I could have believed. The journey north was every bit as crowded and colourful as anything Europe was to provide five or six years later, but of another kind, and it took another eye – which was also mine, but whose visions had not yet surfaced in my mind – to see it.

It was a world of its own, the North Queensland Mail.

People started out formally dressed as on other journeys, insulated, as is proper, behind magazines or the sleeves of sweaters they were knitting. But two and a half days is a long time, especially when you are moving deeper and deeper into tropical heat. More than the superficial upper layers of our clothing were discarded as the journey progressed. By the time we had crossed the Tropic, the carriage, and beyond that, the train, had become a society with its own loose rules and its own subtle adjustments of the private to the communal, the life outside to the life within.

You learned a good deal about people on the North Queenslander, and living in close proximity over so long, and in poor conditions, led to revelations that might not otherwise have been made. For clever young people like myself, who had education but no experience, it was a travelling university offering postgraduate degrees in the stuff of life. I learned to deal with card-sharps, drunks, prostitutes who used the train as a beat, seasonal canecutters, immigrant farmers, bands of rowdy schoolboys going home for the holidays, National Servicemen, young mothers travelling with children who, when the corridor was crowded, had to be held out of the window to pee.

The openness of Queensland houses, in which by convention no door is ever closed let alone locked, has created notions of privacy that are more common, perhaps, in India than in other parts of the Commonwealth. You do not hear what is not meant to be heard in such houses, or see more than you are meant to see. The train extended these conventions.

Couples could make love in the corridor, provided they covered themselves with a blanket; or even, if they were reasonably quiet about it, in the compartment. After all, life had to go on. I saw that often enough. And once, near Ayr, while the train waited at a crossing, I saw a man who had had a heart attack handed down into a yellow ambulance with a red light on top that had been racing us for the last eight kilometres through the thickening dark.

But that first train journey, for all its richness of persons and scene, was not yet a story for me, and it still isn't. The 'story' was my first sight of a place I hadn't heard of till then and have never heard of since, though it exists. It is called the Valley of Lagoons and it lies inland from Innisfail on the far side of the Great Divide. All the major rivers of North Queensland, those that flow south and east to the Pacific, the Burdekin, Burnett, Isaacs, and those that flow away north-west to the Gulf of Carpentaria, have their source there in a chain of waterlily swamps, an area of lagoons and tropical forest the size of a modest republic. It is a kind of primeval garden, and was for me an early vision of nature untouched, a great green place that existed entirely without man but did not resist his appearance, and was neither hostile nor predatory.

It presented a different Australia from the one that is sometimes offered as the real, the harsh, the authentic one. It was not a desert but a vast water park crowded with creatures. I went there for five days on a shooting trip and have never forgotten it. Its paradisiacal light at all times of day, the great flocks of birds that haunted its shores, filled its skies and were reflected in its waters, stayed with me for years afterwards. I could summon them up at will, and knew always that I would write something one day that would owe its existence to them and would try to give that existence back. When I returned to Brisbane I tried to catch the place in poems. It would not be caught. Recently, reading a few paragraphs in a literary review, the whole scene suddenly swarmed about me, I found myself as if at the centre of a marvellously recaptured dream. The suggestion of a plot presented itself, a little complex of characters appeared, and the thing I wanted to write, and had always meant to write, was there complete. I had only to enter the landscape and let it occur.

No piece of writing, of course, is ever so inevitable, so effortless as that first glimpse of it may promise. The clarity of that first view is exceptional. It is not in itself the work. But whenever I wanted, after that, to 'see' what I was doing, I had only to let the light into my mind of what I had recalled of the Valley of Lagoons as it was some twenty-five years ago and all was clear. The landscape of the story and its weather, the tonality and pace of the whole stretch of what I had to write, was immediately before me, though the 'story' was not in fact set there, and what I had in mind had no source in the events of my five days in that extraordinary place, or in the lives of my companions: the owner of the pub at Atherton where I had been staying, who was sufficiently engaged by my youthful enthusiasm and lack of experience to offer me the chance of going; the local major and his son (a boy of my own age, but a country boy, utterly unlike myself), the professional kangaroo hunter who was to be our guide.

I learned something in those days that was relevant to what I have now written, but only indirectly. I learned to live rough. I learned to handle the dogs we had with us, which I had to hold while Cam, the mayor's son, shot his first pig. Most of all, I saw a whole range of native birds – scrub turkey, western bustard, bronzewing and top-knot pigeons, half a dozen varieties of ducks, spur-winged plover – plovers rising out of the early-morning mist, with sunlit drops of water flying from their wings and the swamp water breaking in circles below. The white of them, and the brilliant yellow of their wattles and the scarlet of their feet, is one of the clearest of those images I carry about with me, and one that returns, unbidden, and with a freshness as of something utterly new-made and springing into the world as for the first time, on occasions to which it is in no way relevant but to which it brings, as I see afterwards, an energy that is a source of renewed being.

It means something more than itself, that image. It is the real beginning of this novella, and the work, however far it stands from the original, is an attempt to re-create that meaning, not by wringing the plover's neck but by allowing the landscape it leaps out of to surround me, yield up its events and, through them, its significance.

What I was after in 1955, as this piece makes clear, was the 'exotic'. That is hardly unusual. What was less usual, I think, is that I was looking for it at home.

North Queensland, in those days, at the end of a two days' train journey and more than 1600 kilometres away, was barely known. It was part of the state but on the other side of an imaginary line, the Tropic of Capricorn, that put it in another zone. It was still sparsely inhabited, a lot of it still largely untracked.

I knew people who came from 'up there'. They were like us but had the light of another order of experience in their heads: the wet season, cane toads, crocodiles, and the darkness of impenetrable rain-forests. Even the cultivated land was different. Cane fields evoked the Caribbean, molasses the Deep South. The wisdom, even in Brisbane, was that white men would never live there.

Italians did, and Maltese, and in the rush of migrants immediately after the war, a few Balts and Yugoslavs – only the men. They went up there to work as seasonal canecutters.

Bonded teachers and bank clerks were deployed there and put up in rooms at pubs. They too were temporary. When they had served their time they were brought back – before the climate and the easy pace got into their blood.

Australians still thought of themselves in those days as cool-weather people. Because our forefathers, for the most part, had come from cool-weather coun-tries, they had settled in the parts of Australia that still felt like 'home' and could be reshaped to resemble it. Most of Queensland could not. Even our part of it. The North definitely couldn't.

These days we have redefined ourselves as

hot-weather people. Australia from Kempsey north is now the norm. But when I was growing up, Brisbane, the big, sprawling, one-storeyed wooden town I thought of as mine, the place that was closest and most familiar to me, was too far north to be the norm.

Among the Australian states Queensland's status had always been doubtful, anomalous. Up to the eve of Federation its sugar plantations had been worked by black labourers, Kanakas, from the Pacific. When the Australian government, in 1942, called on American troops to save us from invasion, and discovered that some of these troops would be Negroes, they objected, then reluctantly agreed that black Americans would be acceptable, but only in Queensland. Brisbane was 'segregated' through most of my childhood: black Americans were restricted to the south side of the river. So my hometown already harboured within it a hint of the exotic and would reveal itself, when I looked at it closely at last, as the most exotic (that is, strange and unknowable) place I would ever know. I was just beginning to grasp that in the middle fifties – the period of Johnno, the events of which, at that time, I was still living through. Meanwhile, North Queensland represented our version of the exotic – neat. That is what drew me there.

Over the next three years, I went north on three occasions. Once, it was on a return trip to the Atherton Tableland to see the lakes, Eacham and Barrine, the

Tully Falls, and back to the coast to stay at Innisfail, where in those days half the town gathered on Saturday nights at the Exchange Hotel. Another time, I drove north up the coast road, the Bruce Highway, and back on the inland route via Charters Towers, Claremont, Emerald and the Brisbane Valley with a friend who had been born at Chillagoe in 1933, when it was a rich mining town of some 11,000 souls. We went there in the little two-carriage train that ran from Mareeba, through country stacked with three-metre-high anthills, all built in the same direction along a magnetic line, while great herds of kangaroos raced along beside us in the swiftly falling dusk.

When we got there, Chillagoe turned out to be a single chimneystack sticking up out of acres of ruins under waist-high lawyer vines. There were five surviving buildings, including a pub and a general store, and nine surviving inhabitants, who had different memories of where the street might have been where my friend had lived till he was three years old; of where the Catholic Church used to be, and the site of the oval where his father had played football. All the houses had been lifted off their stumps in the late thirties, loaded onto trucks, and taken to Mareeba, the little tobacco-growing town we had started out from earlier in the day.

Another time, I spent a whole sweltering summer in Townsville – a stony place in dried-out scrub country, not at all a tropical paradise, except on Saturday nights when we went across by boat to the all-night dances beside the beach on Magnetic Island.

Later, of course, the exotic quality that to me was hidden under what I saw as local untidiness – of tumbledown fences, peeling paint, buckled corrugated iron, rampant lantana and lawyer vine and swathes of ineradicable morning glory – was repackaged and commercialised for the tourist industry. Places I had seen as wild, Port Douglas for example, thanks to air-conditioning and architecture and cash, and some imagination, became oases of good living – a fair example of what the wilderness can be when it is nearly contained, and what can be made of the exotic when it is taken out of the realm of mind and made 'real' in the form of ponds and discreetly placed elements of the international post-modern. The Far North, with its profitable tourist industry and its mines, is now a 'resource'.

It is easy to be condescending about this. To pretend that the 'old' North, the one you had to discover on your own, was purer and more authentic because it had not yet been given a public form, had not yet been tidied up and packaged for general use.

In fact, the tidying up, if you look beyond the smoothness and glitter, is not very successful. How could it be when the elements are so extreme, the energy with which things push up and grow so *excessive, the air and the smells, especially the sweetish smell of rotting vegetation, so heavy, the dampness so intrusive as it gets in and causes rust and covers boots and leather belts in a wardrobe with mould, and there are so many Aborigines in the streets and under the trees along the Esplanade who are unwilling to disappear into the landscape, and undisposed to present themselves as happily industrious or indolently picturesque. There are many elements in the North that remain outside control.*

And wasn't it just this, the belief that there might be 'up there' a place that was uncontrolled and uncontrollable, that first attracted me and attracts me still? Isn't that what I meant by exotic? A hope that somewhere close there was a place that belonged to us and was in that sense ours, but that had escaped the laws and the interpretations we like to impose, and remained unknown within us. Darkly mysterious. Overgrown and hard to find our way into. Not yet mapped or fully described. Where we, too, when we entered it, might become other and unknown, even to ourselves.

I see now that that was what I was after when I lined up and bought my ticket on the second division of the Queensland Mail all those years ago and set off hopefully for the North. I found it, too. And then found it again, more powerfully, closer to home, where it had escaped me because I didn't yet have the eyes for it and hadn't discovered where to look. In the familiar streets of Brisbane itself. In the rooms of the house I had grown up in.

The book I began writing immediately after Fly Away Peter *was* Harland's Half Acre. *I was already at work on the first part of* 12 Edmondstone Street.

Griffith Review, *'Up North', Spring 2005*

THE HOUSE OF THE DEAD

THE FATAL SHORE: ROBERT HUGHES

THE MOST ENDURING FACT ABOUT Australian settlement appears at the end of a chapter of *The Fatal Shore* in a phrase that deserves to be quoted early. It concerns the Land. At first deeply alien, itself a confining factor, part of a nature that was 'destined to punish', the land, Hughes says in writing of the bushrangers, was 're-named with the sign of freedom. On its blankness the absconder could inscribe what could not be read in spaces already colonised and subject to the laws and penal imagery of England.'

What Hughes is uncovering here is the point at which newcomers to the Australian continent first recognised, in a place that had been intended only to intimidate and restrict, an area for action, and the sort of experience that makes a wild place home. It is the very heart of his theme.

This detailed and dramatic account of the first

seventy years of white settlement in Australia is not the first book on the subject – the two early volumes of Manning Clark's monumental *History* cover the same ground. But till recently Australians were not much concerned with their own history. Robert Hughes seems to suggest that this has its origin in shame: in an unwillingness to face our origins as a nation founded not in the spirit of Enlightenment but as a place of punishment and despair. He makes a good deal of what he calls The Stain, meaning the shadow of convict blood. But the fact is, these days, that one in every three Australians was either born outside the country or has no British background. For these Australians, the past is elsewhere. And till the last twenty years or so, we were, as a people, too busy coming to terms with the continent itself, its dimensions and distances, to be concerned with the past. You have to be engaged by *time* to be interested in history. The consciousness of Australians has been dominated by *space*. It takes something like a Bicentenary to make people aware that they have also had a life in that other dimension.

The Fatal Shore, then, is a timely book. There are big things still to be said about what happened in those 200 years, and Hughes grasps his subject with great boldness and flair. His writing is full of passion, anger, pity, wit, and it will surprise no-one to hear that he has an eye for the moods of landscape and weather. His theme too is big: nothing less than the meeting of the European spirit, at its most pragmatic and brutal, with a continent that was never intended to receive it; an alternative story both to America's and to that of Europe itself, running from the French Revolution to beyond Auschwitz. What we have here is an example of that peculiar capacity for remaking things in our own image, or remaking ourselves in the spirit of the Other, that is so characteristic of our 'Northern' culture: the making, in an unlikely corner of the world, of what used to be called 'The New Britannia', and which we might see now as a nation of its own, English-speaking but unique.

*

The first Australian settlement had its origins, oddly enough, in an American act.

One of the many inconveniences to Britain of the American Revolution was its interruption to the trade in convicts; the Crown had been used to selling its felons off as slaves, first to private shippers and then to plantation owners in North America. The British expected the intermission to be a short one. But the colonials won, and the new nation (which by 1783 was receiving 47,000 black slaves each year and had no need of white ones) declined the King's offer to go on supplying 'Men unworthy to remain in this Island'. A new depository had to be found. The government, rejecting Madagascar, Tristan da Cunha and several sites in West Africa, decided at last on what was then the remotest spot on earth, the place on the east coast of New Holland that Cook had called Botany Bay. What better repository than the very Antipodes of the Kingdom, its dark opposite on the underside of the earth, for what Bentham was to call an 'excrementitious mass'? – all those thieves, whores, highwaymen and others who had stopped being passive victims of enclosure and unemployment and become the entrepreneurs of their own fortune. A System that Americans would no longer accept was to be established in a new form elsewhere. Transportation was the grand alternative to death. Those whose lives were forfeit under the law were to be bodily removed, not into eternity but to a place where they would be invisible and harmless in *fact* but might still serve as *symbols*. At Botany Bay the Kingdom's excrementitious outcasts would, by the standards of the time, be well used and encouraged to rejoin the industrious part of mankind. This was Mercy. But their fate as exiles suffering all the cruelties of penal labour under an unknown sky would be presented, at home, as hellish. This was the new Terror – as Hughes puts it in one of his many memorable phrases, 'a theatre of horror acted out for a distant audience'.

In May 1787, eleven ships, well appointed and provisioned, set out under the command of Captain Arthur Phillip, who would be, on arrival, the

Commandant of the Penal Settlement and also (since the two intentions were there from the start) the first Governor of the Colony. The original nucleus was 158 marines, who would mostly return to Britain, and 563 male and 189 female convicts, who would not. These latter, as Hughes shows, were not the innocent poachers of Australian legend. None of them was a rapist or murderer, but several had committed crimes of violence and none was a first offender.

The Colony was proclaimed on 26 January 1788 – not, as it happens, at Botany Bay, which proved to have no fresh water, but up the coast a little at Sydney Cove. But Botany Bay had already been established as a symbol and it remained one for nearly half a century. Only those who were on the spot knew there was nothing there.

This is only one of Australia's 'beginnings'. It would begin afresh in other places and at other times: in free settlements at the Swan River (Perth) in 1829, Port Phillip (Melbourne) in 1835, Adelaide in 1836. One needs to be wary of speaking of 'Australian' history. To explain Melbourne or Adelaide by referring to New South Wales is like beginning a history of California with the Salem Witch Trials – possible but far-fetched. Sydney is not Australia. The settlement there just happens to be the first.

*

As befits a colony that was intended to exist in two places, a real geographical antipodes and at the same time an antipodes of the mind, everything that occurred in early New South Wales seems double and ambiguous; yet what was eventually worked out, in the pragmatic English way, by improvisation rather than theory, was a System that in Hughes' words was 'by far the most successful form of rehabilitation that had ever been tried in English, American or European history'.

To be fair to the originators of the scheme, and Hughes is not always fair, this intention was there from the start. The Colony had several purposes, some of them contradictory. The most ambitious, and least likely, was the founding of a new Empire in the south. The penal settlement was to exist within it and was to have a triple purpose: to rid the Kingdom of its criminals, to rehabilitate as many of them as possible in a new and distant place, and to make an example, through Terror, to the rest.

Phillip, who was an astute man, saw from the beginning that the various conditions of his charter were in conflict with one another. 'Convicts,' he insisted, 'must not lay the foundations of an empire.' For that reason they should remain 'forever separated from the garrison and other settlers that may come'.

In fact few settlers came – twenty-three in the first twelve years – and though the penal settlement and the Colony might exist in Phillip's mind as separate intentions and in different places, they could hardly do so in effect. No separation was possible between convict and free. The marines and sailors of the First Fleet took women from among the convicts, and male and female convicts could not be kept apart; and any child of such unions was free. Then, in the starvation years of the early Colony it was impossible to preserve distinctions between the convicts and the garrison, let alone keep them physically separate. They shared the same rations and even the same punishments (flogging or hanging); even, at last, the same rags of clothes. In November 1789, with the Colony less than two years old, Phillip abandoned his original policy and took what was to be a decisive step: he provided a convict whose term had expired, James Ruse, with the means to set up an experimental farm, with the promise, if he succeeded, of fifty acres of Crown land. At a single stroke Phillip had created a new class: the Emancipists.

In this act the System both succeeded and failed: succeeded in its attempt to rehabilitate, failed, as would be proved, in its power to terrify and deter. A new currency was created.

In England it had been property, in the form of land, that gave a man the right to vote and established him as a full member of society; its value was mystical. Australia had millions of acres of land – it was the only commodity here that was not in short supply. Is it any wonder, then, that men who had been cast out of society for having no property, or for being caught in the attempt to acquire it, should have found in Australia a new life in opportunity that no other place could have given them? It was the land itself that broke the old forms of distinction and turned the purgatorial venture from despair to optimism. The principle of 'equality' in Australia is based on the capacity of each man (and woman, recently) to acquire a house-with-land. It is a simple but powerful thing: sixteen perches in the suburbs or a thousand acres in the Gulf Country. To be a property owner is to be your own man. The deep irony that all this land, so easily occupied and doled out in such large portions to officers and ex-convicts, was in fact stolen has only gradually been perceived. No treaty has ever been signed with the natives of Australia. When Cook claimed the land, in 1770, as *terra nullius*, he not only dispossessed the original possessors; he deprived them of their *legal* existence.

Hughes is excellent on the emergence of the Emancipists and their rivalry with the free settlers, noting how early a snobbery that seems typically Australian entered this society, where distinction was based on something other than 'the exaggerated rituals of class superiority', and men who in England would have had no prospects of advancement could now mark themselves off from convicts and ex-convicts both.

'Convicts,' he writes, 'ate salted meat – which signified lack of property, for only the landed could enjoy fresh beef or lamb – and fresh fish. The ceremonial food of the free therefore must be fresh meat and salt fish.' This on a coast with some of the finest seafood in the world.

He is also good on that other development of the System, one that began, quite simply, as a way of getting the convicts 'off the Store' – that is, of getting them fed, clothed and sheltered by private persons, who would in return use their labour. This was the system called Assignment. Women, who were useless for such government work as road-building, were regularly assigned as servants (and bed-fellows) to those who would take them, or married off – sold would be more accurate – to Emancipists and settlers. The men were assigned as shepherds or labourers to big land-owners or as domestics. The statistics speak for themselves. As Hughes gives them: 'In 1790 there were 38 such "assigned" convicts in New South Wales. By 1800 there were 356, and by December 1825 there were 10,800.' Eventually such assigned convicts might be 'on their own hands' – that is, still legally bound, but free on 'ticket-of-leave' to work for themselves.

Once again Hughes has a sharp eye for the social ironies this produced. Servants in Sydney were hard to come by. 'There was a demand,' he writes, 'for city convicts, preferably refined and literate forgers, who might know from which side to pass the roast; or, if not forgers, at least thieves, who would protect their masters' property.'

What all this meant was that rehabilitation was working better than anyone in London had intended; in fact, too well. Alexander Dalrymple, before the First Fleet was at sea, had predicted the result:

> . . . although it might be going too far to suppose This will *incite* men to become *Convicts* . . . yet surely it cannot *deter* men, inclined to commit Theft and Robbery, to know that in the case they are detected and convicted, *all* that will happen to them is, That they will be sent, at the Public Expense, to a good Country and temperate Climate, where they will be their own Masters . . .

By 1825 the news had drifted back to the Old Bailey and to Newgate that 'a great number of the persons who keep carriages in Sydney were once convicts . . . now they, in the course of a very few years, have raised themselves from the situation of convicts into that of the most important persons, in point of wealth, perhaps, in the Colony'.

Conditions in England were so bad in the early decades of the century that it was difficult to sustain the fiction of a more hellish Elsewhere. As a report of 1831–32 puts it: 'If a criminal can conquer the sense of shame, which such degradation is calculated to excite, he is in a better situation than a large portion of the working classes, who have nothing but their daily labour to depend on for a sustenance.' In looking at the plight of convicts, their diet, the hours they worked, we have to remember the conditions under which women and children laboured in the mines and factories in England and the privations endured by those who were 'on the parish'. Transportation was no longer a deterrent.

So, to the extent that the penal colony succeeded in reforming criminals and restoring them to society, it would fail in its darker purpose as a model of Terror. It might even call into doubt the whole philosophy on which the System is based. Perhaps there *was* no 'criminal class'. All it might need to turn hardened criminals into solid and conformist citizens was a change in conditions, a little hope, and *property*. It was not a message the authorities were eager to receive. The Bigge Report of 1820 stated unequivocally, as Hughes puts it, 'that Australia must be "rendered an object of real Terror", and that this must outweigh all questions of the economic or social growth of Australia as a colony'. Once again the two intentions were in conflict.

*

Hughes devotes a great deal of *The Fatal Shore* to this business of Terror. The problem was that it was difficult to sustain. As Phillip had seen, a penal colony and a free one could not exist in the same place. As soon as Sydney developed pretentions to being a centre of civilisation, Terror was driven out: first to Newcastle, then to Port Macquarie, then to Moreton Bay. These secondary settlements were places where second offenders were transported, partly to punish, partly to isolate, most of all to satisfy the need for an exemplary deterrent. Not one of them survived the arrival of free settlers within their bounds. The pattern kept repeating itself; free settlers objected to living in a police state and in sight of the 'necessary' horrors. One after another, Newcastle, Port Macquarie, Moreton Bay (Brisbane) were declared too good for their vile purpose and Terror was pushed out. By the 1840s it had been driven, in all senses, to the limits: to Norfolk Island and to the end of an isthmus in Van Diemen's Land, the notorious Port Arthur.

That it lasted at all, right up to the end in fact, tells us a good deal about the dialectical terms in which decent society defined itself in the nineteenth century. When Alexander Maconochie went to Norfolk Island in 1840, and proved, even to the Governor's satisfaction, that the most 'depraved' convict could be softened by decent treatment, he was universally vilified.

Maconochie spent only seven years in the Colony;

he is a minor figure on the Australian scene, though a major one in the history of penology. But he emerges as the most fully drawn and certainly the most admirable and interesting character in *The Fatal Shore*, which says something for the man himself, but something also of Hughes' emphasis in the book. His account of Maconochie's three years at Norfolk Island makes extraordinary reading.

Maconochie's own words about what he did are modest. It is difficult to see how they could have caused so much scandal:

> Every man's sentence was to imprisonment and hard labour; the island was his prison; and each was required to do his full daily Government task before bestowing time on either his garden or education. What I really did spare was the unnecessary humiliation.

'Education' and 'garden' must have been hard for some people to swallow, but the real catch was in that last phrase. Maconochie's crime was to treat these 'outcasts' as men rather than as irrelevant criminals.

His success was spectacular, as in the case of 'Anderson':

> An orphan, Anderson had passed from the workhouse into the navy at the age of nine. On active service, he

was wounded in the head and suffered irreversible brain damage; after a drink or two, especially when under stress, he turned violent and hostile. During such a bout on shore leave, Anderson smashed some shop windows and was arrested for burglary. Tried and convicted, he was sentenced to seven years in Australia; he was then eighteen. Anderson was so crazed with resentment when he landed in Sydney that the penal authorities isolated him on Goat Island, a rock in Sydney Harbour. Over the next few years he escaped and swam for shore three times, and received a total of some 1500 lashes for such 'offenses' as 'looking round from his work, or at a steamer in the river, etc'. He spent two years tethered to a chain on the rock, naked and sun-blackened . . . Prisoners were forbidden to speak to him, on pain of flogging. The welts and gouges torn in his back by the cat never healed and were infested with maggots. He stank of putrefaction and Sydney colonists found it amusing to row up to his rock, pitch crusts and offal at him, and watch him eat. Eventually Governor Bourke, ashamed by the light this public spectacle cast on the people of Sydney, had Anderson removed to the lime-kilns of Port Macquarie. He escaped again and joined a black tribe; was recaptured and savagely flogged; and killed an overseer, hoping to be hanged. The authorities sent him to Norfolk Island instead, and he was still there – a man of twenty-four, looking twenty years older, relentlessly persecuted by the Old Hands – when Maconochie took command.

Maconochie's therapy for Anderson was simple: 'he gave the poor, crazed man some responsibilities by putting him in charge of some half-wild bullocks . . . He hoped, rather fancifully, that 'bovine' characteristics would rub off on Anderson, making him more tractable. But the man did tame the bullocks, and found himself – for the first time since leaving England – congratulated and spoken kindly to . . . Anderson could never be fully rehabilitated – his earlier brain damage was too severe for that – but when Governor Gipps visited Norfolk Island in 1843, he recorded his amazement on seeing the former wild beast of Goat Island bustling about in a sailor's uniform, open and frank in demeanor, returned to his human condition. (p. 511)

Faced with an open scandal in the Colony, the authorities withdrew Maconochie. He was replaced by Major Joseph Childs, with orders to make the island a place of real Terror again. By 1846 Norfolk Island had been raised to its peak of 'exemplary' horror under one of the few genuine monsters of Australian legend, John Giles Price, and decency, in Sydney and London, was preserved.

Hughes writes with great power and compassion of all this; he is at his most colourful when he is dealing with physical suffering under the lash and with daily humiliations. The horror was real, and we would do an injustice to the men and women who suffered if we were to turn away from its savage cruelties. That the number of lashes administered should be so minutely recorded is itself appalling: 33,727 at Macquarie Harbour between 1822 and 1826, 304,327 in New South Wales in 1836. But we need to remember two things here. One is that floggings of this sort were common amongst free men too, in the contemporary army and navy; it was an age when forms of physical brutality that seem unimaginable to us were entirely acceptable. The other, as commentators have been quick to point out, is that the majority of convicts were never flogged at all. Still, the individual lashes, and Hughes' descriptions of them, are important; they bring us some way toward experiencing these statistics as real men and women felt them. The horror puts us in the scene, and as something more than distant spectators. It is part of Hughes' stance, which is not that of the historian, for all the scholarly apparatus he employs. He respects the facts, but also allows himself, as a professional historian might not, to sketch a view, evoke a character, make us see and hear and feel as well as ponder meanings. He works, that is, like a writer, putting us inside what he writes as a dramatist might. He understands that the *story* in *history*, if we are to experience the thing fully, is as important as the mere recounting of events.

As for the men and women who lived this story: we know the administrators and the important movers in this colonial world from their decisions and the reports and letters they wrote. Few of them were men of intellect or vision, Australia was not a top imperial posting as India was. It had none of the glamour of the great sub-continent. The wars fought by the Aborigines – guerrilla skirmishes followed by massacres – offered no scope to generals and did not demand the presence, as on the North-West Frontier, of crack regiments. The makers of the Colony (like the fathers of Federation when it came in 1901) were at best decent and dull, but along with their other privileges had the power of the word. The view we get, as always in 'history', is theirs. The huge majority of those who endured the System were either illiterate or left no personal record.

We get only the briefest glimpse, in a poorly spelled letter here and there, of the grief a man suffered at being separated from a wife or from his parents, or a woman's plea (the emotion already distorted by its formal expression) that she be allowed to join her husband at the Bay.

These working-class people came from a different culture from their educated masters; they could have seen themselves and all that happened around them in a different light. For the most part, they are mute. They suffered as objects and they *appear* as objects in the records, even when they are objects of sympathy.

Convict women, for example, are very often presented as 'prostitutes', persons naturally depraved. What this means, for the most part, is that since they were intended to be used as prostitutes, either officially or unofficially, it was easier for the men concerned if they were defined that way. A reply to Governor Macquarie's request of 1812 that 'as many male convicts as possible be sent hither, the prosperity of the country depending on their numbers; whilst on the contrary female convicts are as great a drawback as the others are beneficial' offers an insight into the confusions of the Official View.

To this observation Your Committee feel they cannot accede: they are aware that the women sent out are of the most abandoned description, and that in many instances they are likely to whet and to encourage the vices of the men, whilst but a small proportion will make any step towards reformation; but yet, with all their vices, such women as these were the mothers of a great part of the inhabitants now existing in the Colony . . . Let it be remembered too, how much misery and vice are likely to prevail in a society in which women bear no proportion to the men; in the Colony at present the number of men compared to that of women is 2 to 1; to this, in great measure, the prevalence of prostitution is to be attributed; but

increase that proportion and the temptation to abandoned vices will be increased . . .

Manning Clark, Select Documents in
Australian History, p. 117

Convict women were caught between that view and
the opinion of the Reverend Samuel Marsden that
all women who were cohabiting outside wedlock,
however sustained the relationship, were prostitutes.
Only rarely, and then indirectly, do we hear from
one of the women herself, as in this deposition to a
Committee from a settler, W. R. H. Brown in 1819:

These women informed me, as well as others of their
shipmates, that they were subjected to every insult
from the master of the ship and sailors; that the
master stript several of them and publickly whipped
them; that one young woman, from ill treatment,
threw herself into the sea and perished; that the
master beat one of the women that lived with me with
a rope with his own hands till she was much bruised
in her arms, breasts and other parts of her body. I
am certain, from her general good conduct since
she arrived, to the present day, she could not have
merited any cruelty from him . . . In addition to the
insults they were subject to on board, the youngest
and handsomest of the women were selected from
the other convicts and sent on board, by order of the

master, the King's ships who were at that time in the fleet, for the vilest purpose; both my servants were in the number.

Manning Clark, Select Documents in
Australian History, *p. 114*

Writing the truth of what happened in history is a matter of taking the records and then listening hard between the lines, not only for the cries of individual agony and protest, but for the buzz of ordinary conversation and comfort, and humour, and hope. It demands the highest imagination.

The nineteenth century in Australia produced no literature of the convict experience from a man or woman who had actually known it. We have no *House of the Dead*.

A people can face the future only when they have fully recognised their past, and in one form or another relived it. If the literature does not exist, it has – even a hundred years later – to be imagined and made. Robert Hughes' reading of Australian experience belongs to this process, as well as to the simpler one of telling us 'what happened Down There'.

The New York Review of Books, *1987*

PUTTING OURSELVES
ON THE MAP

WHEN I WAS IN THE fourth grade at primary school we spent a lot of time drawing the map of Australia. It was hard to get right. Too often you ended up with something in which, in order to close the outline, the southern tip of Western Australia was like a limb affected by polio and the east coast, perhaps because we knew it better, was suffering a hysterical pregnancy.

We worked on the outline. What mattered was to get the island into its proper shape and then fill in, all round, the names of the natural features, the capes, gulfs and bays. The centre, even when the map was finished, remained empty save for a few dotted lines – some of them rivers, the rest, if the hour was up and geography had become history, the routes of the explorers.

The year was 1942. Australia was at war and under threat of invasion. The scary thing was that our coastline was so extensive and unoccupied that if the Japanese landed it might be several days before anyone knew it. The comforting thing was that if they did struggle ashore the country itself would deal with them. No need to adopt, like the Russians, a scorched earth policy. Geography had already taken care of that. The land was permanently scorched.

All meditations on history in Australia begin as geography lessons. Geography is fate.

Cultures tend to be either time-oriented or space-oriented; they are seldom both. They tend, that is, to measure their experience either in Ages, Periods, Dynasties, all with dates affixed, or by the amount of territory they have covered, the distance they have come by conquering, occupying, settling.

The very nature of our continent, together with our late arrival on the scene, has made our history of the second kind.

If you want to see Australian history there is no point in looking for 'significant events'. It is pretty difficult, in our case, to name an event that is significant in the conventional sense: one, that is, that has struck the Australian imagination and made itself as significant as Magna Carta or the Battle of Crecy or the Restoration or the Bill of Rights in English history, with dates that any reasonably educated person is likely to recall. Our experience of Australia (and one immediately puts it that way rather than saying simply 'our experience') knows no dates, no sharp turning points in time – though I suppose advertising has made it certain that everyone now is aware of 1788.

Australian history is of a quieter kind, and that isn't because ours is *modern* history in which nothing dramatic ever occurs. Other places, France or Germany or Italy or Spain, in the same 200 years, have had more drama, more noisy and murderous events, than anyone in their right mind might care for. In those terms our history is invisible. It consists of happenings so small, so everyday, so ordinary, so endlessly repeatable that they draw no attention to themselves, and so momentary as to defy dating. They are the sort of events that have made up almost the whole of history – if what we mean by that is the lives of all those who have shared this planet. The remains are visible but the individual events and lives are not.

If we want to *see* this sort of history we look out of an aeroplane window, on any regular flight across the country, and take in the pattern of cultivation, the mile on mile of wheatfields stretching to the horizon; or we stand at South Head and try to imagine the view *without* the Bridge, the Opera House, the city towers, the suburban roofs and parklands reaching to the mountains westward and out of visible distance to the south. What we are seeing there is our 200 years.

Two hundred is a paltry number as these things go, and we might be intimidated into believing, if we were to forget the millions of lifetimes that have been crammed into it, that such a stretch of time is insignificant and barely amounts to a history at all. Until we see the achievement in *space*. That is breathtaking.

So we are back once again with Geography.

We measure our life on this continent by how far we have got, at any point, in our knowledge of it, in crossing mountain barriers, uncovering river systems, assaying its mineral resources; how much of it has been felled and fenced and made productive; how far our cities have extended beyond the original cluster of huts into the surrounding countryside. Or, for those who would put it another way, by the amount of land our farming and grazing methods have stripped or soured, the topsoil gone, the forests lost, the species of bird and animal life – and not *only* those – exterminated to make room for us.

These things, rather than ancient monuments or ruins, or the crossed swords that mark a battle site, are the signposts, the mile posts in our story. The land itself is the record of our 200 years.

Still, time does have a part to play in human affairs, and the paucity of it in our case is decisive.

In the Old World, but also in Africa and the Americas, 'culture' means the long association of a native people with their land: the process of coming in out of the wilderness, bringing with them the wild grasses and fruits and beasts that over the years have been improved and domesticated to provide a diet, and which, after long sophistication, may become a cuisine.

This is the culture that is present and renewed at every table at every mealtime, an ordinary sacrament in which man's relationship with the earth he belongs to, and which for that reason belongs to him, is lightly commemorated.

Native Australians have such a culture, though we have learned nothing from it. White Australians do not. We came as immigrants and brought our culture with us – not just a language and the many forms of social organisation, but the crops and animals to feed us and from which, through effort and industry, our economy has grown. There was no need to begin, as others had, from the beginning.

So there is, at the centre of our lives here, a deep irony: that the very industry that gives us a hold on the earth has no roots in the land itself, no history, no past; and *that* sort of past – the experience of having developed along with the land and its creatures – may be precisely what one needs (a sense of continuity, a line passing through from the remotest past into the remotest time to come) if one is to get a grip on the future.

There is, and always has been, something rootless and irresponsible about our attitude to the land. We treat it, we go at things 'as if there were no tomorrow', using, wasting, making the most of everything while it lasts, stripping assets, taking the short view; as if we had no responsibility to those who might come after because we have no sense of what lies behind. We *took* the land, grabbed it by main force, so we miss the sense of its being a gift – something to be held in trust and passed on. Perhaps a deep awareness of history has less to do with the past than with a capacity to hold on hard to the future.

This lack in us – it is a radical one – can also be read in the landscape. If decisions about wood-chipping or sand-mining can be shot home to individual politicians, the basis on which these decisions have been made is general and expresses more than a personal irresponsibility or greed.

There is a rootlessness in us, an anxiety about where and how we belong, that goes beyond such simple questions as what sort of destiny Australia might have, or how we define ourselves as Australians, and which the celebration of a Bicentenary in no way impinges upon. That too has to do with geography, with a disjunction between our immigrant society and the land that sustains it that is still decades, maybe centuries, from resolution.

Isolation: the essential quality of the isle. It created the uniqueness of our flora and fauna and it kept the continent, until only a short time ago, outside history – outside the consciousness, that is, of those who keep records. It has also determined, in us, the angle at which we stand to the world: that timidity, for example, or canniness, which has kept us tied for so long to our mother's apron strings, terrified that if we broke away, or slipped the mind of England, Europe, we might slide right off the world; or more destructive still, that willingness, which shows little sign of diminishing, to suck up to the biggest bully in the playground, with a mixture of truculence and shameless abjection, so long as he deigns to call us his 'little mate'.

This horror of being left on our own, of being left out, has led us, with an eagerness that would be pathetic if it hadn't also produced so much suffering and heroism, to rush off blindly to other people's wars, from the Boer War to Vietnam – happy to bleed ourselves dry at other people's significant occasions because we have no belief in the centrality of our own lives, in what happens to *us*.

In looking at where we stand we have always taken our stance elsewhere, seen ourselves as being at the bottom right-hand corner of things – on the edge, where at any moment we might fly off the globe; at the bottom where, given the laws of gravity, we can only be the passive receivers of what others let fall.

But geography is as much convention as fact. It is a way of seeing. Maps can be approached from any angle, they can be reversed. We have only to turn our minds upside down, stop thinking in terms of our inherited culture, to which we will always be peripheral, to find ourselves standing at the centre rather than the edge of things. Which brings me back, once again, to that classroom of forty years ago; to the idea of Australia which exists in our heads as a map.

If I had tried, back there, to imagine my way across Australia from Brisbane, say, to Perth, I would have run into sand. Once you left the coast and the wheat-lands beyond, there was nothing out there to hang on to. The centre, imaginatively speaking, was blank. Just thinking of it, the distances, the emptiness, made you dizzy. Thought stumbled, became a dotted line – like the tracks of explorers. It snuffed out.

And now?

Now the centre of Australia, the Centre, is fixed, occupied by a vivid symbol, a natural phenomenon so powerful that it rivals and counterbalances our man-made ones, those unmistakable marks of our presence, the Bridge and the Opera House. It is even (if we ignore its previous life in geology and think only of the point at which it emerged, out of nowhere it might seem, into our national consciousness) of the same vintage as those products of iron, concrete and mythological sleight of hand. I mean Ayers Rock – and will give it, for the moment, the name under which it first worked its magic on us.

Still unknown forty years ago, and therefore invisible, its emergence in a thousand forms (as a big hamburger or as the mould that breaks open to reveal the new Ford) is one of the few significant events of our history: the hero as rock. It has become the true navel of our consciousness, the great belly-button of the land. All the rest – that coastline, all those capes and bays – are held in place now by its magnetic pull.

So are we. Just how powerfully was demonstrated by its influence in the Chamberlain case. Would any of that spooky terror, that rage, that runaway desire for public expiation and revenge, have burst forth so irrationally, and from such a deep level of our national psyche, if baby Azaria had gone missing from a caravan park at Eden or a camping site at Burleigh Heads?

We can see the centre now. It has been coloured in. We can even see the people who live there, and are curious enough at last about who they are and how they live to recognise in them, and in *their* relationship to the land, a consciousness so different from our own as to call into question some of our deepest assumptions. Maybe if Burke and Wills had been able to see them they would not have died of starvation in country where others, who were human like them, had known for centuries how to survive: the lines on the map might not be dotted, but double.

Sixty years ago, out there, one of the last of many massacres occurred – not the worst or the most shameful. In the age of the movie camera and the radio! But the place was invisible; in the map Australians carried in their heads it was blank. They had no responsibility for what happened there. Today the blank spaces on that map have dwindled. We cannot so easily let ourselves off the hook. The inside and the outside of the map have got themselves connected and we know only too well where we are, what we have done, and who is in it with us. We are centred in our own lives.

If I had been asked, back in 1942, to draw the line that most strongly connected me to the world, I would have shut my eyes, thought of England and produced the long series of loops between stopping-places of the Orient and P & O lines. Sydney to Southampton or Tilbury. The names of those ports were magic. I could have sung them in my sleep.

The lines themselves of course (not the shipping lines) were *notional*, but then so were the tropics, so was the equator. They were the lines of force that held us in History, that reshaped the globe. When they broke at last and the ships went to scrap, we were on our own. So what remains of that original cord?

By a freak of nature, or perhaps a fated affinity, the colonisers of our out-of-the-way continent had themselves once been on the fringes of the known world.

When it was first discovered by the Phoenicians, Britain was a remote and savage island on the way to nowhere, tucked away in the north-western corner of the map. Colonised at last by the imperial power of the day, its native people were disposed of by waves of immigrants – Anglo-Saxons, Jutes, Danes, Normans – and in the end exterminated, not by policy but by the natural savagery of the more highly civilised. So when our two islands, one small and isolated, the other large and isolated, came together at last in 1788 the colonisers not only brought with them a language, and the ways of seeing and organising of which a language is the most intense expression, but a history as well of having triumphed over a natural disability.

Britain had by then made it to the centre. By 1788 all distances on the globe were measured from Greenwich. What an example! These immigrants, by nature little-islanders, now had to adjust to the biggest island in the world: Lilliputians in Brobdingnag.

It is fashionable to sketch alternative histories of Australia based on the premise of some other colonising presence than the one we got.

Would the Russians, for example, as Bruce Chatwin asks in *The Songlines*, with their long experience of interiors, of endless horizons, have made a better fist of coming to terms with the *whole* of Australia? Would they have learned to live more easily with distances and space?

Would we have found some quicker adjustment between culture and climate if we had been colonised by Mediterraneans, the Spanish for example?

Would we have been saved from Anglo-Saxon philistinism by those bearers of light and learning, the French?

And what about a Catholic rather than a Protestant Australia – with the church producing the same enlightened and civilising influence here as in the Spanish Empire of the Americas?

Idle questions perhaps, but they help define both the limitations and the advantages of what actually shaped us and what we have begun, painfully, to outgrow.

English law, for example, since that is what first set the seal of ownership on the land – the pragmatic English law, and the whole mode of thinking and proceeding that springs from its sample: the distrust of absolutes and codes, the determination to take each case as it comes, as it tests and qualifies or proves the rule. Whole education systems derive from that, whole arts and sciences, and the kind of thinking we apply (as if by nature) when facing problems of ordinary living – adapting an old tool to new conditions, trying this, trying that, until the thing fits. A way of dealing with the world that we do not consider peculiar and *learned*, until we see how other nations do it.

And beyond the law itself, at least notionally, is the independence of the law, and of all our social institutions, from the government of the day – a simple thing, and one that we take for granted as if it too were natural, too obvious to be questioned; except that it has always been rare.

We might remember this when we regret the siesta we would have enjoyed had the Spanish come, since these embodiments of British dullness, plus the absence of a professional officer class, have deprived us of the more interesting history that so many other nations have enjoyed over these past centuries: Revolution and Terror, civil wars, alternating periods of weak democracy and strong rule by thin generals and fat colonels, putsches, soviets, juntas and twelve-year Reichs.

Pity the nation, Brecht said, that needs heroes. Pity even more the nation that needs an 'interesting history'.

So this celebration of a great event goes against the grain with me because it goes against the grain of our real experience as Australians. Anniversaries are not what this particular enterprise is about. The anniversaries of the real events that made us, the millions of small ones – axe-blows, blows with the pick and crowbar, childbirths, first cries, the squeak of chalk across a blackboard – do not need celebrating, or are celebrated already, by repetition each day. This particular event is too ambiguous – and its repetition in fancy dress is ridiculous. It is too blackened with sorrow for some of us (if we really think of them as among us) and with shame for the rest: too loaded with despair, courage, the slow triumph of surviving and creating, for its re-enactment to be any more than a tawdry farce.

The real achievement, and it *is* real – even astonishing – we already celebrated yesterday and will need to celebrate again tomorrow and the day after. I salute *that*.

The Age, *'Bicentenary Extra'*,
Saturday 23 January 1988

THE EIGHTIES,
A 'LEARNING' EXPERIENCE

ONCE AGAIN, WE HAVE ENTERED the silly season. Because we happen to be on holiday we think nothing serious can occur; the world out there, in gracious compliance with our comfort, will produce no disaccommodating event. Still, as we let ourselves off the hook and settle to beach days and a little light reading, there are one or two things we might remind ourselves of.

It is true that we are important and powerful. What we do has an effect in the world quite out of proportion to our numbers. But there are millions of Indians and Chinese – Africans, too – who know as little of us as we do of them. They look about and in the world they see we are invisible. There is a whole other consciousness, Islam for example, in which history – *now*, I mean, but also the future – has a quite different shape from the one we find ourselves in, and keeps no special place for us.

The fact is that for most of the men and women who crowd our planet, even the minority of them who share our calendar, 1 January 1990 isn't a *date*, the beginning of a new year or decade, but a day like any other, belonging to weather rather than history, and to work, the repetitive, monotonous, inescapable routines of a rice crop, wheat crop, dairy herd, or to olive or date or poppy or maize harvests; or it is another twenty-four hours of trying to stay alive on the pavements of Calcutta or Sao Paolo or New York. It takes affluence and leisure (paid holidays), but also a high degree of selfconsciousness, to see your life in the sort of literary perspective that demands a term like 'the eighties'. But here we are.

Of course there is a place in our head, or bowels, where we too live in immediate sensation and event; where we are under the pressure of moments rather than decades; where we exist, not in the twentieth century even but in our ears, eyes, breath, and among the same needs and hopes and panic fears that have moved men and women at all times everywhere.

It is worth reminding ourselves of that, too, since so much of what is created on TV – but also in the part of our consciousness that belongs to dates and decades and bicentenaries – is meant to save us from the reality of our own experience; to make us believe that time, as it opens before us, is not a field of continuous and potentially dangerous being, in which history is what we are doing *now*, but a space for commemorating what others have done, one, two, ten centuries ago.

So 1988 is the bicentenary of white settlement in Australia, 1989 of the taking of the Bastille. Fashion revives the fifties, the forties, the 1890s. Post-modernism – that conservatism in smart modern dress – elects itself the curator of a vast echo chamber or mind museum where the past is ransacked, de-structured, recycled in a brilliant display of allusion that shifts the exhibits into new and striking juxtaposi-tions. Re-enactment replaces being and a selfconscious knowingness the difficult and demanding business of exploring the unknown. We may not know who we are or where we are going, but we do know, when it comes to decades and centuries, what we are at the end of.

This taking of the long view flatters our intelli-gence and gives us a fine illusion of power, because it places us so firmly in the line of those who have made history.

But it deprives us of something, too. It deprives us of a belief in our own lives, our real present and presence in the world, and it robs us of the real past as well by reducing what was, in its own time, open and dangerous (the French Revolution for example) to mere spectacle. A muddled and muddling present that was once a matter of hope and terror and suspense, ideas that had a real form as blood, guts, sweat, acts of emancipation and murder, noble aspirations, deep disillusion – all these are turned into theatre, with everything that is difficult to swallow in them, or refractory or problematical, squeezed out in the interests of a bland consensus that will allow us – 500 million or 600 million of us – to enjoy it all on a 21-inch screen, between the ads for Mitsubishi and Safe Sex.

One of the many astonishments of this past year, when events struck back and showed once again their capacity to run away with us, is the way 1989 was hijacked by men and women who were determined to make it *their* year, and to create history rather than passively commemorate it.

The abiding image of 1989 is not the ideologically safe and trendy one of a black woman, draped in the tricolour and singing at dirge-like speed all three, or was it nine, verses of *La Marseillaise*, but the students in Tiananmen Square, and the vast crowds in all the squares of Eastern Europe, who assembled not to re-experience history as entertainment but to take it by the throat and shake the life out of it.

We need to tread warily when we come to defining 'the eighties'. Which eighties, where?

There are years, 1789 for one, 1989 too as it happened, that have a nasty habit of disintegrating decades and sometimes whole centuries in an explosion of unpredicted and unpredictable action, while all the rest of us were doing was punching out pin-numbers at the Flexiteller or partying on.

Here then is a checklist, for which readers can provide their own notes, of some names and terms that were unknown a decade ago or had quite other associations, a kind of dictionary of the eighties.

Under A: acid house parties, aerobics, AIDS; under C: Chernobyl, child abuse, condom, consensus, corruption . . . and so on through deregulation, 'dob in a you-name-it', Ecstasy, fundamentalism, Gorbachev, insider trading, J-curve; to privatisation, Rat parties, supergrass, Uluru, video-clips, white-collar crime, yuppies. It is, on the whole, a depressing parade, or would be if it wasn't itself such an example of eighties modishness.

One of the paradoxes of the eighties is that in being so resolutely and profoundly superficial it was never quite what it seemed. For all its shoulder-shrugging cynicism, its unapologetic selfishness and cupidity, its Brasserie News and Business News and shabby glitz, this decade has seen some of the most radical shifts of consciousness of any in our century. The open face of the eighties may be docile and conservative but its secret face has been revolutionary. We have been forced, against our will as always, to take the full weight of our experience, which does not lead, as we might hope, to a safe and self-protective knowingness, but to what it always was: muddle and immersion in the immediate, the unknown, the creative/destructive element, none of it optional and none of it to be taken – in a typical phrase of the eighties – as simply a 'learning' experience.

So in what way revolutionary? What 'shifts of consciousness'?

There was a time, not so long ago, when we lived, even the richest of us, in a world where the body was a paradoxical entity, to be treated by modern standards in a rough and ready way, without fuss but with an awareness always of its absolute vulnerability. Ordinary life was full of risk. Women died in childbirth or, as men did too, of blood-poisoning or pneumonia. Children died of whooping cough or diphtheria or polio, and as barefoot kids in Brisbane we kept a good lookout for rusty nails. In the world outside, smallpox was raging and we bore the scars of our immunity. We all knew that more people had died – uncles, aunts, neighbours – in the world flu epidemics of 1919 and 1922 than in the Great War.

This common vulnerability made us see our bodies, and our lives, in a particular way, and the presence among us of killer viruses made us see our relationship to one another too in a particular way: we were vitally connected. A writer like Dickens could use smallpox in *Bleak House* as a secret agent connecting all the disparate social worlds of his novel, a real agent but an image as well of the hidden relationships it was the role of his plot to lay bare. The world Dickens was writing of was the world we were still living in as late as 1944.

But the appearance of antibiotics after the war removed most of the risks – at least where we lived. Death from anything other than old age, or road accidents or domestic murder, came to seem an unnatural thing, a violation of what was orderly and expected. For forty years or so we learned to see our bodies as places that science had made safe for us, areas of play, and our connection with others as socially or sexually optional.

Of course this was true only of some places; elsewhere people went on being subjected to the same old risks, or most of them, so that when AIDS appeared among them it wasn't a new and incomprehensible thing, as it has been with us, but one more of the many ills that might at any moment carry you off.

There is nothing good to be said of AIDS. But the change it has made in our awareness of what the body is, and how we are connected, is worth pointing to. It marks, in one sense, a return to normal. That forty years was an anomaly, it was freakish. The norm is risk. We're back again with mortality and interconnectedness, and the reality of this imposes itself equally on the hard-line moralists among us and the libertarian sensualists. No-one is off the hook. The world of the seventies is gone and seems as remote and exotic now as the age of Pericles.

When the great powers launched their space programs back in the fifties, those new stars or satellites, and later the moon-shots and planet-shots, seemed no more than extensions into an extraterrestrial arena of our global politics; another boyish form – all wars, as Melville says, are boyish – of the Cold War. Even later, when men did actually walk on the moon, it was difficult for most of us to see any more in all this than a playful exercise in human curiosity, ingenuity and love of adventure; it was hard to believe, I mean, that it was a genuine attempt to establish new colonies or new areas of human habitation.

Space-fever has cooled off in this decade, but paradoxically its real importance has revealed itself and is enhanced. What all that swashbuckling was about, or so it now appears, was not *man* in space but our *planet* in space. The real message was in the pictures that came back, those impressive but poignant images of a lonely sphere in orbit out there, seen as from far off, with all its oceans and continents just as we knew them on some schoolroom globe we could set spinning with a finger – as close and familiar as *that*, but seen now as God might see it, so that we could grasp it, finally, in two senses at once: in all its closeness as something we could get our hands around, an object about the same size as a human head, but objectively as well, in all its immensity out there, but with the immensity so diminished by distance that that too was 'graspable'.

Maps, if we can read them, tell us where we are on the surface of the globe. We have got used to that. But what this new thing told us was something different. It did not set us on an extensive surface. It made the planet and our awareness of it co-extensively one.

What we were being prepared for by all that space-adventuring was an apprehension that may be essential now to our survival, and to the survival of the planet itself: a vision of where we are, and all it involves in the way of loyalty and affection and concern, as 'global', and the problems we have to resolve as equally 'global'. The awareness is evolutionary, and the rapidity with which it has occurred is as astonishing, and as indicative of what is human and remarkable in us, as the moon-walk itself.

The other changes we have seen, so many of them in the past six months, in Eastern Europe and the Soviet Union, but also in the relative shift in power between Europe and the United States, are too new and extraordinary – too obvious as well – to be more than pointed at and marvelled over.

Only a crank or madman could have predicted a decade ago what has been happening daily in these past weeks: the work of cranks and madmen pulled down at last by ordinary citizens. History was the privilege of tyrants and their treasonous clerks. Now whole worlds and systems come tumbling down that we had been told were the product of a history that could not be resisted because it was inevitable and necessary. Events have taken care of that as well, and there is more to come. To try to predict what it might be is for cranks, madmen and those who have learned nothing, this past year, of how events can shift the ground under our heels.

Sydney Morning Herald,
'*Summer Agenda*', 27 December 1989

A SPIRIT OF PLAY

THE MAKING OF AUSTRALIAN CONSCIOUSNESS

1
The Island

LOOKING DOWN THE LONG LINE of coast this morning, I see the first rays of the sun strike Mount Warning and am aware, as the light floods west, what a distance it is to the far side of our country – two time zones and more than 3000 kilometres away, yet how easily the whole landmass sits in my head. As an island or, as I sometimes think of it, a raft we have all scrambled aboard, a new float of lives in busy interaction: of assembly lines and highways, of ideals given body as executives and courts, of routine housekeeping arrangements and objects in passage from hand to hand. To comprehend the thing in all its action and variety and contradiction is a task for the imagination, yet this morning, as always, it is simply there, substantial and ordinary.

When Europeans first came to these shores one of the things they brought with them, as a kind of gift to the land itself, was something that could never previously have existed: a vision of the continent in its true form as an island, which was not just a way of seeing it, and seeing it whole, but of seeing how it fitted into the world, and this seems to have happened even before circumnavigation established that it actually was an island. No group of Aboriginal Australians, however ancient and deep their understanding of the land, can ever have seen the place in just this way.

It has made a difference. If Aborigines are a land-dreaming people, what we latecomers share is a sea-dreaming, to which the image of Australia as an island has from the beginning been central.

This is hardly surprising. Sydney, in its early days was first and foremost a seaport; all its dealings were with the sea. Our earliest productive industries were not wheat-growing or sheep-raising but whaling and sealing. It took us nearly thirty years to cross the first land barrier. Right up to the end of the nineteenth century our settlements were linked by coastal steamer, not by road or rail. In his sonnet 'Australia', Bernard O'Dowd speaks of Australia's 'virgin helpmate, Ocean', as if the island continent were mystically married to its surrounding ocean as Venice was to the Adriatic.

As the off-shoot of a great naval power we felt at home with the sea. It was an element over which we had control; more, certainly, than we had at the beginning over the land. It was what we looked to for all our comings and goings, for all that was new – for news. And this sense of being at home with the sea made distances that might otherwise have been unimaginable seem shorter. It brought Britain and Europe closer than 10,000 miles on the globe might have suggested, and kept us tethered, for longer than we might otherwise have been, by sea-routes whose ports of call, in the days before air travel, constituted a litany of connection that every child of my generation knew by heart. Distance is not always a matter of miles. Measured in feelings it can redefine itself as closeness.

And this notion of an island continent, contained and containable, had other consequences.

Most nations establish themselves through a long series of border conflicts with neighbours. This is often the major thrust of their history. Think of the various wars between Germany and France, or Russia and Poland, or of British history before the Union of the Crowns.

Australia's borders were a gift of nature. We did not have to fight for them. In our case, history and geography coincided, and we soon hit upon the idea that the single continent must one day be a single nation.

What this means is that all our wars of conquest, all our sources of conflict, have been internal.

Conquest of space to begin with, in a series of daring explorations of the *land*, which were also acts of possession different from the one that made it ours merely in law. This was possession in the form of knowledge; by naming and mapping, by taking its spaces into our heads, and at last into our imagination and consciousness.

Conquest of every form of internal division and difference: conquest of the original possessors, for example, in a war more extensive than we have wanted to recognise. Later, there was the attempted resolution, through an act of Federation, of the fraternal division between the states; and, longer lasting and less amenable of solution, of the conflict, once Federation had been achieved, between the states and the Federal Government. Also, more darkly, suppression, in acts of law-making and social pressure and through subtle forms of exclusion, of all those whom we have, at one time or another, declared to be outsiders among us, and in their various ways alien, even when they were Australians like the rest.

That early vision of wholeness produced a corresponding anxiety, the fear of fragmentation, and for too long the only answer we had to it was the imposition of a deadening conformity.

In time, the vision of the continent as whole and

unique in its separation from the rest of the world produced the idea that it should be *kept* separate, that only in isolation could its uniqueness – and ours – be preserved.

Many of the ideas that have shaped our life here, and many of the themes on which our history has been argued, settle around these notions of isolation and containment, of wholeness and the fear of fragmentation. But isolation can lead to stagnation as well as concentrated richness, and wholeness does not necessarily mean uniformity, though that is how we have generally taken it. Nor does diversity always lead to fragmentation.

As for the gift of those natural, indisputable borders, that too had a cost. It burdened us with the duty of defending them, and the fear, almost from the beginning, that they may not, in fact, be defendable.

Our first settlements outside Sydney, at Hobart in 1804 and Perth in the 1820s, were made to forestall the possibility of French occupation (and it seems Napoleon did plan a diversionary invasion for 1804). Then, at the time of the Crimean War, it was the Russians we had to keep an eye on. The Russian fleet was just seven days sailing away at Vladivostok. And then, from the beginning of this century, the Japanese.

This fear of *actual* invaders, of being unable to defend our borders, led to a fear of other and less tangible forms of invasion. By people, 'lesser breeds without the Law', who might sully the purity of our stock. By alien forms of culture that might prejudice our attempt to be uniquely ourselves. By ideas, and all those other forms of influence, out there in the world beyond our coast, that might undermine our morals or in various other ways divide and unsettle us. All this has made little-islanders of us; has made us decide, from time to time, to close ourselves off from influence and change, and by settling in behind our ocean wall, freeze and stop what has been from the beginning, and continues to be, a unique and exciting experiment.

*

Australia began as an experiment in human engineering. We should not allow the brutalities of the age in which it took place to obscure the fact that among the many mixed motives for the founding of the colony there were some that were progressive and idealistic. The eighteenth century was as troubled as we are by the nature of criminality, and in dealing with it the need to balance deterrence, or as they would have called it, terror, with the opportunity to reform. Botany Bay was not just a dumping ground for unwanted criminals. It was also an experiment in reformation, in using the rejects of one society to create another.

What seems astonishing when we look about at

the world we live in here, this clean and orderly place with its high level of affluence and ease, its concern for rights and every sort of freedom, these cities in which a high level of civility is simply taken for granted and barely remarked upon, is that it should have emerged from a world that was at the beginning so *un*-free, so brutal and disorderly. It did so because these rejects of society of whom so little might have been expected *made* it happen. Out of their insistence that they were not to be so easily written off.

Charles Darwin, who was not always a sympathetic observer of the Australian scene, has two things to tell us of the colony as he first saw it in 1836, not quite fifty years from the beginning. 'Here,' he writes in his *Journal of the Voyage of the HMS Beagle*, 'in less promising country, scores of years have affected many times more than the same number of centuries has done in South America.'

That is a tribute to the pace of development in Australia, and also, no doubt, to British efficiency and moral fibre as opposed to Spanish and Portuguese fecklessness. But he has something else to say as well. 'As a means,' he tells us, 'of making men honest – of converting vagabonds the most useless in one hemisphere into active citizens in another, and giving birth to a new and splendid country – and a grand centre of civilisation – it has succeeded to a degree perhaps unparalleled in history.'

When we think of our beginning, we are inclined to emphasise what is sensational in it, the many horrors, and this is understandable. They were real, and indignation at injustice does credit to us – so does a passionate sympathy for its victims. Fellow-feeling for the weak and for those who fail, out of bad luck or bad judgement or ordinary human hopelessness, is one of our strongest national characteristics and has its beginning here. Our attitude to welfare, for instance, and to those who need it, is very different from the way these things are seen in some other places.

But victims, and sensational brutality and misery, are easy to imagine and identify with. What is harder to think our way into is ordinariness, the day-to-day routine of lives that, however brutal they may have been by our standards, were unremarkable except in the astonishing capacity of those who lived them (and we need to think hard about what this must have meant to individual men and women) to endure, but even more, to change; to take hold of the opportunities offered by a second chance in a new place.

Eighteenth-century playwrights and novelists often made their hero a criminal, a highwayman or confidence trickster or thief. Gay's *Beggar's Opera*, Defoe's *Colonel Jack* and *Captain Singleton*, Fielding's *Mr Jonathan Wild*, all play with the interesting and subversive notion that the qualities that go to the making of a successful criminal – entrepreneurial egotism, an eye for the main chance and for the weakness of others – may be the same qualities that in other circumstances make a politician or businessman. Botany Bay in some ways puts this cheeky proposition to the proof.

John Locke claimed that men join a civil society or commonwealth 'for mutual protection of their lives, liberty and estates, which I call', he says, 'by the general name of property'. Now, if it is the need to protect property that makes men join together and become citizens, mightn't it be possible to make citizens out of vagabonds, as Darwin calls them, by *giving* them property, that is, land, but in a place so far off that they would not be tempted to return; a place where possession of property would lead them to *settle*, even when their term of exile was up? Land, that real yet mystical commodity of measured dirt that can raise a man (or as it happened, a woman) from a mere nothing to an individual of status and power, and eventually, since this is what land usually ensured in the days before universal suffrage, the right to vote and have a voice in the making of the laws.

It was the promise of land, fifty acres for a man, thirty more for his wife, and thirty for each child, that was the new element in this experiment and a defining one in our history, not least because of the conflict it involved with the original owners. That is another story, another and darker history interwoven with our more triumphal one, and the conflict over land that is at the centre of it is not just about occupation and ownership; it is also about what land means. For Aboriginal people land is the foundation of spiritual being. For Europeans it represents security and status, or it is a source of wealth.

The desire of ordinary men and women to become property owners was the making of this country. To own a piece of Australia, even if it was only a quarter-acre block, became the Australian dream. The desperation that lay behind it, the determination of poor men and women to grasp what was offered and raise themselves out of landless poverty into a new class, was the source of a materialism that is still one of our most obvious characteristics.

It has taken us 200 years to see that there might be another and more inward way of possessing a place, and that in this, as in so much else, the people we dispossessed had been there before us. But the fact is that for those convicts who did succeed, all this was a fairy tale come true. Samuel Terry, for instance, was transported in 1801 for stealing 400 pairs of stockings – he seems always to have done things on a large scale. He served his seven years, and when he died in 1838 owned 19,000 acres, more than some of the greatest lords in England.

Of course, opportunity, however great, was

also limited. Not everyone ended up as a merchant prince. But when all the savageries have been taken into account – and the disruption and pain of leaving loved ones and a life, however unsettled, that in their mind, and in their hearts too, was home – transportation worked for most of these men and women. To suggest otherwise is to deny the extent to which so many of them *did* change and become the active citizens who made our world. And there must have been some among them – Simeon Lord and Mary Reibey, for instance, or Esther Abrahams – for whom Botany Bay was not just the underside of the world but the realisation of that dream of radical English thinkers in the seventeenth century, the world turned upside down. Esther Abrahams, who was transported in the First Fleet for theft, set up with, and later married, Major George Johnston, and was for a time the First Lady of the colony.

It is the poet Mary Gilmore who has given us our most memorable statement of all this. The convict in her poem 'Old Botany Bay' gives a voice to many thousands who have no other voice in our history.

I'm old
Botany Bay;
Stiff in the joints
Little to say.

I am he
Who paved the way
That you might walk
At your ease today.

I was the conscript
Sent to hell
To make in the desert
The living well.

I bore the heat,
I blazed the track –
Furrowed and bloody
Upon my back.

I split the rock;
I felled the tree;
The nation was –
Because of me!

Old Botany Bay
Taking the sun
From day to day ...
Shame on the mouth

That would deny
The knotted hands
That set us high!

I would want to add that it wasn't just muscle and dumb endurance that these people brought, and which we enjoy the fruits of, but also native wit, inventiveness, imagination, and most of all the amazing human capacity to re-imagine and remake themselves.

*

One surprising detail leaps out of the various accounts we have of the First Fleet voyage. It is this: on the night of 2 January 1788, some of the convicts on one of the ships, the *Scarborough*, as their contribution to the possibilities of diversion and simple enjoyment in the place they were coming to – and in defiance, it seems, of the misery of cramped conditions and whatever terror they may have felt at their imminent arrival on a fatal shore – got up a dramatic entertainment, some sort of play.

So, smuggled in on one of those eleven ships, along with their cargo of criminal rejects and all the necessary objects for settling a new place – the handsaws and framesaws, the steel spade and iron shovel, and three hoes and an axe and tomahawk for each man, and woollen drawers and worsted stockings for the men and linsey-woolsey petticoats and caps for the women, and Lieutenant George Worgan's piano, and the rights and obligations that, in being argued back and forth between authority and its many subjects, would make the new place they were coming to so different from the one they left – was the spirit of make-believe, of theatre, of play. And along with it, an audience's delight, and practiced skill no doubt, in watching and listening.

The fact is that the whole of a culture is present, in all its complexity, in small things as well as large. What arrived here with those eleven ships was the European and specifically *English* culture of the late Enlightenment, in all its richness and contradiction, however simple the original settlement may have seemed. From the moment of first landing, a dense, little new world began to grow up here.

Out of the interaction of Europeans with a new form of nature that put to the test all their traditional assumptions about farming methods and how to deal with weather and soil.

Out of the interaction of authority with the mass of convicts around questions of right and obligation, force and consent – these were open questions in some ways because the status of convicts was different here from that of convicts At Home.

Out of the interaction between men and women in a place where women were freer than men (they did not have to perform government labour for their food), and freer than women were at home – a good many of these women became independent traders and land holders.

Out of the interaction between all these newcomers and those, the original possessors, who were already on the ground.

Before long, and well within the first two decades, all the amenities of an advanced society had been conjured up. Craftsmen of every sort – furniture- and cabinet-makers and long-case clock-makers – had got to work using Home designs but local woods; only some of them are known to us by name. John Oatley is one. He made the turret clock that can still be seen in the tympanum of Francis Greenway's Hyde Park Barracks.

Then there were the brass-founders and tinsmiths, the pottery makers like Samuel Skinner, whose wife, Mary, took over the business when he died; and quality silversmiths, many of them Irish and most of them transported for forgery, a common crime in that profession.

John Austin and Ferdinand Meurant, for example, were both transported from Dublin in 1802 and pardoned two years later, Meurant, it is alleged, for knocking £50 off the price of a necklace he made for Governor King's wife. Austin, in a nice colonial irony, went on to become an engraver for the newly established Bank of New South Wales.

All these many artisans and makers of fine goods were convicts. They got conditional pardons quickly because the colony needed their skills.

There is something very moving, something we can feel close to, in all this. It speaks of inventiveness and industry beyond the level of mere making do; of a determination to create a world here that would be the old world in all its diversity, but in a new form – new because in these new conditions the old world would not fit. But what is newest of all is the opportunity that was offered to those who might have believed that, in being transported, all future opportunity had been closed to them. In the more relaxed conditions of this new world even convicts had a kind of power they could never have exercised at home. The System had holes – air holes through which a man could catch a second breath and through which a new form of society could be breathed into existence, a society that was rough perhaps, but full as well of the raw energy that comes with opportunity. If I settle on this occasion on just one of this little new world's many recreations, it is because it seems to me to look forward more evocatively than most to the future, and in a particular way.

In January 1796, just eight years from the beginning, a playhouse was established, a local habitation for that spirit of theatre smuggled in on the *Scarborough*.

It was a real theatre. Georgian in design, with a pit, a gallery and boxes. Entrance to the boxes cost five shillings, to the pit two and six, to the gallery a shilling, and those who had no ready cash could pay in kind; that is, in meat, flour or spirits. It was a convict enterprise of the colony's baker, Robert Sidaway, and seems to have established itself (this too might tell us something about the kind of society we were to become) rather more easily than the first church. The Reverend Johnson had to build that for himself, and his first Christmas service in 1793 drew only thirty-five worshippers. Sidaway's theatre, presumably, did better than that.

An audience is a mysterious phenomenon and subject to mysterious and unpredictable forces. Made up of individuals who shift their attention and their sympathies from moment to moment, under the influence of strong emotion or an appeal to their imagination or their sense of humour, but under the influence as well of a sharpened critical sense in the matter of watching and listening, it is a little society of its own, reconstituted at each performance inside the larger one, and for the most part beyond its control. Not a mob but a cohesive unity with its own inter-ests and loyalties, but unpredictable, and therefore dangerous. And this must have been especially true of *this* audience, composed as it was of convicts and their guards but in convict hands. Fascinating to wonder how far such an audience might constitute the begin-nings here of an integrated community, one in which, given the differences – of status as between convicts and guards, bound and free, of origin, English and

Irish, of education, religion, fortune – a various crowd could nonetheless become one.

On 8 April 1800, Shakespeare's *Henry IV Part One* was played. It must have had a special appeal, a special relevance for this audience – one wonders how the authorities allowed it: political rebellion presented as a falling out between thieves; a tavern underworld of sublime exuberance, where a light-hearted attitude is taken to highway robbery and the picking of pockets; a Lord Chief Justice openly insulted; every sort of high principle roundly mocked. Old hands might have recognised, in the improvised play in which Falstaff and Prince Hal alternately plead for mercy to the King, a version of the mock trials that had been one of their chief entertainments in Newgate, a training-ground for first offenders in how to defend themselves in front of the 'beak'. (And Shakespeare's scene may have had just such occasions as its reference.)

The play's language must have been a particular delight, with its thieves' cant so like the convicts' own 'kiddy' language. And how comically liberating to see lordly authority taken out of the realm of the distantly sacred and brought up close – as they must have seen it every day in the streets of Sydney, in the form of Lieutenant-Governor King for example – blustering, wrangling, breaking out in the same bad language as themselves.

An extraordinary achievement so early in the

piece, this alternative stage for action, this exercise in audience-making, society-shaping in the spirit of play. But risky. Dangerous.

Governor King must have thought so anyway. In one of those about-turns that are so common a feature of our history, when all that seems given is abruptly taken back, in September 1800, when his own authority was confirmed, the Governor closed the playhouse and had it razed to the ground.

2

A Complex Fate

Writing more than a century ago, when Americans had not yet settled the question of their 'identity' or discovered for themselves an independent role in the world, and when Made in America had not yet become a mark of imperial authority, Henry James spoke of the 'complex fate' of those who are children both of the old world and the new, and of the 'responsibility it entails for fighting against the superstitious valuation of Europe'. What James was concerned with was how, in the face of all that Europe represents in terms of achievement and influence, we are to find a proper value, neither brashly above nor cringingly below its real one, for what belongs to the new world;

for what is local but also recent, since part of what is 'superstitious' in our valuation of Europe has to do with the reverential awe we may feel in the presence of mere age. We speak of these places we belong to as new worlds, but what they really are is the old world translated: but *translated*, with all that implies of re-interpretation and change, not simply transported.

Our ways of thinking and feeling and doing had been developed, and tested, over many centuries before we brought them to this new place and gave them a different turn of meaning, different associations, a different shape and weight and colour on new ground.

But the relationship to 'Europe' is only one part of our complex relationship, here, with an anterior world and the intimidating weight of the past. There is also, for us, the example, like a shadow history to be reflected or avoided, of the United States itself.

Australia and the United States are variations, though very different in tone and constitution, on the same original. This means that we share qualities that will always lead us to make comparisons with our American predecessor, forms of social and political thinking that are peculiar enough to keep us close, however we may deviate in practice, and rare enough to be worth noting.

Australia and the United States derive their legal systems from the English Common Law – that is, a system based on precedent rather than principle. Each case, as it comes up, is referred back to a previous one, and a judgement arrived at by comparing the two. This preference for the particular over the general has affected more than just the workings of the law. It has kept thinking in both our societies close to example and fact; made it pragmatic and wary of abstractions, and if this has remained stronger in our intellectual life than in the American, it is because we missed the influence of Continental Europe that came early to the United States with successive waves of migration in the nineteenth century and especially with the exodus of so many European intellectuals to America between the World Wars. It was an influence we did not feel until the middle 1950s.

Equally important to our two worlds has been the separation of powers we inherited with the British system; and, most important of all, the fact that since the dissolution of Cromwell's New Model Army in the 1650s, no political power has ever been accorded in our system to the military. When Australians occasionally play the game of alternative beginnings, of imagining an Australia that might have been French, for example, or Spanish, it is worth reminding them of something. That in failing to be French we missed out on four bloody revolutions, as well as French cuisine and Gallic stylishness and wit, and in failing to be Spanish spared ourselves an almost continuous history of coups by army factions and the rule of a series of brutal juntas. Stability may be dull, and our society may lack passion – fire in the belly as Manning Clark used to call it – but it does allow people breathing space – and if what this results in is a history without 'interest', it also produces fewer graves. There are not many nations in the world where authority has passed without bloodshed from one administration to the next for more than 150 years, as in our case, and more than 200 in the case of the United States. We owe this to the dullness of our British origins.

This shared heritage has made the example of the United States an unusually close one. When it came to Federation, the American model was clearly one of the possibilities we might have followed, and for our Upper House we did take some elements from it. In recent arguments about the republic, the American model of a popularly elected president has seemed to many Australians the one we should in our own way reproduce.

This use of American experience as a reference point for our own goes back to the very beginning.

It was, for example, the British experience of convict transportation to Virginia that determined the new and very different way convicts were dealt with in New South Wales, and the British Government took great care at the beginning, but also later, not to reproduce in its relations with their Australian colonies the mistakes that had led to the loss of the American ones. This meant the establishment of freer conditions here, both for convicts and colonists.

So did the decision, again a lesson learned from the United States, to use convict labour to do the hard work of establishing the colony rather than the labour of slaves. We were saved something in that. A convict, once he has served his time, is free; his children are *born* free. If the convict stain has remained hard to forget, and the brutalities, for some, even harder to forgive, it has not been carried down from generation to generation like the stain of slavery.

But if the American model was there as one to be avoided, it also, in other ways, provoked expectations, a good many of which have proved delusory.

The long search in the nineteenth century for an inland river system that would water the interior and provide a cheap means for the transportation of goods was based on the analogy of America. So was the idea of an Australia Unlimited, the confident expectation that by the end of the twentieth century Australia would rival and maybe even surpass the United States both in population and power. The hope died hard. When Professor Griffith Taylor, in 1911, made the abominable suggestion that by the year 2000 Australia might have a population of no more than twenty million, he was greeted by howls of patriotic rage and driven out of the country.

Almost from the start, our relationship with America and Americans was a special one, a kind of fraternal twinship. The earliest contact was through the shared industries of whaling and sealing. Later, during the two decades of the gold rushes, there was the movement back and forth between here and California of an army of hungry gold-seekers.

This meant not only an extraordinary exchange and mixing of populations, but the introduction into what had been a predominantly English and Irish place of American ways of speech, and folk songs come to us in their American version rather than in the original Irish or Scots. All this is part of a continuous cultural relationship, especially with the West Coast, that out of loyalty perhaps to our British origins we have allowed, in our accounting of these things, to be forgotten or suppressed.

San Francisco and Sydney in the nineteenth century were already twin cities. The Lyster Opera Company for example, which for more than two decades after 1861 provided Sydney and Melbourne with regular opera seasons, had its home base in San Francisco. Australian vaudeville, which was still very much alive here until the late 1950s, was closer in style to American vaudeville than to English music hall; and American Country and Western music, after nearly a century of acclimatisation, has become in both senses of the term one of our liveliest indigenous arts. As early as 1827, Peter Cunningham, the convict-ships' surgeon whose *Two Years in New South Wales* is one of the best accounts of life in the colony, writes of the many foreigners who had taken up residence in Sydney. He speaks of French and Germans and Italians, and goes on, 'I had almost said Americans, but kindred ties prevent my ever proclaiming *them* as such'. The kindred tie persisted. When, not long after Federation, the new Australian Government invited the American Fleet to visit, the British had to be assured that this was not, as it clearly was, an attempt on our part to form our own Pacific ties.

There is a sense in which the Australian East Coast and the West Coast of America can be seen as opposite banks of a shared body of water. The reflection back and forth is a strong one, as it has always been, especially if we look these days at the demographic make-up of the two places (the strong presence of Asians, for example, in both populations), or at the lifestyle – surf culture, gay culture, food. (What we call 'modern Australian' cuisine is very like what the Americans call Californian.)

Once again the idea of ocean has been essential to how we define where we are and who it is we are most closely related to. In that shrinking of distance that is a characteristic of our world, even the Pacific, largest of oceans, has become a lake.

All this complicates any argument we might need

to make about the 'superstitious valuation' of Europe, or of our colonial link to Britain.

Our fate has been more complex than the American one, as Henry James defined it, and was so from the start. The tension for us is not simply between the old world and the new, or even, as I have been suggesting, between new and newer.

Unlike the Americans, we found ourselves in an opposite hemisphere to Europe, with contrary seasons, different plants and animals and birds, and different and disorientating stars overhead. This has meant a greater tension, for us, between environment or place on the one hand and on the other all the complex associations of an inherited culture. We have our sensory life in one world, whose light and weather and topography shapes all that belongs to our physical being, while our culture, the larger part of what comes to us through language for example, and knowledge and training, derives from another. This is indeed complex, though complexity is not an intolerable burden to minds as flexible as ours – or oughtn't to be. We are amazing creatures, we humans. Our minds can do all sorts of tricks and somersaults. And this form of complexity, the paradoxical condition of having our lives simultaneously in two places, two hemispheres, may be just the thing that is most original and interesting in us. I mean, our uniqueness might lie just here, in the *tension* between environment and culture rather than in what we can salvage by insisting on either the one or the other.

*

One of the 'superstitious valuations' I wanted to point to in Henry James' definition of 'complex fate' was that of age as opposed to newness; a valuation, as we have experienced it here, that has sometimes made our 210 years seem too small a purchase on time to constitute a genuine history.

But 210 years is not so short. Not if we think of it in terms of lives lived and of all the events and activities and passionate involvements that went into those lives: the things bought and sold, the ideas developed and given a new form, the work, the talk, all that is part of a single life in any single day and which, if we were to grasp the whole of it, we would have to multiply a million times over. Sometimes the only way we can get a sense of those lives, and all who lived them, is through the objects that they made and handled. An ancient midden, an axe-head, a fragment of wall painting: it may be no more than that, as we know from the way such survivals bring alive for us the 40,000 years of Aboriginal presence in this place.

The truth is that history, as we commonly conceive of it, is not what *happened*, but what gets recorded and told. Most of what happens escapes the telling because it is too common, too repetitious to be worth setting down. Even in places like this one where records *are* kept, the history that is in objects may need to be excavated and made visible before we can experience the richness it represents.

When I was growing up fifty years ago, what I think of now as the iconography of Australia – the visual record of all that has been done and made here – had not yet been gathered and made visible. Compared with Europe, the local world we had come out of seemed empty and thin.

Now, largely through the work of scholars and museum curators and editors, we can see that that world was not empty at all, but crowded with a making and doing as dense and productive as that of any other offshoot of an advanced civilisation. The evidence now is all about us. In town and country houses and grand public buildings; in country pubs and court houses and fire stations and old stone bridges, in barns, shearing sheds, bark huts; in the working landscape of ports. In all those necessary objects that make up our sort of living; bookcases and chaise longues and silver trophies and cast-iron railings and shoe buckles and biscuit tins. These things speak to us. They also speak *for* us, and for the many lives that lie behind us and lead up to us.

And 200 years is not so short a time in the life of a city, if we set Sydney and Melbourne, for example, beside Washington or Chicago or Leeds – or, to choose European cities that had their major growth in much the same period, Budapest or Berlin.

This business of making accessible the richness of the world we are in, of bringing density to ordinary, day-to-day living in a place, is the real work of culture. It is a matter for the most part of enriching our consciousness – in both senses of that word: increasing our awareness of what exists around us, making it register on our senses in the most vivid way, but also of taking all that *into* our consciousness and of giving it a second life there so that we possess the world we inhabit imaginatively as well as in fact. This has been especially important in the case of the land itself, and I mean by that everything that belongs to the land: its many forms as landscape, but also the birds, animals, trees, shrubs, flowers that are elements of its uniqueness; and most of all, the *spirit* of the land as it exists in all these things and can be touched and felt there.

Painting can do that for us – we have a long history here of landscape painting. So, with its subtle response to light, can photography. But it is in and through the written word, and especially poetry, that the process works best. This perhaps is because reading is itself an interiorising activity, a matter of 'taking things in'; perhaps because language, with its combination of image and rhythm, its appeal to the eye and to the way

152

our bodies move, is continuous with some activity in us that involves, in the most immediate way, mind and body both.

But the process is not always a simple one. Subtle adjustments may have to be made in the way we look at things before we can bring them within the range of our feelings and then, through words, give them a new life as consciousness.

One of the most eloquent of our early writers is the explorer John Oxley. His *Journals of Two Expeditions into the Interior of New South Wales, 1817–18* is the work of a man of real literary sensibility and an exuberant, if sometimes thwarted tendency to the romantic.

So long as what lies before him is desolate plains, 'deserts' he calls them, we see him struggling to find words for their undifferentiated dullness and for his own disappointment in them both as explorer and writer.

Country of this sort does not need the language he has brought along to describe it. It is unworthy of his generous range of 'feeling'. Each night, like a dutiful schoolboy, he writes up in his journal the landscapes he has crossed. It is heavy going. Then his party gets into rugged mountain country. They see a river that 'entered the glen', he writes, 'in a fall of vast height . . . A kangaroo was chased to the fall, down which it leapt and was dashed to pieces – like the hero', he adds, 'of Wordsworth's "Hart-Leap Well"'. This is on 14 September 1818.

Next day, Oxley's whole literary apparatus swings into action at last, and it is the appearance in the landscape of that literary ghost, the enabling image of Wordsworth's hart, as much as the landscape itself, that brings the land he has encountered into the realm of what he can now express.

'Quitting this place,' he writes, 'we proceeded up the glen, into which many streams fell from the most awful heights, forming so many beautiful cascades. After travelling five or six miles we arrived at that part of the river at which, after passing through a beautiful and level though elevated country, it is first received into the glen. We had seen fine and magnificent falls, each one of which excelled our admiration in no small degree, but the present one so surpassed anything we had previously conceived possible, that we were lost in admiration at the sight of this wonderful natural sublimity.'

And there it is at last, the Australian sublime. No sense here of that ironic limiting of Australian possibility (which is also, oddly enough, associated with a kangaroo) in which the earliest of our poets, Barron Field, discovers that the only rhyme our language provides for the continent is 'failure'.

What Oxley reveals is as good an example as we might find, and one that is especially useful because it comes so early, of the way a landscape that at first seems unfamiliar and estranging, to lie outside any possibility of response, can be brought into the world of feeling so that it belongs at last to the man who has entered it, comes to exist for him, through the power of words, as a thing *felt*, and therefore fully seen at last, fully experienced and possessed.

Writing in the 1960s, Judith Wright, who is our best reader of poetry as well as one of our finest poets, pointed out that 'except for the wattle . . . there is very little mention of trees, flowers and birds by name or by recognisable description in Australian verse during the nineteenth and early twentieth century'. This is not because they were not there in the landscape, to be seen and appreciated, but because there was as yet no place for them in the world of verse. The associations had not yet been found that would allow them entry there. They carried no charge of emotion. They had as yet played no part in the unfolding human drama. As we saw in the case of Oxley we may need to *bring* something to natural phenomena before they can reveal themselves to us. As Coleridge puts it, speaking of Nature itself: 'Lady, we receive but what we give'.

In writing of Christopher Brennan and the flowers he uses in his poetry, Judith Wright notes that they have a purely literary provenance. These roses and lilies are the flowers of Swinburne and Tennyson, 'not the familiar and unsung flowers of his new country – flowers which had as yet no ritual or symbolic significance and no meaningful associations in literature, even in the minds of his Australian countrymen'.

In fact, by the time Judith Wright was writing this, in 1963, it was no longer true. But only because the poets of her generation – she herself, pre-eminently, but also Douglas Stewart, David Campbell and Roland Robinson, and, when it comes to sea creatures, John Blight – had created a body of poetry in which all the common phenomena of our Australian world – flowers and trees and birds, and helmet shells and ghost crabs and bluebottles – had been translated out of their first nature into the secondary and symbolic one of consciousness, in that great process of culture, and also of acculturation, that creates a continuity at last between the life without and the life within. It is one of the ways – a necessary one – by which we come at last into full possession of a place. Not legally, and not just physically, but as Aboriginal people, for example, have always possessed the world we live in here: in the imagination. And I should just add that I am not suggesting this as yet another and deeper move in the long process of appropriating the continent and displacing its original owners, but as a move towards what is, in effect, a convergence of indigenous and non-indigenous understanding, a collective spiritual consciousness that will be the true form of reconciliation here. The convergence will take place in the imagination, and imagination is essential to it, as Judith Wright saw more than thirty years ago. And poetry is one of the first places where we see it in the making.

Earlier Australian poetry, even the best of Henry Kendall, had scarcely attempted this. The *Bulletin* writers of the 1890s, to quote Judith Wright again, had turned poetry here away from the possibilities of 'philosophy and interpretiveness towards simplicity, vigour and colloquialism', or towards 'sociable yarning', as another critic puts it, 'with a group of mates'. This was poetry of the outward life, of the soul in *action*, of Paterson's *Clancy of the Overflow* and *The Man from Snowy River*. It took another forty years, and a poet of great originality – and considering what had gone before, of extraordinary daring – to write a poem that broke out of these manly restrictions and dived inward, claiming for poetry the *right* to be inward, to be difficult, even obscure, so that the poem might speak for itself at last and get into words what had not yet come to consciousness, what was still 'feeling its way to air'. The poet was Kenneth Slessor; the poem 'South Country'.

After the whey-faced anonymity
Of river-gums and scribbly-gums and bush,

After the rubbing and the hit of brush,
You come to the South Country.

As if the argument of trees were done,
The doubts and quarrelling, the plots and pains,
All ended by these clear and gliding planes
Like an abrupt solution.

And over the flat earth of empty farms
The monstrous continent of air floats back
Coloured with rotting sunlight and the black
Bruised flesh of thunderstorms.

Air arched, enormous, pounding the bony ridge,
Ditches and hutches, with a drench of light,
So huge, from such infinities of height,
You walk on the sky's beach.

While even the dwindled hills are small and bare,
As if, rebellious, buried, pitiful,
Something below pushed up a knob of skull,
Feeling its way to air.

Landscape in this poem finally gets inside. It would
be difficult to say whether what is being presented
here is the image of a real landscape – precisely
described, objectively *there* – or an interior landscape
just breaking surface, just coming into existence, into

apprehension, of which the external one is a reflection. The poem in fact makes no distinction between the two, and part of its beauty and the pleasure it gives us is that it allows us to enter this state too, in which all tension between inner and outer, environment and being, is miraculously resolved.

'South Country' is an important moment in the development of consciousness in Australia. It is a poem that grants permission to us all to be men and women for whom the inner life is real and matters. And it has a special significance for writers: there is a sense in which the whole of modern Australian writing is 'feeling its way to air' in this poem – and not just poetry either, but fiction as well – in the same way that a whole line of Russian writers, as Turgenev tells us, came out from under Gogol's overcoat. But on this occasion what I want to point to is the resolution of that tension between inner life – mind – and the world of objects; between consciousness and environment.

It is in moments of high imagination and daring like the writing of 'South Country' that what Henry James called our 'complex fate' is most clearly visible, but as a tension that has been embraced, as a complexity that has been put to use, a condition made available to all of us as an agency for grounding ourselves both in a particular world and in our own skin.

3

Landscapes

Towards the end of the sixteenth century, the rich, hardworking little republic of the Netherlands, which was already on its way to becoming the largest economy in Europe, was struck by a craze, which became a mania and led to a second or black economy that threatened to overwhelm the first. It was a craze for tulip bulbs, the rarest of which, by the 1620s, were being exchanged at the rate of a single bulb for a good-sized country estate. At its peak, as on a real stock exchange, only the name of a bulb was needed for a transaction, and a General Bol or an Augustus could change hands for fantastic sums a dozen times in a single day.

This extraordinary phenomenon came about because the tulip, which now grows in vast fields around Lisse and has become, in the popular mind, along with windmills and clogs, a symbol of all things Dutch, was at the time an exotic, brought in, like so many of the plants we associate with the European garden, from the East, in this case from Turkey, via Vienna and Venice, and before that from Persia. Most fruits also came from the East – cherries, peaches, plums, mulberries, apricots – along with a good' many of the trees that now make up the recognisable landscapes of the various regions of Europe:

the poplars of Lombardy and central and northern France; the umbrella pines of the Mediterranean coast; the cypresses and olives of Provence and Tuscany; the plane trees that shade the streets of London and so many other cities. Imports all, that over the centuries have made the journey west and been acclimatised to create landscapes so deeply associated with particular scenes as to appear essentially and eternally European.

The European landscape is a *made* landscape, a work of 'culture' in both senses of the word.

We need to remember that in the five or six millennia before there were schools of agriculture or bio-technicians, or institutions like the CSIRO, the sophistication of plants and fruits and grasses through which modern foods came into existence was the business of ordinary farmers working with an altogether different form of science: the knowledge that comes from tradition and the questioning of tradition; by trial and error, on the ground.

This is art as well as work. We are makers, among much else, of landscapes. The land under our hands is shaped by the food we eat; by farming methods and ways of preparing and rotating fields; by the ways we hedge or wall or fence them; and by the laws we make for passing them on. We remake the land in our own image so that it comes in time to reflect both the industry and the imagination of its makers, and

gives us back, in working land, but also in the idealised version of landscape that is a park or garden, an
image both of our human nature and our power. Such
making is also a rich form of possession.

Fertility is the essence of it; greenness, both as an
actuality and as a metaphor for growth and fruitful-
ness; a feeling for green seems to be universal in us.
And why shouldn't it be? The new leaf, the return of
greenness, is a seasonal fact of the world we live in,
part of a cycle that gives shape to our lives and to
the way we see living itself. Even for desert people an
eye of green is the promise of continuity and rebirth.
Anyone who has seen an oasis in the desert will know
what a miracle it seems, how immediately it lifts the
spirits: a garden, which, to make maximum use of
the space, is arranged vertically – pomegranates and
peaches under stately date-palms, and, in their shade,
all mixed in together, every type of herb and salad
vegetable, and geraniums and stocks and daisies. The
idea of God's unpredictable bounty, of Grace as some
religions conceive it, is only an extension into the spiritual realm of a vivid fact.

And nature in Australia?

Over and over again, what the early settlers and
explorers have to say of the landscape they encountered here – Cook and Banks in 1770, Tench in 1788,
Oxley on the Western Plains in 1817, Mitchell in
Victoria in 1836 – was that it resembled, with its half

dozen trees to the acre and its rich grasses, a 'gentle-men's park'. This was the highest form of praise.

What they were referring to was the eighteenth-century style of English landscape-gardening practised by Capability Brown, as opposed for example to the regimented paths and geometric garden beds of Le Notre and the Italian gardens of the time, all playful fountains and mythological fantasy.

The English garden was an open woodland, planted or 'improved' to look like nature itself, or rather, nature as it appears, in idealised form, in the paintings of Poussin and Claude. What our gentlemen explorers found remarkable was that what, in England, Nature merely aspired to was in this new place Nature itself.

They were mistaken of course. What they did not see was that this nature, too, was a made one. They did not see it because they did not recognise either the hand of the maker or the method of making. Which was not, as in Europe, by felling with axes what was already there, but by forestalling new growth with the use of fire; by using fire-sticks to create open forests where new grass would attract grazing animals and make spaces wide enough for easy hunting. As Eric Rolls put it in *A Million Wild Acres*, 'Australia's dense forests are not the remnants of two hundred years of energetic clearing; they are the product of one hundred years of energetic growth,' because indigenous people were no longer there to manage them.

The landscape the first settlers came upon was, as we now recognise, a work of land management that native Australians had been practising for perhaps thousands of years. They had, over that time, created their own version of a useful landscape, a product of culture, and a reflection of it, every bit as much as the Italian or French or English; and they may earlier, we now believe, have changed the elements of the continent's vegetation; not by importing new and more competitive species, as Europeans did, but accidentally, and once again through their use of fire.

Before their coming, a large part of Australia had been covered with dry rainforest; the Araucarias (bunya and hoop-pine) that still cover large areas of southern Queensland and northern New South Wales, and the Antarctic beeches of which a small stand still remains at Springbrook in the hinterland of the Gold Coast. The eucalypt, though it was already on the move, was a minor component of the ancient landscape. The wider use of fire destroyed the rainforests and favoured the species that were resistant. The eucalypts and sclerophylls took over.

If you drive north from Sydney to Brisbane you come to a natural border, some way south of the political one, where the first bunyas and hoop-pines and silky oaks begin to appear. For me this is always a kind of homecoming to the spirit country of my earliest world, the familiar green, subtropical Australia that was for a long time the only Australia I knew. A world that was always lush green, evergreen.

In a continent as large as ours, there are many kinds of landscape, each of them typical of a particular region, no one more authentically Australian than another. I mention this because I am always taken aback when I hear Australians of a certain turn of mind claim that we will only be fully at home here when we have learned to love our desert places. My Australia, the one I grew up with, and whose light and weather and range of colour shaped my earliest apprehensions of the world, was not dry or grey-green: it was dense and luminous. The old idea that everywhere in Australia looks the same, the myth of the great Australian uniformity, was just that, a myth that was meant, I think, to confirm an Australian need, as if in this too the landscape was to be our model, for a corresponding conformity in the body social and politic. You need perhaps to believe in the *idea* of diversity, before you develop an eye for it in the world about you.

We can all learn to appreciate kinds of landscape other than the one we grew up with, to see what is unique and a source of beauty in them. But the landscape we most deeply belong to, that connects with our senses, that glows in our consciousness, will always be the one we are born into.

What indigenous Australians passed on to us, or

rather, what we took from them, was not untouched nature, or at least not in the places where we and they settled, but a *made* nature, which we went on to remake in our own way.

The land had received the imprint of culture long before we came to it. It had been shaped by use and humanised by knowledge that was both practical and sacred. It had been taken deep into the consciousness of its users so that all its features, through naming and storytelling and myth-making, had a second life in the imagination and in the mouths of women and men.

Here are two visions from that world. The first is an extract from one section of the best known of all Aboriginal song cycles, the Moon Bone Cycle, known, among so many that are not, because it has been so vividly translated for us by the anthropologist, R. M. Berndt:

Up and up soars the Evening Star, hanging there in the sky.
Men watch it, at the place of the Dugong and of the Clouds and of the Evening Star.
A long way off, at the place of the Mist, of Lilies and of the Dugong.
The lotus, the Evening Star, hangs there on its long stalk, held up by the Spirits.
It shines on that place of the Shade, on the Dugong place, and on the Moonlight clay-pan.

The Evening Star is shining, back towards Milingimbi,
and over the 'Wulamba people.

The second part of Song 30 from the Djanggawul
cycle was also translated by Berndt.

We walk along making the country, with the aid of
the *mauwulan rangga*.
We put the point of the *rangga* into the ground and
sing all the way along, swaying our hips.
Oh, *waridj* Miralaidj, our heads are lolling in
weariness!
Our bodies ache after our long journey from Bralgu!
We are making country, Bildjiwuraroiju, the large
sandhill at the Place of the Mauwulan.

What we did when we came here was lay new forms
of knowledge and a new culture, a new consciousness,
over so much that already existed, the product of many
thousands of years of living in and with the land.
This supplemented what was already there but did not
replace it, and cannot do so as long as any syllable of
that earlier knowledge exists in the consciousness of
even one woman or man.

A land can bear any number of cultures laid one
above the other or set side by side. It can be inscribed
and written upon many times. One of those forms
of writing is the shaping of a landscape. In any place

where humans have made their home, the landscape will be a made one. Landscape-making is in our bones.

*

I want to go back now to those eleven ships of the First Fleet and turn to another part of their precious cargo: the seeds and cuttings, all carefully labelled and packed, that were to be the beginning of a new landscape here; all of it the work of one man, Joseph Banks, President of the Royal Society, founder of the great gardens at Kew, Cook's companion on the voyage of 1770 and the man who first suggested Botany Bay as the site for a colony (he had the advantage of having been there).

If Lord Sydney and Governor Phillip were the fathers of the new society that grew up here, Banks is the father of the new natural world that came with it; not just the gardens that Grose saw as early as 1792, 'that flourish', as he says, 'and produce fruit of every variety – vegetables are here in great abundance', but, in time, of the wheatlands of the Darling Downs and the Western Plains, the orchards of Tasmania and the Riverina and the Granite Belt in Queensland, the vineyards of the Hunter and the Barossa and Margaret River in the west. Of the tree plantings, too, in country towns, some now so old and established as to form part of our national heritage; of our Botanical

Gardens, and of that special fondness we have here for exotic imports from South America and South Africa and Asia: the jacarandas we like to plant so that they will bloom in vivid combination with our native flame trees, the bauhinias and poincianas and African tulip trees of our suburban streets, the camphor laurels and Benjamani figs and deodars of older gardens.

We can imagine Banks, the 'amoroso of the Tahitian Islands' as Manning Clark called him, fifteen years after he had last been there, stepping back in imagination to the far side of the globe to play a godlike little game with himself, and with a whole continent, by doing what no man in history had ever done before: telescoping into a few hours and a single occasion what might have taken centuries – millennia even – in the natural course of things: the equipping of an arkload of plants suitable for a place, as he recalled it, with 'a climate similar to that of southern France' – apples, cherries, apricots, nectarines, red and white beets, early cauliflower, celery, sainfoin, nasturtium, broccoli, York cabbage – the makings of a very practical little garden of Eden, with due care taken for the good health of those it was to feed and with nice problems to be solved on the ground, since only trial and error, and a flair for inventiveness and guesswork, would determine which of the several varieties he had chosen would actually 'take' in a place where the soil and seasons were as yet unknown. Where the soil, as it turned out, lacked minerals and large animals to manure it, and the seasons were not an alternation of hot and cold, as in Europe, but of Wet Season and Dry.

Some of these plants had already made the slow journey westward from China and Persia, and had travelled on from Europe to the new Europe of the Americans. Others – tomatoes and maize and peppers and potatoes – had made the journey in the other direction, from west to east. Now they were to feed the even newer Europe in Australia. They were to make the landscape we all live in here – and live off as well – and whose produce we have sent out for the best part of 150 years to feed the world.

All this once seemed a bold and triumphant exercise, typical of the belief, which has been central to our culture, that nature is there for our delight and use, to be adapted and improved and made fruitful; the belief that intervention in the workings of Nature – by divine injunction in the seventeenth century, out of civic duty later – is part of what it is to be *human*.

These days we are less sure. This is because we have begun to be aware at last of what such radical intervention may mean, especially in a continent like ours that has turned out to be more fragile than we first understood and less naturally suited than we believed to the kinds of farming and pastoralism we have imposed upon it.

Eric Rolls, a poet as well as an historian, who writes better about the Australian landscape, with more affection and a keener eye for its intimate life than any other man here, describes what the earliest settlers found when they first came upon it. 'The surface was so loose that you could rake it through your fingers. No wheel had marked it, no leather heel, no cloven foot – every mammal, humans included, had walked on padded feet. Our big animals did not make trails. Hopping kangaroos usually move in scattered company, not in damaging single file like sheep and cattle . . . Every grass-eating mammal had two sets of teeth to make a clean bite. No other land had been treated so gently.'

The damage since has been severe: the breaking up of the soil and the trampling of the grass by hoofed animals, indiscriminate clearing, erosion, the draining of swamps that has led to salination through a rise in the water table, the damage to our rivers through excessive irrigation and through chemical pollution.

This degradation of the environment is one reason why we no longer feel triumphant. Another is the doubt many of us have about whether our particular way of doing things is the *only* way, the only human way – a doubt, by the way, that would not have occurred to our predecessors: it only occurs to us because we began, a few decades ago, to interest ourselves in comparative anthropology; in the way other cultures see the world and interact with it.

We live in close proximity here to a people whose way of looking at things is quite different from ours; and while they have not lived entirely without intervening in the workings of Nature, they have, in fact, dealt gently with it, and, in their long experience of the place, have learned a thing or two about how to live in cooperation with its strange and unpredictable ways. We now recognise this.

Nature once seemed all-powerful, a force before which man, with his puny strength, was entirely vulnerable. These days, in one of those odd reversals that occur in human thinking, it is Nature itself that seems vulnerable – fragile, precarious, constantly in need of our protection and care. Its resources no longer seem infinite. We need to preserve and protect them if we ourselves are to survive, and to do this we need to listen carefully to what the experts have to tell us, and to both sides when they disagree. To many people who care about these things it is already too late to save the continent and, as some of them insist, the planet itself. Eric Rolls, in his quiet and pragmatic way, is more reassuring. 'It is not too late,' he tells us, 'to make corrections, the knowledge is available.'

It is partly because Rolls is by nature so reasonable, partly because he has himself been a farmer, that he is unwilling to ascribe all that has been done here to contempt for the land or to simple greed; nor does he put Nature's needs at every point before our need to feed ourselves. 'The greatest song of the land,' he writes, 'is the food it produces. One cannot blame European settlers for bringing in the livestock and plants that have done so much damage here, it would have been unnatural for them to settle in a new country without the feed that they knew.'

Rolls is passionate but he is neither evangelical nor apocalyptic. The important thing for him is that the way we use the land should be sensible and informed. But there are many people for whom nature in these last years has become the last repository of the sacred. Saving it, saving every last scrap of it, every species, every tree and plant, is a religious duty. The struggle between farmers and conservationists, loggers and conservationists, has become for them another and later version of the old fight between moral and spiritual purity on one hand and on the other the devil's work that is inherent in the day-to-day business of being in the world. Evangelical and apocalyptic language, and a hectoring self-righteousness, powers their energy and gives shape to their rhetoric.

The fervour is understandable and may even be necessary; but self-righteousness is not a pretty phenomenon. Neither is religion when it develops an edge of fanaticism. I am thinking of those holy vandals of the late sixteenth and early seventeenth century who, out of pure Protestant zeal, knocked the heads off statues in Lady Chapels and smashed every stained-glass window in East Anglia. Our culture is subject to these waves of purifying zeal, and Australia has not been exempt in the past from outbreaks of radical purity.

Wowserism at the end of the nineteenth century led a crusade against drink, sex and every form of pleasure, and imposed a censorship here that lasted for more than sixty years. A fanatical racism once seemed inseparable from the very idea of nationhood. It would rigorously have excluded Asians, blacks, Jews, and such 'inferior' southern Europeans as Italians, Greeks and Maltese, in the attempt to preserve a purity of race that would guarantee for Australians an eternally white and, if possible, eternally Protestant history.

In their latest incarnation these puritanical exclusionists have chosen Nature as their sphere. Their aim is the expulsion from our parks and gardens and foreshores of every bush, plant and flower that is not a *bona fide* native. Not so much out of concern for the health of the environment, the need to conserve water, for example – though that is sometimes a part of the argument – as for the health of the nation, our sense of ourselves as Australians. Only when the last non-native shrub and flower has been grubbed out of the earth, and our hearts no longer leap up at the sight of a daffodil or a bed of tulips at the Canberra Floriade, will we have broken free at last of the old superstitious nostalgia for Europe and be ourselves natives, at least in spirit, of our Australian land. This is the most fundamental form of an argument that only what belongs uniquely to this place, that derives all its elements from the *life* of the place, can be authentically Australian. That Australia must be kept free of all alien pollutants and influences. That if we, as individuals and as a nation, are to be unique, only the uniqueness of the land can shape us.

This may present itself as an authentically local passion, but is more culturally determined than its adherents suspect. What is new in it is the strong associations carried by the word 'native'.

Once applied only to Aborigines, it was appropriated by the first generation of the native-born as a sign of their difference from settlers and other imports, and as a claim to belonging. We have long since given up that claim to it; we no longer speak of ourselves as 'native'. Perhaps, as some of our radical conservationists use the term, we are meant to see in the exclusive claim of 'natives' to a place here, not only an argument about the land but a restorative gesture towards its original owners. The gesture may be a noble one, but is not, in its exclusiveness, in the spirit of Aboriginal practice in dealing with the world, which seems more concerned, in its pragmatic way, with what is present and on the ground; with re-imagining the scene to include all that is now in it, rather than looking back nostalgically to what was there twenty or even 200 years ago.

This capacity to re-imagine things, to take in and adapt, might be something we should learn from, something that comes closer than a nostalgia for lost purity to the way the world actually is, and also to the way it works. It might remind us as well of something we need to keep in mind: which is the extent to which Aboriginal notions of inclusiveness, of re-imagining the world to take in all that is now in it, has worked to include *us*.

Writing of an early moment in our history, Alan Atkinson, in *The Europeans in Australia*, speaks movingly of Bennelong's relations with Phillip, and suggests that Bennelong may have made a larger leap in incorporating Phillip into his world, in opening his view of things to include all that Phillip stood for, than the Governor or any of his officers had to make to find a place for *him*.

They had come here *expecting* to find natives. They had an impeccable document that outlined how they should deal with them, and knew, either from previous experience or from their reading in Montaigne and Shakespeare and Rousseau, and from Defoe's *Robinson Crusoe*, what a native might be, and from Cook and Banks what *these* natives might be. But Bennelong was not expecting this meeting.

He had no preparation for it but his own capacity to observe, open his imagination, and respond.

What he made of Phillip, the room he made in his world for Phillip's authority and for Phillip's house as a 'sacred site' (he was eager, for example, that his daughter should be born in its grounds), speaks for an act of accommodation, of inclusiveness, that is an example to each one of us, and, considering all that followed, a shame to each one of us as well. But Bennelong, however weak he may have been in physical power, had behind him the strength of a culture that in being old had developed, in its long view of things, an extraordinary capacity to accept change and take in what was new and must be adapted to. It is in terms of that long view that what we have made here will be judged; and in the shaping of a collective consciousness, mixed but truly native, Bennelong's inclusive view, his imaginative leap, may turn out to have been the most important element in that first and fateful meeting of two worlds.

4

Monuments to Time

The Brisbane I grew up in in the late 1930s and early 1940s was a sprawling, subtropical town with a style of domestic architecture that was all its own, and which comes as close as we get here to an urban vernacular. One-storeyed weatherboard, with a tin roof, verandahs, and, since the house sits high on stumps, an under-the-house closed in with lattice, it is a style that is directly responsive to the climate and to the city's hilly terrain, and makes use as well of local timbers: hardwood for the weatherboard exterior, hoop-pine for the interior tongue-and-groove. The same materials were also used, on a larger scale, for churches, including some high-pitched, turreted affairs that are their own form of antipodean Gothic.

If anything made me aware of being Australian, and specifically a Queenslander, it was the house I grew up in. I have written elsewhere of how its spaces determined early habits of living, of mapping the world, as well as my first sensory responses; of the way that living, as we did, in weatherboard houses on high stumps, creates a certain sort of consciousness.

They have about them the improvised air of tree houses. Airy, open, often with no doors between the rooms, they are on such easy terms with breezes, with the thick foliage they break into at window level, with the lives of possums and flying-foxes, that living in them, barefoot for the most part, is like living in a reorganised forest. The creak of timber as the day's heat seeps away, the gradual adjustment in all its parts, like a giant instrument being tuned, of the house-frame on its stumps, is a condition of life that goes deep into consciousness. It makes the timber house dweller, among the domesticated, a distinct subspecies.

But the truth is that most people in my youth were ashamed of this local architecture. Timber was a sign of poverty, of our poor-white condition and backwardness: it made 'bushies' of us. Safe houses, as everyone knows, are made of brick – think of the *Three Little Pigs*. Timber is primitive. The fact that you could, on any day of the week in Brisbane, see a whole house being carted through the streets on the back of a lorry suggested that there was something impermanent, makeshift, about these dwellings, but also about the places where they were set down. Queensland was full of ghost towns whose houses had been carted off to make a new town elsewhere. It wasn't until the late 1960s that our shabby weatherboards got a new lick of paint, a new name – Old Queenslanders – and Brisbane's beautiful inner suburbs, with tin roofs flashing in the gullies among paw paw, mango and banana trees, or on hilltops among the original hoop-pines and bunyas, were recognised at last as 'interesting', even unique, and our comfortable weatherboards as one of the distinctive forms of a domestic architecture that, variously produced from state to state, represents one of our most original achievements as Australians and a happy addition to the local scene.

Even when the basic style is imported, as in the case of the Sydney terrace, the up-and-down nature of the streets gives it a different rhythm from the British original, and the decoration a new and less formal accent. A Sydney terrace is not at all like a terrace in Liverpool or Newcastle upon Tyne. Not least in the profusion of the decoration and its sense of fantasy – lions rampant and couchant, and urns, Welsh dragons, flame-like filials – and the flamboyance with which its cast-iron balconies celebrate local flora in the form of ferns and lilies, or ethnic identity in thistles and Irish harps.

If we need a reference for such originality in the adaptation of an imported style, we might find it in the colonial houses of the United States, whose lovely incongruity lies in their being built in a correct Queen Anne or Georgian style but in timber rather than brick, and then painted bright yellow or emerald green or burgundy. It makes them, if we know the original, look problematical and wrong – a mistake, it might seem, or a provincial joke. But because of their lightness, the confidence with which they are set down in the new place and the rightness of their colours in the watery light, the old style translated becomes something fresh and original.

I took our weatherboard house for granted. I didn't

think it particularly beautiful – I barely thought of it at all. It was simply where we lived, the only sort of house I had ever known. What I did think about, and puzzle over, when I looked at Brisbane and asked myself what sort of city I was growing up in, was our public buildings.

Built for the most part between Separation, in 1859, and the late 1880s when Brisbane was not much more than 20,000 souls, they *were* of stone, local sandstone. Big, imposing monuments to – to what?

In a variety of styles – Italian Renaissance, French Renaissance, Palladian – that had little to do with the real history of a place that had only recently been reclaimed from densely wooded, subtropical rainforest, they were, it seemed to me, incongruously and pretentiously plonked down where they simply did not belong.

They were impressive, certainly, you could not miss that. Or their confidence. Solid gestures towards the future, they were landmarks of a city that had not yet come into existence, the 'grand centre of civilisation', to steal Darwin's phrase, that would one day grow up around them and, leaving behind at last the memory of tin-roofed stores and weatherboards and verandahed pubs, be equal at last to what their buildings had in mind. They belonged to Time rather than Space. To a city that even in my youth had not yet seized the occasion to appear.

If our flimsy wooden houses were the product of

geography, of a response to climate and to the peculiar topography of the place, these grand public buildings were the product of history, of that form of it called culture. But to what extent could one think of them as local and Australian rather than as impressive reproductions of a more real and authentic Over There?

That others of my generation shared these doubts is revealed by the number of these grand old buildings that were pulled down in other places in the 1950s and sixties to make way for architecture that was more modern, more 'appropriate'.

The results, in Sydney for example, were devastating. Half the nineteenth-century city was destroyed. It might just as well have had its heart ripped out under the fury of aerial bombardment. The line of buildings that still remain along Macquarie Street and around Bent and Bridge Streets, and the single block of the Queen Victoria Building, show us something of what was lost.

Other places were barely touched. In Adelaide most of King William Street has survived, and so has North Terrace. And until the oil and mineral boom of the late 1960s, Brisbane too escaped. Brisbane and Adelaide were poor. Sydney, in the decade of the Southern Vandals, had the misfortune to be rich.

So what I have to say is in some ways an attempt at reparation, a late tribute to what, forty years ago, I did not recognise because I did not have the eyes as yet to see what was there.

I had known these buildings for as long as I could remember. A nervous ten-year-old, I had stood in the middle of the big empty ballroom at Old Government House on a cold winter's afternoon and bowed my way through the studies and solo pieces I had chosen for the AMEB music exams. On hundreds of afternoons on my way home from school, I had waited for the West End tram outside the old Treasury Building on North Quay. Among so much that was merely patched together, and rotting and peeling, they had such an air of permanence, these old buildings: the Customs House, the Post Office, the State Parliament. They were the nearest thing we had to something ancient and historical.

What disturbed me most, I think, was that I had always found them beautiful, even moving, but I distrusted their beauty and could not understand why I was moved. If I do now, it is because I have liberated myself from the narrow assumptions about what is appropriate, or authentic, that prevented me then from seeing what these buildings were doing, what they were for. To see that I had to look elsewhere.

*

In the early eighteenth century Lord Burlington and his followers had begun to build country houses in England in the style of the Venetian architect Palladio, a style that was already 100 years out of date when they took it up, and itself a kind of folly; a fantasia, though a very restrained one, on Classical themes, which Palladio had translated from an imaginary South, all bosky groves and warm honeyed light, and set down among the misty valleys and hills of the Veneto. Burlington translated the style a second time, to the Home Counties, where it established itself so thoroughly, in the form of winged villas and arcaded loggias, that it became the prevailing British style for the next century and a half.

That the style did not at first sit easily with the English climate is suggested in Pope's gentle mockery of those who built, as he says:

> Long arcades through which the cold winds roar,
> Proud to catch cold at a Venetian door.

What were the English Palladians doing with this late Renaissance version of the Classical? That it *was* Classical gives us the clue.

The late seventeenth and early eighteenth centuries in England were a time when the Classical world, and particularly Augustan Rome, the age of Virgil and Horace, represented the ideal of elegance and achieved order and beauty, and a model of what the civilised and civilising spirit might achieve, not only in poetry but in all the arts. Palladianism was the equivalent in architecture of the heroic couplet – of Pope's *Moral Essays* and *The Rape of the Lock*, works whose tone might be playful, mock-heroic as well as heroic, but whose intention was always serious. It was an attempt to claim for eighteenth-century England a continuity, not an historical continuity, but one of the spirit, with Augustan Rome, that would encourage Roman ways of thinking and feeling, Roman virtues, on English soil. In this the particulars of climate and place were irrelevant. It was a matter of mind, of imagination, and Palladio had already shown the way. If Classical forms could be translated from the heat and glare of the South to misty Venice, then why not to misty Buckinghamshire?

The point of these pedimented villas and domed rotundas was not to *express* place but to redefine and transcend it. By setting a Palladian building down on English soil, what might be coaxed from the English landscape were the qualities of an Italian one; not as they existed in any real place, even in Italy, but as they appeared, along with the usual Virgilian and Arcadian associations, in the idealised landscapes of Poussin and Claude.

It is in the light of this view of architecture, this way of using it to exert a force on the sites it occupied, that I came to look again – but really for the first time – at my Brisbane buildings.

To take the immediate example of Old Government House. Far from being yet another example of servile colonialism, a nostalgic glance towards the Home Counties, its Palladian pretensions quite out of place in subtropical Queensland, mightn't we see it as doing just what the same style had done for Burlington – claiming for this new place a continuity with the Classical world and its values (Governor Bowen, who built it, was a renowned classicist); imposing on the local land-scape – in this case Brisbane's old Botanical Gardens with their bamboos and Moreton Bay figs and hoop-pines and bunyas – the aesthetic order of Poussin and Claude, and in this way legitimising, domesticating within the arcadian world of those classical painters, Brisbane's exotic flora and tempestuous late-afternoon skies?

Governor Bowen, who was fond of drawing a comparison, both topographical and climatic, between Queensland and Naples, might even have seen it as restoring the style to an original, 'Mediterranean' envi-ronment where it was more at home than it could ever have been in either southern England or the Veneto.

Of course, this kind of thinking is very far from the theories about building that have prevailed in our own century, in which architectural forms are related, in an organic way, to the landscape they stand in, or emerge directly from it. Only recently has Post-modernism, with its eye for the playfully eclectic, raised the possi-bility of a different way of looking at things; one that has allowed us to regard our older buildings with renewed interest, as products of an age when architectural design was a matter of spirited play – between landscape and culture, style and history, history and function; but *strong* play. Play with a purpose. Play as an act of bold appropriation.

I am speaking here of a time, the mid-nineteenth century, when Australia saw itself not as a primitive outpost of the known world but as a participant in all that was happening in an exciting and expansive age. It was remote certainly, but not for that reason either behind the times or out of competition with what was being done on the international scene. If public buildings in our cities presented a set of variations on past historical styles, this was not out of nostalgia for someone else's history, or because the place lacked a history of its own, but because it saw itself as being up with the contemporary. Men built here as they were building at the time in Paris and Vienna and Budapest. On the same principle and in pretty much the same styles.

This feeling for period, and for period styles, was something new.

A sense of history, of what is still alive and accessible in past times and past objects, has not always been part of our sensibility. Until well into the nineteenth century, things were either ancient – that is, classical – or they were modern. Only the antique was capable of eliciting a romantic response, and this was almost entirely literary. Greek and Roman ruins were eloquent. They spoke to the heart, because they belonged to the world of Virgil and Homer.

No such associations were evoked by the gothic. The medieval world of heraldry and castles and tournaments and chivalry had not yet become, as it would be later, the repository of everything noble and picturesque, the great spiritual escape from industry and steam. Gothic buildings, which were invariably in a poor state of repair, were merely decrepit and old. Relics of a dead past and an age that, for modern taste, was primitive and barbaric. They were leftover rubble, taking up space that might better be filled with the living, with what belonged to the new world of light and speed.

When Victor Hugo began *The Hunchback of Notre Dame*, in 1829, the great cathedral that stood at the centre of his book was a dilapidated ruin. Solemn and neglected, in a style that spoke too clearly of ancient unrefinement and a brutality for which modern people of cultivation could feel only a fastidious revulsion, it was an embarrassment, an ignominious wreck. It was Hugo's extraordinary imagination that restored its grandeur and mystery and made Notre Dame, with its fantastic waterspouts and gargoyles, its buttresses and high inner spaces, the embodiment, for a later generation, of the very spirit of Paris. The vast popularity of Hugo's novel made Gothic (with a capital letter now) the high point of all that was finest in the recent past, and French Gothic the highest achievement of French civilisation. This was one of the great revolutions of the age.

But for the men who remade Paris and London in the 1840s and 1850s, the old was simply old: filthy alleys that clogged the city with foul odours, tenements that were the breeding ground of crime and every sort of infectious disease. They had no compunction about clearing away such rubbish so that these great cities could be what every city aspired to be – that is, modern.

Balzac had written evocatively of the old Paris, as Dickens did of London, but very little of what they describe survived their lifetimes. The wooden galleries of *Lost Illusions*, the original of Tom-all-Alone's in *Bleak House*, the nightmarish bridges and walkways across which the Artful Dodger leads Oliver in *Oliver Twist* – all were swept away by the new science of town planning to make apartment blocks or residential squares for the expanding middle class, and thoroughfares, boulevards, for traffic, or to clear a path for the railways and a space for those temples to Progress, the big new terminal stations, the Gare de Lyon, the Gare d'Orsay, St Pancras, Euston. As late as 1871, when the Tuileries and the Hôtel de Ville were damaged during the Paris Commune, the authorities thought them not worth preserving, though they were by no means beyond repair.

To have none of these old relics to deal with was to a city's advantage. The Australian cities, along with such newly laid out, post-industrial cities as Leeds, Manchester and Newcastle upon Tyne, which until recently had been little more than large villages, had the good fortune to be modern already, and Melbourne thought of itself as having the edge on Sydney because it had been planned from the start, whereas the elder city had grown up higgledy-piggledy and had much early rubbish to remove.

Vienna offers a good example of the way the age looked at things.

When the medieval walls of Vienna were pulled down in the late 1850s to make way for the Ringstrasse, most of what remained of the pre-Baroque city went with them. What was raised in its place was 'modern'. That is: the Opera House was neo-Baroque, the National Theatre and the two great Museums, as befits houses of culture, were neo-Renaissance, the Town Hall and the University neo-Gothic, and the Parliament Greek.

Now the Austro-Hungarian Empire, in point of fact, has no more direct relationship with ancient Greece than Australia has, or the United States; but classical Greek in the Kaiserlich and Königlich nineteenth century seemed as proper a gesture towards liberal democracy as it had been earlier for the Capitol in Washington and the Assemblé Nationale in Paris.

In the same way, Gothic, on the model of Oxford and Cambridge and Marburg and Göttingen, seemed proper for a university, not only in Vienna but all over the world.

I have gone this long way about to create as precisely as I can the contemporary context – the idea of a city, and specifically a modern city – in which we need to place Australian buildings of the period if we are to see what their makers had in mind; the claim these government offices, and banks and stock exchanges and galleries and museums, were making for Australia as an internationally up-to-date place and as Europe translated. The claim was to the continuation of an ideal rather than an actual history. It was the same claim that was being made in Paris or Vienna, where after all a real history, if that was what you wanted, was already available on the ground.

What we are dealing with here is an Australia that saw itself, in cultural terms, not as colonial but as confidently provincial, standing in the same relationship to London as Dublin or Leeds or Edinburgh, or, to put it another way, as Palmyra or Baalbek or Leptis Magna did to second-century Rome. A lack of history can free you from history by leaving you free to play with the historical and construct an ideal history of the spirit or mind.

When I look again at Brisbane's most triumphant building, J. J. Clark's Treasury – it is now the Brisbane

191

casino; we too have our playful mode – what I see is an attempt, a bold one, very forward looking and ideas-driven, to claim for this site above the river, and for what till then had been a town of unsealed streets and only the most modest timber dwellings, the sort of Italianate possibilities that go with its grandeur of design; the entrepreneurial energies of Italian Renaissance bankers, the independence and enterprise of the Italian city-states. It is a matter of using style, conjoined with function, to exert force on a site, and to open up within it a whole range of social and economic possibilities. It would be quite wrong to see such a building as offering no more than a comfortable evocation of the European and familiar – to see it, I mean, as nostalgic. It is too commanding for that. It exerts too strong a force, establishes too many tensions, speaks too boldly of ambition and local power. Like the gem-like Customs House in the next bend of the river, its aim is to redefine the site by deepening its associations in a way that will make the building's uses seem natural, sanctioned by long association, and in that way to appropriate a future for it. But its aim is also to make the site itself more complex and open to possibility, adding to climate and vegetation a cultural dimension, and shifting what can be seen – the site's natural history – in the direction of what is there as yet only in potential, a future that will be determined not by nature or past history but by the calling of new forces on to the scene.

*

The scene.

If there is something of the theatrical, something of the stage-set about these buildings, then that surely is part of their intention. They are, like a stage-set, meant to be both a proper scene for action and an inspiration and guide to action, encouraging, by their very size and assurance, but most of all by the references inherent in their style, a grandeur and confidence of gesture that might push a man towards illustrious performance. In the same way, Gothic halls of residence, Gothic cloisters and quadrangles, were meant, by a kind of associative process, to encourage a devotion to scholarly excellence. The set was there – it was up to those who entered it to fill the scene with appropriate action.

These buildings have an air of magic as well as theatre about them. They were magic boxes, a good part of their function as galleries, banks, city halls, treasuries, parliaments being to give those who entered them access to power, which they would acquire by setting themselves in the line of a powerful continuity.

What I have been looking back to is a time when culture, as it was embodied in our long European inheritance, was the determining factor in the creation of our Australian world. In the choice between culture on the one hand and geography on the other, the nineteenth century comes down firmly on the side of culture; on what belongs to mind. Arguing from there made nineteenth-century Australia confident because powerful. Even over-confident. The idea grew up that if we could only keep ourselves pure, it would one day be our privilege, as a nation, to carry forward into history the British ideal.

But this ambition for empire, for a manifest destiny, came at a price. It introduced a note of anxiety, which deepened and has never gone away.

Strange as it may seem at this distance, we were most confident, most sure of where we stood, both as regards space and time, when we saw ourselves in a provincial relationship to a world that was itself central and stable. The desire to stand alone, to have a destiny and a history of our own, was inevitable of course, and necessary, but it destabilised us, introducing first a resentful sense of being marginal, of being colonial and irrelevant to the main course of things, then an endless worrying back and forth about how we were to ground ourselves and discover a basis for identity. Was it to be in what we had brought to the place or what we found when we got here? Was cultural inheritance to define us, even in the radically changed form that being in a new place demanded, or the place itself?

But the belief that we must make a choice is an illusion, and so, I'd suggest, if we are to be whole, is the possibility of choosing. It is our complex fate to be children of two worlds, to have two sources of being, two sides to our head. The desire for something simpler is a temptation to be *less* than we are.

Our answer on every occasion when we are offered the false choice between this and that should be, 'Thank you, I'll take both.'

5

The Orphan in the Pacific

The 1950s, precisely because they mark a watershed in the life of modern Australia, have become a disputed area. They are for some the last time in our history when old-fashioned frugality and a sense of duty mattered to people; when you could still leave the front door open while you slipped down to the shops; when it was still shameful to be divorced; when gentlemen still gave up their seats to ladies on the tram; when backyards in the cities still had a vegetable patch and a wire-netting enclosure for chooks that kept city folk in touch with country matters and made city kids aware of where eggs come from and that the chicken they were eating had once had a head – though not perhaps what any four-year-old today could tell them, which is where they themselves had come from, unless it was from under one of the cabbages their dad grew down the back.

It was the last time, too, when most Australians shared the same culture; that is, when there was no significant divide between high and low culture and none, certainly, between youth culture and the rest. When families had their own seats at the Saturday night pictures and were loyal to the Regent or the Metro whatever film happened to be on. When the races dominated the radio on Saturday afternoons and everyone had the number of an SP bookie. When rodeos were still a city spectacle, and English comedy shows such as *Much Binding in the Marsh* and *Take It from Here*, and vaudeville houses with their strong flavour of vernacular humour, had not yet been replaced by American sitcoms; when we still told Dad and Dave or Dave and Mabel jokes, most of them dirty.

At sixteen, as I was in 1950, I could mix Tex Morton, big band jazz, and Gladys Moncrieff in *Rio Rita*, with the Top Twenty, the Amateur Hour, the Lux Radio Theatre and the Borovansky Ballet, the surf every weekend, and the last episodes of *The Search for the Golden Boomerang* – all with no sense that I was doing anything but responding to what most interested and amused me. High culture was there – Australia in those years was still on the international concert circuit and in the late 1940s I heard almost every great conductor and instrumentalist of the day – but it was simply part of the mix. So were we. I had not yet discovered that names I had known all my life like Uscinski and Rasmussen and Reithmuller were 'foreign', or that my own name was as well. It didn't feel foreign and was so common around Brisbane that most people did not take it that way. All very comfortable, it sounds, and secure and cosy. Still, I have other memories of the time that are none of those.

Like most young people, I saw the world as excitingly new and full of possibility, but what struck me in the adult world around me was a kind of anxiety at the centre of people's lives, a sense of resentment, of disappointment or hurt; a prickliness, too, that could easily become mean-spirited mockery and contempt for anything 'different' – large gestures, extravagant emotions; a suspicion of everything 'out there' that might challenge our belief that the world we had here, however ingrown and pinched it might seem to outsiders, was the biggest, the fairest, the sunniest, the healthiest, the best fed.

What was it that had scared us? What were we afraid of?

Communism, of course. Reds, both outside and, more insidiously, within. The infection of Europe: all those recent horrors that we imagined might be brought in, like germs, with those who were fleeing from them. The sick disorder and obscenity of Modernism, and especially of *modern art*, whose cleverness and assault on traditional beliefs and values, we thought, were meant to make fools of us – well, we were *not* fooled! American culture and commercialism. But there were some of us who were also in love with it: American pop songs and musicals. American writing, American style in the way of Levi jeans and Cornel Wilde hair-cuts, American films – though much that we took to be American, as it came to us from the Hollywood dream factory, was shot through with the darker tones of Europe. It was in the popular and commercial form of the movies, held in such contempt by local intel-lectuals, that we had our first contact with forms of Modernism – contemporary music, for example, or German Expressionism – from which we were other-wise protected.

It seems to me now to be a world that was forever crouched in an attitude of aggrieved and aggressive self-defence. Closed in on itself. A stagnant backwater and sullenly proud of the fact. A world that had not come to terms with wounds, deep ones, that some-thing in the national psyche, or our Digger code, did not allow us to speak about or even to feel as deeply as we might need to do if we were to be whole again.

The lack of tradition in our writing for dealing with anything but the external life – manly action in the open – meant that the experience of the trenches, that moment in Western history when a break occurred in our long-held belief in progress and the benign nature of technology, went unexpressed here. There was no local equivalent of Wilfred Owen or of *All Quiet on the Western Front*. The horror, the deep pain of that experience, was not recreated here in the kind of imaginative form that allows a society to come to terms with itself by taking what it has suffered deep into its consciousness and reliving it there in the form of meaning rather than as muddle and shock.

We began to think of ourselves as having been betrayed – of our willingness, our good nature, as having been taken advantage of. At Gallipoli. In the last days of the war in France, when we had made so large a sacrifice but received so little acknowledge-ment of it. At the Peace Conference afterwards, where the British had thwarted our attempts to acquire the German possessions in the Pacific, and granted those that lay north of the equator to the Japanese, thus bringing one step closer what most Australians saw as a potential aggressor.

Events out there seemed to have developed a quality that reduced us, for all our larrikin know-how and swagger, to victims. There was the death overseas, among strangers as we thought of it, of Phar Lap and Les Darcy. There was the swamping of our cinema industry, which had begun so strongly and was so lively and confident, by the superior power, the *money* power, of Hollywood. There was the Bodyline series. All these blows, large and small, had shaken our confidence, made us draw back in distrust of the world, but also of ourselves and of one another.

There was also the censorship. On books, on films, on any idea that might corrupt us morally or shake the society up by questioning values so firmly entrenched, so universally accepted, that to go against even the least of them might begin a fragmentation that could never be repaired.

To read *Ulysses* you had to get permission from the State Librarian, who kept it under lock and key in his office. It was not for sale. And it was still forbidden to advertise condoms (men and boys got them 'under the counter' at the barbers) or to publish information of any kind about birth control.

In Queensland, where I lived, in an odd reversal of what everywhere else in the world is regarded as civilised behaviour, the law forbade us to eat and drink on the same premises.

It is easy to laugh at these foolish restrictions. But they were only the visible sign of something larger and more insidious – more disabling, too. A sense of embattlement against life itself, a fear not just of the threat from without but of the even darker forces that lurked within. We were terrified, I think, of discovering that the body, for all our shame and fear of it, was harmless and that pleasure too might be harmless; that ideas, even dangerous ideas, ones that put us at risk, might be as essential to our wholeness and good health as cod-liver oil or Vegemite.

Meanwhile, it seemed, only the acceptance of a strict conformity would save us from ourselves and society from a collapse into total degeneracy: National Service, a vote for Mr Menzies, moral and legal restrictions backed up by a system of official and unofficial pimping and prying that used nice-looking young policemen to entrap homosexuals in public lavatories, and divorce agents, hired by the 'aggrieved party', to burst into hotel bedrooms and expose adulterers in the act of being what the newspapers on Sunday called 'intimate'.

Comfortable, secure, cosy?

*

What is most striking about earlier periods in Australian history – say the 1830s to the 1880s – is the sense of openness and optimism the place generated, in spite of droughts, economic slumps like the one that shook the country in the early 1840s, or the disappointing discovery that the continent had no great inland river system like that of the United States.

As early as 1810, Lachlan Macquarie, newly arrived as Governor of NSW, speaks in a letter to his brother of the 'flourishing condition' in which he found the colony. 'Indeed the whole country,' he writes, 'is much more advanced in every kind of improvement than I could have supposed possible in the time it has been settled.' He did not add that this was the more remarkable because for all but three or four of those years Britain had been engaged in a major Continental war.

Peter Cunningham, in 1828, writes of 'gentlemen foreigners, tempted by the fineness of our country and climate to take up permanent abode among us. Frenchmen, Spaniards, Germans . . . all add to the variety of language current among us . . . In the streets of Sydney, too, may often be seen groups of natives of the numerous South Sea Islands with which we trade . . . a considerable proportion of the Othesians [Tahitians] and New Zealanders are employed as sailors in the vessels that frequent our ports.' This reminds us that Sydney at this time was still mainly a seaport, and that Australia was still a place open to nationalities other than the British.

Cunningham also remarks on how a passion for the outdoors in all classes of Australians already marks them as quite different from Englishmen. 'Young men,' he writes, 'think no more of swimming out a mile or more, and back, than a stranger would of taking a walk the same distance' – although the great Victorian respectability, which was introduced here two decades before its time by the Macquaries, and in some ways never receded, soon decreed that mixed bathing was unacceptable, and for the sake of decency restricted all bathing to the hours before six in the morning and after six at night!

By 1870 Australia was importing one third of all books printed in Great Britain; we were already a nation of voracious readers, and not only of pulp fiction. As Michael Cannon shows from library records in Victoria, the average borrower from the Sandhurst Mechanics Institute read forty books a year, ten of them history or biography or political economy.

Sydney and Melbourne had a lively theatrical life: vaudeville, melodrama, the dramatisation of popular novels like *East Lynne* or *The Three Musketeers* or *A Tale of Two Cities*, but also of such local works as *For the Term of His Natural Life* and *Robbery Under Arms* – the same fare that was available in English and American cities.

German immigrants (Germans were, until the First World War, our largest non-British group; at the time of Separation, one in ten Queenslanders was German speaking) introduced musical clubs – Liedertafel – to all the capital cities and to dozens of smaller towns all over the country, importing their own conductors and performing locally composed pieces.

The Lyster Opera Company from San Francisco gave 1459 performances in the eastern capitals between 1861 and 1868.

An English visitor, Henry Cornish, whose *Under the Southern Cross* is one of the classic accounts of nineteenth-century Australia, found Sydney in 1870 'not at all the dull second-rate English town of my expectations'. Archibald Michie, a member of the Victorian Legislative Assembly and author of *Readings in Melbourne*, writing of the southern capital in the 1860s, when it was larger than Sydney by 45,000 people, speaks of it as 'a great city, as comfortable, as elegant, as luxurious (it is hardly an exaggeration to say it) as any place out of London or Paris'. When young Australians of talent went overseas they were not fleeing a cultural desert. They were doing what ambitious young people from Manchester did, or Boston or New York: taking their genius, if they had one, to where it could be put to the test. And London, even for Australians, was not always the Mecca. They were provincial not chauvinistic. For painters it was Paris, where John Peter Russell and Hugh Ramsay went to study, for musicians like the young Henry Handel Richardson it was Leipzig, as it was also for the composer Alfred Hill, who played in the Gewandhaus Orchestra at the first performance of the Brahms Fourth.

So what went wrong? Where did it all go, that early self-confidence and ebullience, that bouncy belief of the clever lad from the provinces, the seventh son, in the world's infinite possibilities and his own abounding good luck?

Some of it disappeared into the sand with those inland rivers; much more in the downward turn of the economy that began in the 1890s and lasted right up to the Second World War. More again was drained away in the horrors of the trenches and the 62,000 deaths in a population of less than four million that robbed the country of so much vitality and talent, struck at the heart of country towns and left so many women for the rest of their lives without men. The big houses of my Brisbane childhood, the old patrician houses, were inhabited by lone women, the widows and sisters and fiancées of those who had been killed, and whose names were everywhere: on the honour boards at school, on war memorials in suburban parks, in the lists of employees who had served and been killed at the post office and at railway stations and banks. It was a psychic blow from which the country in some ways never recovered, and which it suffered, for the most part, in silence.

Added to this was the long agony in the 1920s and 1930s of the soldiers' farms, where men who had survived the trenches and taken up what turned out to be marginal farming land found how harsh the land could be, and how little reward they had received for their years of sacrifice. Then, when the Great Depression struck, the bitter lesson that however hard you might be, however you clung to the bushman's code, the Digger code, of mateship and stoicism and hard-won independence, your life was not in your own hands. The country was at the mercy of outside forces, overseas banks, and market trends that neither you nor the government, it seemed, could control.

Add again the shock of discovering, as was brought home to Australians again and again in the new century, that loyalty to empire did not necessarily assure you a special place in the priorities of the British Government.

Even more alarming, that the wholeness of the society you thought you lived in was an illusion; that Germans, your good, hardworking neighbours, were really the enemy within – or so it appeared – and then, when things settled again, the shameful discovery, or recollection, of how those old friends and neighbours had been treated: the attacks against them in the streets; the law that had prevented them from hiding the disloyalty of their origin by changing their names; the deportation of those who had been interned, and with them their Australian wives and children. So what *was* it to be an Australian? What did it mean to be loyal – to the nation, to your own people? Who could you trust?

Involvement for the first time in a total war had changed things. That was what it was all about. And they could not be changed back.

Emergency restrictions that had been imposed under the extraordinary conditions of war, on pub hours for instance, the famous six o'clock closing, tended to establish themselves, become permanent. Then there was the setting up of a counter-espionage bureau in 1917, an internal spy system to keep a watch on aliens and dissidents and other wartime undesirables, and which, in the decades after the war, became the agency of a growing paranoia about the presence among us of un-Australian elements whose aim was the destruction of everything we stood for. And the emergence, as a reaction to the presence of Wobblies, anarchists and local Communists inspired by the Russian Revolution, of secret armies, mostly of ex-Diggers, the White Army, the Old Guard, the New Guard, who were ready if necessary to seize power and set up their own version of Australianness and order.

Then in 1942, as a final blow, came the fall of Singapore, and the end of the old belief that we might be left to make our own life here, away from interference by a larger world. Nearly 30,000 of our men were marched into captivity in darkest Asia. It was the fulfilment at last of what had been from the beginning our great nightmare; that those borders that nature itself seemed to have established with just us in mind might not hold. Two hundred and forty-three dead in a single raid on Darwin. Two weeks later, seventy-three more at Broome. Nineteen dead in the midget submarine raid on Sydney. The Americans arrived to protect us from invasion, and some of our saviours, despite our protests to the United States government, turned out to be black.

After 1928, black jazz musicians had been banned from entering Australia on the grounds that they were a moral threat to our women. When the American government insisted that blacks must be included in their forces here, we insisted in turn that they should be used only in Queensland and must not be landed either in Sydney or Melbourne.

*

In the dark days after Singapore, Australia, which had put so much faith in the goodwill of the British and the power of the British Fleet, was mocked in Nazi radio broadcasts as 'the Orphan in the Pacific'.

Once again we had been too trusting. Or – another temptation of living on an island – too sleepily closed off in our own little world to see how completely the world around us had moved on.

Through most of the 1920s and 1930s we seem to have been too stunned to take any sort of initiative. It had taken us eleven years to ratify the Statute of Westminster which recognised us as an autonomous nation, and we were thirteen years behind Canada, and eleven behind South Africa, in having our own rather than British representatives overseas – even in

Washington. We drew in behind our ocean wall and sulked. We turned our back on everything foreign or new or contemporary.

One or two of our painters, Margaret Preston and Grace Cossington Smith for example, who studied outside the country, did work that was modernist, and Kenneth Slessor might be called a modernist poet; but this was rare. Most of our writers were still devoted to bush realism and later to socialist realism. Even Nettie Palmer, the most internationally aware of our literary critics, was anti-modernist. So were Stewart and Hope and McAuley. A. D. Hope, in one of his most frequently quoted poems, speaks from the very heart of educated Australian philistinism, of 'the chatter of cultured apes, which is called civilization over there'. Who are these cultured apes, one wonders, who have failed to pass the test of civilisation as we Australians understand it? Wittgenstein, Benedetto Croce, Walter Benjamin, Jung, Ortega y Gasset, Simone Weil, Thomas Mann?

A fair indication of the cultural climate of the 1930s can be seen in the response of local experts to the *Herald* art show of 1939, when Australians first had the chance to see paintings by Picasso, Braque, Matisse and other twentieth-century masters.

For Lionel Lindsay, as for the Nazis, the School of Paris was a 'Jewish conspiracy'. Australia, until now undefiled, was, he tells us, 'threatened by the same

aliens, the same corrupting influences that under-
mined French art'. Explaining why the Victorian
gallery would not be buying any of the show's works,
the director, James MacDonald, told journalists: 'The
great majority of the work called "modern" is the
product of degenerates and perverts . . . As the owner
of a great Van Dyck, if we take a stand by refusing to
pollute our gallery with this filth, we shall render a
service to art'.

This is the same J. MacDonald who believed that if
we kept ourselves pure, and free of taint from inferior
types like Asians and southern Europeans, we might
become 'the elect of the world, the thoroughbred
Aryans in all their nobility'.

One sees here, in the language as well as the attitudes, why Australia did not benefit from the exodus
of European intellectuals in the mid to late 1930s that
created, in America, the new disciplines that would be
so influential for the rest of the century. In this sense,
too, Australia was closed. Between 1936 and 1940
just 3828 migrants landed on our shores.

James McAuley's great phrase, 'the faint sterility
that disheartens and derides', seems to me to express
most clearly the mood of Australia in the 1920s and
1930s and it was still there, along with all the old
terrors of life both within and without, and with tea
and butter and petrol rationing, at the beginning of
the 1950s.

And then?

Sheer panic at our lack of numbers, at a birthrate that had fallen 25 per cent since 1870, made the Labor government, after the war, embark on an ambitious migrant program.

No Asians, of course. As Minister for Immigration Arthur Calwell is reported to have put it in 1947: 'Two Wongs don't make a White'; our agents were to give preference in Europe to people with fair hair and blue eyes. But the important thing was, we were open to the world again.

These people would bring more than themselves. They would bring the world and new ways of looking at it; new models of what an Australian might be, might care for, aspire to, sell his soul for; new notions, whatever the demands of local conformity, of how one might want to live one's life.

But the real source of change was another newcomer that we let in at last in 1956, and not just into the country but into our homes. Television. That little black box was also a mirror. Looking into it we would see our real faces at last, and how many and various we were: women who argued and had opinions, blacks, homosexuals, young people whose tastes and ideas were different from those of their elders.

Television taught us to look and listen. It gave us a new image of ourselves and a new version of local culture – a popular, commercial culture that we too, these days, export to the world. Most of all, it got us to open up and *talk*. To break the great Australian silence. To break out of a disabling tradition of close-lipped devotion to the unspoken, the inexpressible, that had kept so much pain – and so much love, too, one suspects – unacknowledged because it could not find words.

*

One of the ways in which we deal with the random-ness of what happens to us is by seeing it as a story, imposing on it the *shape* of story. Perhaps this is why folk tales and fairy tales mean so much to us. They offer a range of story-shapes – Cinderella, Sleeping Beauty, Hansel and Gretel, Beauty and the Beast, Puss-in-Boots, the Joseph story – that are models for turning the muddle of living from one day to the next into something with a middle and an end. Novels do the same: picaresque novels like *Don Quixote*; the growing-older-and-wiser novel the Germans call a *Bildungsroman*; love stories like *Jane Eyre*; the novel of the divided self like *Dr Jekyll and Mr Hyde*; novels of self-reliance and salvation through work like *Robinson Crusoe*. And national myths, too, follow these prototype narratives. That is why the represen-tation of us as the 'Orphan in the Pacific' was so cruel.

Two elements are worth noting here: our tendency

to see ourselves as childlike, forever in the process of growing up or coming of age, and the self-pitying sense of being unloved and abandoned by a bad step-mother in a place far from home.

Anxiety about where we are, what we are to be, an endless fussing and fretting over identity, has been with us now for more than a century. Perhaps it is time we discovered a new shape for the story we have been telling ourselves.

Identity can be experienced in two ways. Either as a confident *being-in-the-world* or as anxiety about *our-place-in-the-world*; as something we live for ourselves or as something that demands for its confirmation the approval of others.

Perhaps it is time to stop asking what our Asian neighbours will think of us, or the Americans or the British, and try living free of all watchers but our own better and freer and more adventurous selves.

6
A Spirit of Play

One of the things we seem to find difficult is to see our history – all that has happened and was done here – as a continuity, a whole. And this for more than the usual reasons; that historians differ in their reading of what happened and why – on the reasons, for example, for the founding of the colony – or because we have, each one of us, an emotional or ideological investment in such questions as why the Aborigines died out so quickly after we came, whether by accident through the spreading of disease or through deliberate extermination, and the extent to which the way we acted towards them may have departed from British Government policy. Disagreements of this sort are common to historians everywhere. Our problem is different. It is one of selective memory. We remember the bits that speak well of us, the freedoms we have achieved, the good life we have created for so many here; the dark bits we suppress.

The truth is that our history has not been one of unbroken progress, either materially or socially. It has been a continuous shifting back and forth. Between periods of economic boom and long periods of depression. Between a confident openness to the world, to our own capacity for experiment, and a cautious drawing in behind defensive walls. Between a brave inclusiveness and a panicky need to make distinctions and exclude. But it *is* a continuity, and we need to take it whole.

What each of us takes on, at whatever point we enter it, is the *whole* of what happened here, since it is the whole of our history that has created what now surrounds and sustains us. We cannot disassociate ourselves from the past by saying we were not present. It is present in us. And we must resist the attractive notion that the past is, as they say, another country. It is not. It is this country before the necessities of a changing world changed it.

As for the wish to return to the past in the belief that it was somehow simpler and more truly 'Australian' because less diverse – all one can say is, there *are* no simplicities, there never were. Life is always more complex than the means we have for dealing with it. It always has been. We change, but not fast enough. That's the way things are. As for our Australianness, that has always been a matter of argument, of experiment. What is extraordinary in the society we have developed here is the rapidity of the changes it has undergone, and we feel this all the more when we see them tumbling in, one upon the other, within the span of our own lives.

Some of these changes are changes of attitude, of the way we see the world; others, more radically, are changes in the way we see ourselves.

*

When Europeans first came to this continent they settled in the cooler, more temperate parts of it. This was where they could reproduce to some extent the world they had left, but it was also because they saw themselves as cool-climate people. The wisdom, fifty years ago, was that white men would never live and work in the north.

Well, we seem to have re-invented ourselves in these last years as warm-climate people. Not only do we live quite comfortably in the north, it is where a great many of us prefer to live. If present population trends are anything to go by, a large part of our population in the next century will have moved into the tropics, and Queensland, our fastest growing state, will be our local California.

This is a change of a peculiar kind: a change in the way we define ourselves and our relationship to the world that is also a new way of experiencing our own bodies. And the second change I have in mind is related to this. It is the change in the living habits of Australians that we can observe any night of the week in Lygon Street in Melbourne, in Rundle Street, Adelaide, in various parts of Sydney: people eating out on the pavement under the stars in a style we recognise immediately as loosely Mediterranean, a style that has become almost universal in these last years but which fits better here than it does in Toronto or Stockholm.

It seems to me to be the discovery of a style at last that also fits the kind of people we have now become, and that fits the climate and the scene. And the attitudes it expresses, also loosely Mediterranean, make the sharpest imaginable contrast with the way we were even two decades ago, the way, in that far-off time, we saw life and the possibilities of living.

Look at these diners. Look at what they are eating and drinking. At the little dishes of olive oil for dipping their bread; the grilled octopus, the rocket, the tagines and skordalia, the wine. Look at the eye for style – for *local* style – with which they are dressed, and their easy acceptance of the body; their tendency to dress it up, strip it, show it off. Consider what all this suggests of a place where play seems natural and pleasure a part of what living is *for*; then consider how far these ordinary Australians have come from that old distrust of the body and its pleasures that might have seemed bred in the bone in the Australians we were even thirty years ago.

These people have changed, not just their minds but their psyches, and have discovered, along the way, a new body. They have slipped so quickly and so easily into this other style of being that they might have been living this way, deep in the tradition of physical ease, a comfortable accommodation between body and soul, for as long as grapes have grown on vines or olives on trees.

But half a lifetime ago, in the 1950s, olive oil was still a medicine and spaghetti came in tins. Eating out for most Australians was steak and chips at a Greek café if you were on the road, or the occasional visit to Chinatown. We ate at home for the most part and we ate pretty much what our grandparents had eaten, even those of us whose grandparents had come from 'elsewhere': lamb chops, Irish stew, a roast on Sundays. It would have seemed ludicrous to take food seriously – to write about it in the newspaper for example – or to believe that what we ate might constitute a 'cuisine' (something new and original), a product of art as well as necessity, an expression, in the same way that 'Waltzing Matilda' or 'Shearing the Rams' might be, of a national style and of the local spirit at play.

As for those other changes – of attitude, ways of seeing ourselves in relation to one another and to the world – I shall mention only two. Both were once so deeply embedded in all our ways of thinking here that they might have seemed essential to what we were. We could scarcely have imagined an Australia without them.

The first was that belief in racial superiority and exclusiveness that went under the name of the White Australia policy, but was really, until the end of the Second World War, an exclusively British policy. As *The Bulletin* put it with its usual brutal candour: 'Australia for the Australians – the cheap Chinese, the cheap Nigger, and the cheap European pauper to be absolutely excluded'.

These sentiments, this sort of language, which was common to *The Bulletin* and to later popular papers, like

Smith's Weekly, right up to the early 1950s, expressed the policy of *all* political parties, left and right, and seemed not only acceptable but unremarkable. Both the attitudes and the language were inextricably tied in with our concept of nationhood. Or so it seemed.

Yet the White Australia policy, when it disappeared in the 1960s, did so almost without argument. This great tenet of the Australian dream, of a single superior race on the continent, had grown so weak and theoretical by the 1960s that it simply vanished as if it had never been, and despite recent rumblings shows few signs of revival.

So, too, amazingly, did what had been from the beginning the strongest of all divisions among us, the sectarian division between Protestants and Catholics.

When I was growing up in Brisbane, in the late 1930s and early 1940s, Catholic and Protestant Australians lived separate lives; they might have been living in separate countries. The division between them, the low-level hostility, was part of the very fabric of things; so essential, so old and deeply rooted, as to seem immemorial and impossible of change.

Catholics and Protestants went to separate schools and learned different versions of history. Secondary students even went to different dancing classes, and when they left school they played football with different clubs, joined different lodges (the Order of Ancient Buffaloes or the Oddfellows if they were Protestant, the Hibernians if they were Catholic), and debutantes 'came out' at different balls. People knew by instinct at first meeting, by all sorts of tell-tale habits of speech and attitude, who belonged to one group and who to the other, just as they knew which corner shops or department stores they should patronise. And these divisions functioned institutionally as well as at street level. Catholics worked in some areas of the Public Service, Protestants in others. In Queensland, the Labor Party was Catholic; Protestants were Liberals. In the two great referenda over conscription, in 1916 and 1917, the country divided not on party but on sectarian lines – Protestants for, Catholics against – although in the end the 'no's' won and one should add that serving soldiers were as likely to be Catholic as not.

Part of the bitterness behind this was that Catholics were almost exclusively Irish, so that the division had an ethnic and historical element as well as a religious one. It was a continuation, on new ground, of the history of Ireland itself, based on ancient resistance to English invasion and tyranny, and on the English side on fear of Irish disloyalty, subversion and a deep-rooted contempt for Irish superstition and disorderliness. All this created its own mythology. The suggestion, for instance, that bushranging in Australia was a new version of Irish rebellion. Now it is true that most of the best-known bushrangers, real and imaginary, have Irish names, but as so often, what is told and strongly felt is not necessarily what is true to fact. The Kelly gang was Irish, but so were Kennedy, Scanlon and Lonigan, the three troopers they killed at Stringybark Creek. So were the police who hunted them.

And what exactly was at stake in all this? To a Protestant militant like John Dunmore Lang, the continent itself.

For Irish Catholics in Australia, Protestants were not only in the 'ascendancy' as they had been At Home, but in the majority. For Protestants the fear was that this happy condition might one day be reversed. That they might wake up one morning and find they had been outnumbered and this great continent had fallen overnight to Rome and to Mariolatry.

That Catholics did become the majority at last in the late 1980s, and nobody noticed, is a mark of how large the change has been. Young people today not only feel none of the old hostility, for the most part they have never heard of it. And this is not only because of the increasing secularism of our society, although that too is part of it. It is because these differences no longer matter. The whole sorry business is worth recalling now for only one reason, and it is this. If Australia is basically, as I believe it is, a tolerant place, that tolerance was hammered out, painfully and over nearly 150 years, in the long process by which Catholics and Protestants, the Irish and the rest, turned away from 'history' and learned to live with one another, and in a way that, for all its distrust and resentment, was never actually murderous as it had been elsewhere, even in times of the greatest stress: during the Easter uprising of 1916, for example, and the Irish Civil War of the early 1920s; or, before that, during the Home Rule controversy of the 1880s, or before that again, in 1868, when a suspected Fenian named O'Farrell tried to assassinate the visiting Alfred, Duke of Edinburgh, at Clontarf.

This rejection of the move from hostility to murder is important. The smell of blood is not easily forgotten. The stain of it is hard to eradicate and the names of the dead are always there to be reiterated and to become the source of a new round of violence.

Something in the tone of Australian society has been unwelcoming of extremes, and if this makes for a certain lack of passion, a lack of the swagger and high rhetoric that begins as theatre and ends as terrorism and war, it has also saved us from something. In contrast to some other mixed societies – Ireland itself, central Europe in the 1930s, and, more recently, Lebanon and Bosnia – some final sanction has always operated here against the negation of that deep psychological work that over something like six millennia has made it possible for us to live with strangers and, however different they might be from ourselves, make neighbours of them.

And isn't this, finally, what holds civilised societies together? The capacity to make a distinction between what belongs, in the way of loyalty, to clan or sect or family, and what to the demands of neighbourliness; what belongs to our individual and personal lives and what we owe to *res publica* or Commonwealth, the life we share with others, even those who may differ from us in the most fundamental way – skin colour and ethnicity, religious and political affiliation, customary habits. It is the capacity to make and honour these distinctions, out of a common concern for the right we have, each one of us, to pursue our own interests, that is essential to the life of cities, and beyond that, to their more precarious extension as states.

On the whole, we have done well in this. Not only in creating a society in which these distinctions *are* recognised and honoured but in creating a tone that those who come here from places where they are not, soon learn to value and accept. There is something to be said for mildness. It leaves people the breathing space, and the energy, to get on with more important things. As George Nadel puts it in speaking of the fight for decent working conditions in Australia: 'The fact that it appeared within reach of everyone made democratic experiment safe, and the working classes were satisfied to secure their share by enjoying a greater return for less labour rather than by political radicalism'. That is, there have been no revolutions in Australia. No blood, at least in this cause, has stained the wattle.

The world these days is global. Australians have

not escaped the pressures of an even more complex future. In daring to become a diverse and multi-ethnic society, an open experiment, we run more risk perhaps than most places of breaking up, of fragmenting. But we have faced that danger before. What got us through on those earlier occasions was neighbourliness, the saving grace of lightness and good humour, the choice of moderation over temptation to any form of extreme. These characteristics of our society are still visibly alive in the present; in occasions we take for granted, and so much so that we fail sometimes to see how rare they are.

Consider the atmosphere in which election days are celebrated here. A spirit of holiday hovers over our election boxes. As the guardian angel of our democracy, it is preferable, surely, to the three or four bored paratroopers who descend to protect the ballot-boxes in even the smallest village in a place as politically sophisticated as Italy.

Voting for us is a family occasion, a duty fulfilled, as often as not, on the way to the beach, so that children, early, get a sense of it as an obligation but a light one, a duty casually undertaken. And it *can* seem casual. But the fact that voters so seldom spoil their vote, either deliberately or by accident, in a place where voting is compulsory and voting procedures are often extremely complicated, speaks for an electorate that has taken the trouble to inform itself because it believes these things matter, and of a citizenship lightly but seriously assumed.

I ended my first lecture with the description of an audience, a mixed convict and military one, at a performance in 1800 of Shakespeare's *Henry IV Part One*. What I wanted to see in it was a first attempt here at a society in which all sorts of divisions between groups, but also between individuals, might be resolved by the fact that, in becoming an audience, this heterogeneous crowd had also, for the duration of the occasion, become an entity – and perhaps a single occasion (single occasions) is the best we can hope for and is enough. A recognition that unity is there as a possibility. It does not have to be sustained so long as it is available when we need it to be.

Let me end with another such audience, one in which what was promised in that earlier audience seems to me to be marvellously fulfilled, under more complex conditions and on a vastly larger scale.

An audience comes together of its own volition, unlike a rally, for example, where there is always some element of compulsion, if only a moral one of commitment or duty. An audience simply appears, as the 700,000 or so people do who turn out each year for the gay Mardi Gras procession in Sydney. They have no reason for being there other than interest, curiosity, pleasure, and they are an audience, not simply a crowd; an audience that has been created and shaped by the society it is drawn from, and in which the faculty of watching, listening and judging has been to an extraordinary degree sharpened.

What impresses me about this audience is its capacity to read what it is presented with and come up with an appropriate response. To greet extravagant glitter and camp with delight and a degree of humorous mockery. To see that deliberate provocation is best dealt with by a shrug of the shoulders or live-and-let-live indifference, but that a more sober note is being struck when people incapacitated by AIDS are being wheeled past, and that what is called for by the large throng of their nurses and carers is the acknowledgement of service with respectful silence or applause.

No-one has trained this audience in its responses. They come naturally out of what has been picked up from the society itself, they reflect its 'tone'. It is, as an audience, as mysterious in the way it appears and reconstitutes itself for each occasion as any other. No-one twenty years ago could have predicted its arrival, but there it is.

As for the actors in this street theatre – could anyone have guessed, back then, that it would be just this group that would call a popular audience into being?

What seems extraordinary here, is that what, until recently, had been a marginal group, mostly invisible, has not only made itself visible but has made the claim as well to be central – that is, as central as any other – and has created that audience for all of us.

Open, inclusive, the parade is made up of virtually every strand in our society: the various ethnic minorities, including Asian and Pacific people and Aborigines; members of the armed forces, the police, and of every other profession, including sex-workers.

In being multiple itself, such a parade offers the crowd a reflected image of its own multiplicity, and all within a spirit of carnival, a form of play that includes mockery and self-mockery, glamour and the mockery of glamour, social comment, tragedy and a selfless dedication to the needs of others; as if all these things were aspects of the same complex phenomenon – as of course they are. It is called life.

Carnival deals with disorder by making a licensed place for it, and with the threat of fragmentation by reconstructing community in a spirit of celebratory lightness. It takes on darkness and disruption by embracing them. Forces that might otherwise emerge as violence, it diverts through tolerance and good humour into revelry and sheer fun.

Such carnival occasions have ancient roots. They go back to the pagan world, and to medieval festivals, days of licence, Fools' Days, when the spirit of mockery was let loose and a place found for disorder within the world of order and rule. For all its contemporary glitz and high jinks, our version of Mardi Gras retains much of its ancient significance. As a popular festival it reinforces community. It recovers for us, within the complexities and the divisiveness of modern living, a sense of wholeness. And there is a connection here between the carnival world it celebrates, its vulgarity, its flaunting of the flesh, and that first convict performance of *Henry IV*.

Falstaff, the randy, disreputable anti-hero of that play, is the great embodiment in our literature of the spirit of carnival, the direct descendant of the Vice that larked about at the centre of the old morality plays, and before that of the Lords of Misrule who presided over medieval Fools' Days. Falstaff, and the disorder he represents, is what has somehow to be included in the world of Rule. 'Banish plump Jack,' he tells Prince Hal, 'and banish all the world.'

Falstaff, with his shameless insistence on the flesh, his dirty jokes and phallic shenanigans, is a necessary aspect of what it is to be alive. So is the challenge his non-conformism offers to the coldness and impersonality of the law. Finding a place for Falstaff, acting imaginatively in the spirit of lightness he represents, is the way to wholeness; and wholeness, haleness, as the roots of our language tell us, is health.

The Boyer Lectures, 1998, first broadcast on ABC Radio, later published in A Spirit of Play, *ABC Books, 1998*

THE PEOPLE'S JUDGEMENT

THE REFERENDUM ON THE REPUBLIC

GEOFFREY BLAINEY'S GREAT PHRASE 'the tyranny of distance', when it was formulated nearly forty years ago, offered a powerful explanation of the problems of being Australian and of Australia's relationship to the world. It pointed to geography, seen in terms of position and distance, as a determinant of what we call history, that is, of our daily lives as they are lived through events and conditions.

The Australia Blainey was placing was nineteenth-century Australia, six weeks' sailing distance from Europe, in the age before international cables had made possible the wonder of instant communication; and of course by the time he formulated it the conditions it described had already changed. Air transport had reduced travel time to a single day, satellite images were about to make every event on the globe instantaneously visible. And it was never quite true, even before technology intervened to change forever how we see the world and where we stand. We live in feelings as well as in conditions and events. Distance is also measured by the heart. In those terms, Europe – Britain – was close, not far off. As for now, and the century to come, the new communications systems mean that mere geography will never again determine our sense of where we stand.

In space as the net defines it – *language space* – El Paso Texas, Aberdeen and Longreach are equidistant from what can only be an imaginary centre: some forms of international business can be conducted as easily from Longreach as from Los Angeles. Once again the fact that our language is English has made us powerful well beyond our size. This is the new form of geography we live with, and if it collapses the distance between hemispheres it also collapses the distance between, say, Longreach and Sydney. The space they exist in now belongs to mind, imagination and the new skills that make them function, and this has meant a redefinition, a radical one, of what we do and who we are. No wonder that some of us need time to catch up.

Australians, and especially Australian men, have traditionally defined themselves by the sort of work they do. This is where their pride in themselves, their sense of worth and honour resides. That work had until recently been on the land. It depended on muscle, on hard physical labour and endurance.

The new economy is based on softer skills. The predominance now of service industries such as teaching and tourism means that we have had to redefine what we think of as real work, and this is a psychological change as well as a change in 'conditions'. At this level, the level of feeling, it involves real pain, a strong sense, especially in the bush, that older Australian values, like the older skills, are no longer wanted and for that reason no longer respected; a sense of fracture, of alienation. And this has been intensified by the belief that those who manage our lives are driven by theories that take no account of how people actually live; that they have no ear, behind what sometimes appears as truculent opinion, for the pain, the anger, the frustration and foiled pride of individual lives. But people, in our system, always have the last word. Policies that take no account of feeling inevitably fail.

Take the attempt to convince Australians that they are really part of Asia. It failed because it was based on a 'fact' of geography that had no life in what people actually felt. Asia, of course, is a loose concept, but even when it was translated into something particular – India or Thailand or Vietnam – people still could not feel the tie; even those who had been to Phuket or Bali, were interested in zen or yoga, or had neighbours from one of those countries that they had been to school with; neighbourliness is about sharing things *here*. Neither did it touch us that we had strong trading links with these places. There was only one place in Asia that we felt close to: Timor. That closeness was based on events that went back half a century but were still alive in our consciousness as real experience, and on a debt of gratitude and responsibility that we also feel, and for similar reasons, to the people of Papua New Guinea; a bond of feeling based on shared suffering and sacrifice, in which any difference of culture or skin colour is cancelled out by our common humanity. Bonds of this sort are not easily forgotten and not honourably shrugged off. They are the only ones that really move us. In the case of Timor, there was a gap between what most Australians felt and what politicians thought was practically good for us, but in the end it was feelings that won out.

Then there is 'our link with Britain'. It upsets many among us that after 150 years of de-facto independence this link should still be so strong.

A bond of emotion, of spirit, that for the vast majority of those who feel it has no hint of colonialism, and in no way compromises their sense of themselves as wholly Australian, it has to do with family – identity in that sense; personal identity rather than their identity as Australians. It is no coincidence that so many Australians have a passionate interest in family trees, and understandable that they might be curious about where their ancestors lived, for centuries in some cases, before they found themselves here. It is a link of language, too, and of culture in the sense of shared associations and understanding, of shared objects of affection, and a history of which we are a branch – a growth quite separate and of itself, but drawing its strength from an ancient root. We will know that this link has been broken when we hear an old hymn such as 'To Be A Pilgrim', a folk song like 'Waly Waly' or a ballad like 'Comin' through the Rye' and are no longer moved, or when we no longer laugh spontaneously at old jokes from *The Goon Show* or *Fawlty Towers*.

The fact is that the part of ourselves in which we live most deeply, most fully, goes further back than one or two generations and takes in more than we ourselves have known. To have no roots in time is to have no roots in place either.

We admire indigenous people for belonging deeply to time and drawing from it. We encourage non-English-speaking Australians to hang on to their language, accepting that in doing so they will also hang on to what is inextricably one with language, the culture it embodies: not just in song and story but in patterns of thought that are inherent in syntax and idiom. How odd that when it comes to those among us who are of British origin we feel they will only be fully Australian when they have cut themselves off from what we see in others as the nourishment of a complete life.

This, I suspect, had more influence on the recent referendum than we care to recognise; not because Australians are still colonial, or have a weak sense of national identity, or have not yet come of age, but because the case for the republic was put in terms that people had no strong feeling for, or which ran counter to what they felt.

An Australian republic can only be argued for convincingly at the level of feeling – on what we feel towards the place and for one another. When it comes at last, some time in the next century, it had better be a true republic, one that is founded not on the loyalty of its citizens to their head of state but on their loyalty to one another: on bonds, which already exist and which we already recognise, of reciprocal concern and care and affection. A republic based on loyalty only to a head of state is a monarchy in disguise, even when the monarch is elected and temporary. An elected monarch, as in too many republics one might name, can very easily become an autocrat.

Perhaps, after a century of theories and ideas and ideologies, some of them murderous, we might try listening at last to what the people have to say; paying attention to what they have to tell us; accepting, too, and without resentment, that in being human they are imperfect, and that theories, even the most beautiful and idealistic, are for angels of the imagination, not real men and women. We might grant people the dignity of a life determined not by cold principle but by what they will recognise as true to what they are.

Sydney Morning Herald, *1999*

THE ONE DAY

I DON'T THINK ANYONE THESE days would deny that Anzac Day has established itself in the minds of Australians as the one day that we celebrate as a truly national occasion; a day, that is, when we look around and observe who we are; in the sense, first, of who is present, but also in the larger sense of what it is, in the way of experience, but also of shared attitudes and affections and loyalties and concerns, that brings us together, whatever our individual differences and divisions, as a single community, a single people involved in a common enterprise.

I say 'the one day' because our official National Day, 26 January, the anniversary of the first day of settlement, Australia Day, seems to me to have no general claim on our affection and to be seen by many of us as an occasion that is not fully inclusive – as it never can be while for indigenous Australians it is seen, and more importantly felt, as a day of conquest and dispossession. Australia Day has been declared our National Day, imposed officially from above, and Australians on the whole are pretty resistant to choices they have not made for themselves. Anzac Day has been chosen, and part of the strength of that choice is that it has happened slowly, over time, and with many changes both in what the day represents and who has the right to define and manage it. Over time and through long and sometimes bitter argument.

How has all that happened, and why? What has changed? Is it us, or the day itself? What has Anzac Day come to mean that is different from what it meant, say, fifty years ago? And what does that tell us about the way we now see ourselves? The day has a history, and its history is in some ways our history over the past fifty years.

The present status of Anzac Day is astonishing to those of us who remember the way things were in the fifties. Back then, it was, officially, a holiday – that is, theatres were closed, so were the shops, but not, significantly, the pubs – and it was pretty well accepted that Anzac Day was a dying institution. The numbers that turned out for the Dawn Service were small and dwindling. Many of the men who had served in the two world wars, especially those who had served in the second, had become disaffected with the RSL; a lot of them no longer marched, and had always, in a very Australian way, a good many of them, been non-joiners. The day had no appeal to young people, and for a good many in my generation was a source of actual hostility.

The RSL, which claimed ownership of the event, was one of several pressure groups that in those days were battling, pretty openly, to determine the way Australia might go in the early years of the Cold War, and one of their declared enemies was what was loosely referred to as 'the Students', the first generation of young men and women in Australia to get to the university in large numbers. Many of them working class, and some of them returned soldiers, they made up the first generation in Australia of a noisy and articulate *youth*, a generation of rebels that was university-educated rather than bohemian, as the rebels of the twenties and thirties had been, though it was bohemian as well: university-educated, bohemian and radical, having discovered Hegel and Marx and alienation and the scrap heap of history rather than Hell as a place to which people they no longer agreed with could be consigned, but also Existentialism and Sartre and Camus, and Modernism in all its forms, from Joyce, Faulkner and Dylan Thomas to Stravinsky and Picasso – the same Modernism that the Australian bohemians of the 1920s, for all their non-conformism, had rejected. Student unions had become the training ground of emergent politicians, and the university newspapers of emergent writers and intellectuals.

It was inevitable, in all this, that Anzac Day should become the focus of bitter argument about Australian aims and values.

In 1950, Gallipoli and the trenches were still close. They were part of every family's immediate experience. The men who had fought at Gallipoli, at Pozières, at Villers-Bretonneux, and later on Crete and in New Guinea, were the fathers and uncles and grandfathers of those of us who were growing up into a post-war world that for another decade, after 1945, kept hovering on the brink of a new war to which the new generation might be called. We sometimes forget that no generation of Australians after 1870 had at that point escaped the call to arms. This made the sort of military virtues that were celebrated around Anzac a source of real anxiety and resentment to the young. Anxiety because the fathers had already met their test – which was why Anzac Day belonged to them and was so jealously guarded.

Some of this was just the usual struggle between

one generation and the next given a particular focus. But there were other elements as well that were local. A strong feeling in some cases – and this was a new idea altogether – that by insisting that the masculine virtues were to be discovered only through war, a previous generation had failed to consider the virtues that might be needed in the more ordinary war that we call peace. It was in effect an argument that the old notion of what it meant to be male, and especially an Australian male, was too narrow.

The attempt on the part of the fathers as I've called them to make their experience exemplary, to give it a legendary value, a sacred aura that would put it beyond criticism or challenge, was seen by the generation of the fifties as an attempt to take possession of a history that they felt was theirs to make.

The fathers had two forces on their side: silence, and C. E. W. Bean.

This silence was deeply established. Men used it as a form of self-protection; it saved those who had experienced the horrors of war from the emotional trauma of experiencing it all over again in the telling. And it saved women and children, back home – or so they felt – from the terrible knowledge of what they had endured and walked away from.

It was this old habit of silence about what was most deeply felt, a tendency to understate it or turn it aside with wry humour, that had been both the strength and the limitation of Australian writing, which till this point had excluded virtually everything introspective or inward. One result of this was that the men who had actually lived through Gallipoli and the trenches did not write about it. They had written letters, and a few of them had kept diaries, but they produced no account, either in fiction or poetry, of what they had seen and suffered. Australian writing offered no place in the years immediately after the Great War for the sort of savage introspection that experience of trench warfare demanded, or for the satirical challenge to patriotism that we get in Siegfried Sassoon or e. e. cummings.

As for C. E. W. Bean, his journalistic articles before the war, his vivid and inspiring account from the various 'fronts', the definitive history he wrote after the war, all created the Anzac legend as an extension of the national character, an exclusively male one as it had developed in the bush, and as it was vividly recreated in the 1890s in that central organ of Australian publishing, *The Bulletin*. In Bean's vision of things, this national Australian character had actually needed a war to find its highest and noblest form.

The generation of the fifties did not reject the virtues of Bean's legendary Australian: toughness, good humour, stoicism, irreverent irony in the face of officiousness or 'side', mateship, the dedication to a fair go. What they rejected was the suggestion that these were the only virtues, or the only ones that were necessary; and that for their fullest expression they needed a war.

In fact, the stereotype had never gone quite unchallenged, even by Henry Lawson who might be seen as its originator. It had been hard pressed by the ambiguities and the ironies we get in Joseph Furphy, and pilloried in the savage picture of the Australian bush male – cowardly, lying, lazy, exploitative, irresponsible – that we find in the stories of Barbara Baynton. The attack by the new generation was a more diverse and plural, a more paradoxical view of what it might be to be an Australian; one that would include women, and present a less rigid version of what it might be to be an Australian man.

A good deal of this is at issue in a play, written in the late fifties but first performed in an atmosphere of violent controversy in 1961; Alan Seymour's *The One Day of the Year.*

Hughie, its passionately earnest hero, is that new figure in Australian society in the fifties, the working-class boy who has got to university. He is an angry young man who feels that if he is ever to be himself, and independent, he must break with his family, reject their narrow pieties and proclaim what he sees, with the uncompromising certainty of youth, as the 'truth'. The area in which he sets out to mount his challenge is Anzac Day, 'the one day of the year'.

Filled with youthful scorn for the gap he perceives between the myth of Anzac, especially as it is exploited by those who were never there, and the sordid reality of the day itself – the descent from solemnity and commemoration into drunken buffoonery – he takes a series of photographs for the university paper that will present, as he sees it, the real picture of the heroic Digger: as a drunk sprawled in the gutter and covered with vomit.

The play makes a clear distinction between the real Diggers, who have nothing to say because their experience is beyond words, and those who were never there but are full of the legend and its windy rhetoric. It is very much aware, as people were in those days, of how the men who came back were betrayed by broken promises, and that the Great Depression, which in the early fifties was still close in most families, had been more destructive to many of the returned men – because it was unheroic and humiliating – than the war itself.

The One Day of the Year is very much a play of its time. Full of the cautious questioning of the late fifties, the hostility to suburban values that goes into the early work of Barry Humphries, the breaking up at last of that comfortable, self-protective, timid and sleepy world that some nostalgics among us look back on as the true Australia – a time of mythical wholeness that was already, in fact, under pressure of change.

The One Day of the Year is very accurate in its feeling – its mixed feelings, I'd put it – about family, about fathers, about maleness of the stereotypical Australian kind, and about the pieties of Anzac. But looking at it again, it's hard to feel much sympathy for its rather priggish hero.

Hughie is a bit too full of his own moral superiority, too personally aggrieved; not at all sensitive to shades – as we tended to be back then, and as the young often are. He misses an important point, as Seymour himself does I think, and as I might have missed it too, in 1959. It is that the disjunction he makes so much of between the ceremonial dignity of the first part of the day, the Last Post, the Dawn Service, the words of solemn remembrance, and the disreputable orgy, as he sees it, that follows – the grogging on, the brawling drunkenness and rowdyism – may not be a disjunction at all, but two sides of the soldier's world that are linked, and even necessary to one another: the position of attention – battle and all that goes with it of psychological tautness, of fear that has to be mastered, and the possibility of instant extinction – and the relaxation from that into the bacchanalian celebration of restored life. A classic pairing, we might think, and very human.

Perhaps what we need, if we are to comprehend that, is a more complex and contradictory view than poor Hughie can come up with – one we were not ready for in the fifties, though it is worth pointing out that the Diggers themselves had already grasped it. Intuitively, and with no need for a classical justification, as a response to brutal experience.

The 1950s is itself a period now that belongs to history, as 1915 did then. To be considered from this side and that, and interpreted and argued over. For a younger generation, the original experience of 'the Day' no longer involves their fathers and uncles, or even their grandfathers or any living persons they know and might resent or be in rivalry with. It is neutral ground.

It belongs now to a period – the early part of the last century – that is just beginning to pass out of first-hand human experience, and develop the glow of a reality softened, relieved of the rich contradictions through which personal witness challenges and contradicts received views. It has about it now an aura of mystery that we cannot penetrate and which, precisely for that reason, has a strong pull on our feelings.

Hence the cult – and I use the word with no suggestion at all of slight or condescension – of our remaining First World War veterans, old men now, most of them well over a hundred, who are I suspect rather bemused, in these last years of a life of ordinary works and days that till now went unnoticed, to find themselves the subject of national interest and large and general affection. For some of them, there is embarrassment too in that their actual deeds in the war were undistinguished. They feel, some of them, that the aura they have acquired belongs to other and braver men. Their achievement is survival itself.

And in fact that is the source of our awed affection for them. That they survived the battles, but also the more ordinary dangers of war – flu and fevers and all the other accidents that young men are prone to. That they survived the years *after* the war; the bitterness of betrayal that so many returned men felt, the soldier's Resettlement schemes that went bung, the long years of the Depression. Australians generally have begun to have a clearer sense now of how hard the first part of the twentieth century was for their parents and grandparents. The tribute we pay to these few survivors is in some ways a tribute to all those men and women who lived through that rough patch in our history – a way, I mean, of recognising history itself as lived and accumulated experience; of recognising that we *have* a history, and that it is of this lived and personal kind; that the time behind us as Australians is not short but begins to be long, and that our roots in it are deep, not shallow.

That the lives of these old fellows we see on television, and whose names we now know, go back more than a century, touches us – and it may add to the power they project that they are not especially heroic and do not represent themselves that way. Do not posture or make use of any of the rhetorical clichés, but are modest survivors of the ordinary circumstances and perils of living. Very young people, I suspect, who find themselves living in a dangerous and chaotic world and with their own lives fearfully before them, feel a special affection for these old fellows who have indestructibly battled through – and even a small sense of reassurance.

There is also what these old men once touched back there, when, as young men – just seventeen some of them – they responded to the call to dangerous service (adventure is how many of them thought of it) and discovered horror and sacrifice.

The tragedy of doomed youth continues to hover around the First World War as it never has around the Second. In these days when we know so much, and are so visually sensitive to what we know, there is a kind of horrified fascination with the wholesale slaughter of the First World War battlefields, and how some men endured it, and came back, when they did, to ordinary lives.

Futility and the waste of youthful sacrifice, human folly on a scale almost unimaginable in these days of precision weapons, distant engagement, small losses – this is how we now see the First World War. But we also see aspects of it that we were unaware of fifty years ago, or unable to look at. Women, for example, as victims of war. Rape as an element of war – a fact that would have been seen, in 1950, if anyone had dared mention it, as an insult to fallen heroes and to the fathers and uncles among us who had come back. So too the reality, the ordinary human reality, of the enemy. Gallipoli is now a shared occasion between Australians and Turks. The dead seem inseparable, as on the spot their bones have always been.

All this informs the way that Anzac Day, as an idea, has expanded and become more inclusive as it has passed out of the hands of its original custodians, the Diggers, the RSL, into general ownership, where we have remade it according to present understanding and present affiliations and needs.

So what does Anzac Day mean now? What does it commemorate that so many Australians, and especially so many young Australians, feel that it is ours, that it is theirs? And how has what was once seen as a celebration of military virtues, even if it was in the context of a military defeat, managed to establish itself, and so strongly, in a period that is so passionately dedicated to the idea of peace?

There is, first of all, the strong sense of the tragic – of

the loss, the waste, of young lives: 62,000 in that First War, in a population of just on four million.

A society that does not recognise and mark with awe the presence of death, that has no sense of the tragic, is a poor one. Dying is a solemn fact of life; it is something we all understand and must come to. There is for all of us a close and personal mystery in it that touches us darkly – even the young feel that. And the death of a young person, the brutal fact of a life cut short, brings the possibility poignantly home; and especially if the death happens in the chosen and public context of service.

The idea of service is an important one to Australians. A good deal of what adds most to daily living in Australia comes from voluntary service – in bushfire brigades, surf-lifesaving clubs, in social and charitable organisations like Rotary, the Lions, the Country Women's Association, the RSL, and through what parents contribute, in the way of time and energy, to sports clubs and school tuckshops and fair days. All this is an acting out of neighbourliness, of what we share with those we live among; a bond that is stronger in the end, in everyday working Australia, than ethnic or denominational ties, and takes up much of the feeling that in other places goes out to extended family. Australia is a secular place. A dedication to voluntary service has become the good works of a secular religion among us. A dedication to neighbourliness is understood, if not quite proclaimed, as what holds the country together and makes us, loosely, one.

Perhaps there was from the beginning something in the accidental nature of an accident-prone world in Australia that made this sort of mutual concern and obligation a condition of survival in the place. And of course the supreme form of service, because it includes the possibility of the ultimate sacrifice, is service in war. The solemn acceptance of dying in battle as the highest form of service – not chosen, but accepted if that is what it comes to – remains central to the idea of Anzac, and to the power we feel in the day.

The fact is that Anzac Day has never been in any way triumphalist. The march is a civilian march, by men in suits, its keynote comradeliness, and a sorrowful awareness, as men walk in their platoons and battalions, of those who are missing. Increasingly, as part of its growing inclusiveness, it has become a family affair, with small children marching with a grandfather, or marching alone and carrying a grandfather's photograph, or young men and young women marching in place of a relative who can no longer manage it, and wearing his medals. This reminds us that the losses were always losses to family as well as to the ranks, and as so many war memorials up and down the country remind us, to community. All this makes it easy for the community at large, and especially young people, to see the day as one for dealing in a very open and emotional way with loss, with communal wounds; it is a day for meditating on the waste of young lives, and of all – combatants and non-combatants – who die in war. For some, it is a way of meditating on the folly of war itself.

The fact that Anzac Day is now in the hands of Australians at large, and their day to shape as they please, to make a focus of whatever feelings they need to express, privately or in common, means that what it is now is not what it is likely to be fifty or even twenty years from now. It has become a dynamic phenomenon, and in so far as it matters to us, in so far as we need what it can offer, will go on changing as we do.

Perhaps, since I have done so much looking back, it might be best to pause there, at the edge of a future that will go its own way, and about which we can have nothing very useful to say.

Already this year, there are no surviving Gallipoli veterans and just a handful of First World War Diggers. The numbers of Second World War survivors is thin. Quite soon, the largest numbers of marchers will be the descendants of the original Diggers, and it will be the photographs of long-dead soldiers and their medals paraded like tribal relics or fetishes that will endure to be the stuff of continuity.

*Official Anzac Day address
in Washington, DC, 2003*

MADE IN ENGLAND

AUSTRALIA'S BRITISH INHERITANCE

A FINE CLEAR DAY IN early May. Outside, in the streets of Washington, sedate, uninsistent, half genuine neo-classical – the proper democratic style – half fake, there is no sense that we are at the centre of the world's single great imperium; one, too, that is in the aftermath of a swift and seemingly successful war.

For all its 'magnificent distances' and imposing monuments, Washington is unshowy, seems unpeopled, has none of the residual triumphalism of London: the clatter of the Horseguards each morning down Birdcage Walk, sword-hilts and breastplates flashing; the ceremonial changing of the Guards at the Palace to stirring march-tunes and an invocation of Lysander and Hercules. Washington, named for a revolutionary democrat, lacks altogether the colour and circumstance of empire. Freedom Plaza, off the Mall near the White House, is an austere space, all quotations carved in capitals, a reminder of how essential rhetoric is to the style of this country – and a particular rhetoric at that; one that insists, in a way that seems more European than English, on magnificent abstractions.

The White House itself, almost within spitting distance across its impeccable lawn, is, compared with the Elysée Palace or the sort of extravaganzas preferred by the Saddam Husseins of this world, a very modest residence for the most powerful ruler of the day. And this *is* English. One thinks of Queen Victoria at the height of the British Empire referring to Buckingham House as 'my little palace in Pimlico'.

One also recalls, at this moment when the special relationship is at its closest, that in 1814 this same residence was burned to the ground by a British army of occupation.

These observations on the play, in this New World, between British beginnings and their Transatlantic modifications, seem especially pertinent in an Australian context and at a time when the tripartite relationship between our three countries – General de Gaulle's old fear of an Anglophone alliance – has assumed its most open and aggressive form under a new rubric, 'the coalition of the willing'.

With two fellow Australians, one a writer like myself, the other an art historian, I am four storeys below ground in the vaults of the Folger Library, one of the iconic monuments of our culture – I mean the culture that belongs to the language we speak and have our life in, English.

A hundred metres away, soaring into the blue empyrean, is that symbol of worldly power and influence the gleaming white dome of the Capitol, its name suggesting republican or imperial Rome but its form a later reference, to Michelangelo's St Peter's. And here, in perfect balance with it, in the artificial air of a below-ground shelter, the world's most complete collection of Shakespeariana: priceless quarto and folio editions from the days when the man himself was above ground and working, and later versions from every period and in every language: Pope and Dr Johnson and Malone's editions of the Complete Works, prompt-copies once used by Garrick and Edmund Kean and the Kembles and Booths, and by Sir Henry Irving and Ellen Terry, the seventeen-year-old Mendelssohn's piano-score of his overture to *A Midsummer Night's Dream*.

The librarian who shows us through, and takes down from the shelves and handles some of the priceless books, and allows us to handle them, speaks of how, if there were some sort of biological or nuclear disaster, she would take refuge down here and survive along with the collection. For her this is the real centre of the city and what it stands for. The power of what is embodied here is what will survive should the surrounding empire, like so many before it, crumble and blow away.

It is odd, uncanny, to be standing, eighteen hours' flying time from where history has washed us up, in the light of this woman's conviction and the real presence of these texts, which belong equally to all four of us because *we* belong to the language that produced them. Finally it is language we come home to, and nowhere seems more like home than here.

Outside, because Britain, the United States and Australia all share it – not just the language itself but a particular habit of mind and all that goes with it – an affinity that has been hovering in the ether for more than a century, and has twice already become a power-field, has now broken surface in an actual alliance. Not so much a coalition of the 'willing' as, more exclusively, of those who have an insider's understanding of one another because they inhabit the same language culture. Who, in their exchanges with one another, can take it for granted that a good deal of what is being left unsaid, or exists in shades and nuances under what *is* said, as half-heard echoes out of plays, poems, novels, or out of the *obiter dicta* of occasions great and small in a shared history – 'once more unto the breach', 'Thy need is greater than mine', 'England expects', 'Praise the Lord and pass the ammunition'; phrases that contain whole worlds of experience and philosophy – will not go unrecognised, and may even be left to bear the burden of much that is subtly intended.

The close relationship with the United States that this embodies has for Australians been there from the start. Our relationship with Britain has always been one in which the third term, either open or unstated, is 'America'. Any approach on our part to the one has *always* involved a shift in our dealings with the other, and our relationship with each has been modified over the years by their relations with one another.

Of course we, like New Zealand and Canada, have always been minor rather than major players, as we are in the present alliance; but to be, on the basis of 'family', the member of a powerful club, even a junior member, offers incentives to ambition, and the opportunity to push them through, that you would not have, at the same weight and size, if you were not. The family link is the language we share. Though it is worth pointing out that a *shared* language is not necessarily the *same* language.

All this, hovering in the air in those humming vaults on that peaceful afternoon in the midst of what was still an unfinished war, was the beginning of what I am writing here.

The Rising Child

The first fact of our being as Australians is that the colony was founded in 1788 not by the French or the Dutch, as was quite possible, or by the Spanish or Portuguese, as was at least conceivable, but by two small, damp, divided islands in the far northern corner of the globe – a mixture of Celts, Anglo-Saxons, Danes and Norman French, plus all kinds of refugees and immigrants from other places – that just happened, by the end of the eighteenth century, to be the world's major maritime power, and the richest, most politically stable and technologically advanced nation of the day. A large part of what we are follows from that, and how we have regarded the British at every point in our history has been determined by how we read that act of founding and how we value the society and culture of which we were, at least at the start, a translated re-creation.

But regard goes both ways. When we look at the British we see both what we were to begin with and what we have turned out *not* to be; we also see the way *they* see us.

Sometimes this is condescendingly or with contempt. It was certainly the way we *felt* their regard in the nineteenth century and for much of the twentieth, and the way some of them, we feel, see us still. Think of all those opportunities for a cheap laugh, in Oscar Wilde for example, simply by dropping the word Orstralia or Orstralian into an otherwise ordinary conversation. The point of the joke is almost always the extraordinary presumption on the part of Australians to be taken seriously. That, and the immediate association of Australia with the kangaroo, a comic creature if ever there was one, not least in *its* presumption in rising up, in an almost human way, on its hind legs and begging like a dog or offering to box. We get an early glimpse of this in that occasion when 'the Great Cham', Dr Johnson, in a mood of extravagant high humour, hauled himself up on to a table-top among a party of friends, and with his great haunches lowered and his paws tucked neatly under his chin, made hopping motions in mimicry of the curious beast that had been described to him by his acquaintance Mr Banks.

We reacted to this in different ways. Some of us tried to disguise what we were and win the regard of the English by practising as complete an imitation of them, including their prejudices, as we could manage – not excepting their prejudice against ourselves. Or, filled with resentment at the injustice of being disregarded and misread, we practised a reciprocal contempt and did everything we could to be as little like them as rationality allowed – given that what we had inherited from them was for the most part rational and good, including, not least of all, a high opinion of rationality itself. Or we settled, very sensibly, for what we were; always with a certain awareness of their scrutiny and their eagerness to criticise, but in the determination to do better than *they* had done. That is, we needed our awareness of their scrutiny to keep ourselves up to the mark. The one thing we did not do was pretend they were not there and looking.

They too reacted in different ways. Australia would always be, from their point of view, an offshoot and imitation. The question was whether, as a variation, it was inferior or 'improved'. And increasingly in the nineteenth century, for good family reasons, Australia was in their thoughts. Dickens, when all else failed, sent his characters there – the Micawbers and the Peggottys in *Copperfield*, along with little Emily and poor Mrs Gummidge, and that lovelorn youth Augustus Moddle in *Chuzzlewit*. He also sent two of his sons there, one of them at the tender age of sixteen, and Trollope sent one of his sons as well. Odd to think how often, and how poignantly, Australia, far off in the other part of the day, must have been on the mind of these very English writers; in the morning as they settled to their daily quota of words, and in Dickens' case, late at night as he set out on his gloomy wanderings through the town.

The judgement in the nineteenth and early twentieth centuries, except among those who themselves expected to be improved, was that Australia was inferior.

Charles Darwin, who arrived in 1836 on the *Beagle*, is impressed by the country's extraordinary development in just five decades of settlement. 'It is a magnificent testimony,' he writes, 'to the powers of the British nation . . . My first feeling was to congratulate myself that I was born an Englishman.'

But his *second* feeling, as an Englishman, was that for all that Australia was 'a new and splendid country – and a grand centre of civilisation' – it wasn't as yet so civilised that he could imagine living there. 'My opinion,' he writes, 'is that nothing but rather sharp necessity should compel me to emigrate.' And his final assessment is devastating: 'Farewell Australia! you are a rising child and doubtless will reign a great princess in the South: but you are too great and ambitious for affection, yet not great enough for respect. I leave your shores without sorrow or regret.'

The balance in the past two or three decades seems to have shifted. The difference is, that when the British look at us now, what they are seeking is another and different vision of themselves: themselves caught in a new light; under new and warmer skies and after 200 years of another and less disappointing history. And this is equally true of the thousands of young backpackers who flock here on working holidays and those older visitors, themselves too old to change, who come to spend a month or two with sons or daughters who have married and settled here and made lives for themselves of a kind their parents could scarcely have imagined.

Not long ago, during a visit to Edinburgh, I decided to take a couple of days off and look at somewhere else in Scotland. I chose Dundee. I got in late at night, and stepping out of my hotel after breakfast next morning found myself stopped dead on the pavement, overwhelmingly flooded with a Proustian feeling of time regained. I was back in Brisbane in, say, 1941. The smells, the bodies and faces of the people around me in the street, something indefinable in the whole atmosphere and style of the place, had taken me back. And that was the clue, of course: style. I hadn't stepped back in time, or into a place where time had simply failed to 'move on'. What I had encountered was something that was continuous in this place but which Australians had long since abandoned – when? sometime in the fifties, perhaps – and so completely that this, the original, which I found so immediately recoverable, must for most of us be no more now than a distant memory, and for young people so entirely foreign that they might feel no connection with it at all.

We get some sense of this from Max Dupain's famous photograph of women in a meat queue: the uniform black straw-hats, and the grim determination with which they are clamped down over the brow; the whole shape and expression of these weathered faces, the mouths either toothless and sunken or filled with dentures so ill-fitting they can barely be managed. This is how a poorer age looked, a time of pinched horizons and few amenities, of gas or chip-heaters in unheated bathrooms, a single cold-tap over the kitchen sink, an ice-chest with a daily delivery by an ice-man who was always on the run, with a great dripping block at the end of steel claws and yesterday's soggy newspaper-wrappings to be got rid of.

It is a time but also a style. It is Brisbane or Sydney or Melbourne in the late thirties and early forties, but it might equally be Scunthorpe or Cork. A time of boils and chilblains and whitlows, and mouths open wide each morning in the winter for the daily spoonful of cod-liver oil and malt, with a block of camphor in a flannel scapula round our necks.

All this, along with Milk of Magnesia, castor oil in its own blue bottle, and Antiphlogistine plasters to be boiled up and slapped on the chest, is so ancient and unimaginable, so unlike any Australia that most Australians have a personal experience of today, that we might be talking of galingales and syllabubs or the relics of saints. It is my childhood.

*

We went away most weekends, piled into our huge '27 Hupmobile, with its reinforced canvas top and snapped-down celluloid windows, to a caravan 'down the Bay' that my father had built in our backyard with the help of an ex-ship's carpenter called Old Pop. To Scarborough, a quiet still-water beach with a wooden slippery-slide at either end and the sandhills of Moreton Island on the not-so-distant horizon.

At Redcliffe, a mile away by road (two if you walked it the Beach Way, round the cliffs), there was a skating rink and an English-style pier with big silver weighing machines, flipper games with two little teams of footballers in painted jerseys and shorts, and a row of peep-shows. On the other side of the road, the Redcliffe Pictures: Abbott and Costello and Rita Hayworth, but also Gracie Fields and George Formby, and from the Redcliffe Newsagent's our weekly supply of comics. English of course: *Radio Fun* and *Film Fun*.

At low tide we play beach cricket or Red Rover – a game known in other states as British Bulldog – and on Saturday nights we go with our parents to the Saturday Night Dance at the School of Arts, where we do the Progressive Barn Dance, the Albertina, the Modern Waltz, the Gipsy Tap and the Pride of Erin.

This is the old world translated – rather imperfectly, of course, as any English person recalling the *real* Scarborough might have told us. Perhaps because there were so few signs in it of modern times, the Americans when they arrived, in 1942, found it oddly

'British' and quaint. For us it was neither. It was Australian and where we *were*.

Modern times began for us with the end of the War. The Surf, bringing with it an awareness of ocean rather than bay – the Pacific and its culture of Casben swim-shorts for men and bikinis for women, sun-tan oils, thick-shakes, beer gardens, drive-ins – replaced the old still-water sea-side world of the English watering-place.

Southport, near Brisbane, as its name suggests, had been such a place since the early years of the century, its sleepy waters closed in by The Spit, its pier ending in a vast picture-house where you could see the water glinting through the floorboards as you watched a Tarzan or Bette Davis movie.

Almost overnight it became a backwater. Now it was the surf-beaches that ran south of it that were all the go. Over the next decade their dunes were reclaimed and levelled; the little settlements of one-storeyed fibro houses along the coast linked up and became continuous; the swamps behind were drained to create canals and islands. New and more exotic names – the Isle of Capri or Florida Keys – replaced older ones like Brighton and Ramsgate.

What was under way was the move from an English to a West-Coast/Mediterranean style – outdoor café-tables, espresso coffee, gelato, octopus, rocket and parmesan salad – and that obsession with 'look' that is about as far as you can get from the joyless austerity that still hangs on, in some parts of modern Britain, as a last grim assurance of non-conformist virtue and moral seriousness.

The danger is that 'look' can become all there is, and there are times when Sydney especially comes perilously close. But the look is there and has become recognisably Australian enough to have travelled back to the UK under that label: as Australian cuisine, Australian clothes, Australian interior design, the Australian 'lifestyle' as it is exhibited daily in *Neighbours* and *Home and Away*.

Peter Conrad has recently marked the distance Australians have come in the thirty years he has been in London from a bit of dialogue in the English series *Queer as Folk*. '*Me* though,' a bemused Vince says to his mate Stuart of a new boyfriend. 'I can't be the best shag 'e's ever had. 'E's *Australian*.'

For the English these days Australians have got away and become sexy.

How far this has gone in Australia itself I judge from an exchange, not long ago, with a laid-back waiter in a bistro in Perth.

'Do you do an espresso?' I ask innocently enough, having recently had experience of Bermuda.

There is just a flicker of pain in the blue-blue-eyes at this suggestion from an East Coaster that he might have washed up in some corner of Hicksville.

'*Ristretto*, sir?' he asks with a slight curl of the lip.

'That'd be great,' I say.

'*Coretto?*'

Put thoroughly in my place, I tell him meekly: 'I don't think we need to go that far.'

Songs My Father Sang

A good deal of the energy of an advanced society like the one we live in goes into diverting people; filling their time and their heads with whatever they need in the way of entertainment; some of it enlivening, most of it trivial. What *mass* entertainment means is that there should be something on offer, pretty well twenty-four hours in the day, for every taste. But none of it any longer has precedence, none of it exerts such a dominating influence as to constitute a mainstream: in that sense there *is* no mainstream. There is simply more and more variety, and with each year that passes, more and more specialisation: a many-stranded mix from which we are free to take whatever pleases us, whatever we please.

It wasn't always like this. When I look back on the world I was growing up in, in the late thirties to the early fifties, what I am struck by is how homogeneous the culture was, how little it offered, beyond its own particular kind of riches, to specialist or divergent taste; the degree to which all the members of a family, for instance, young and old, shared the same social occasions and enjoyed the same interests: card-games like Euchre or Five Hundred or Auction Bridge; the pictures on Saturday night. There was, as yet, no separate 'youth culture', though by the mid-fifties, the first signs of it – with Rock 'n' Roll and the growing beach culture – were beginning to emerge.

Families sang together round the piano on Sunday evenings, and gathered round the household's single wireless – in those days a sizeable piece of furniture – to listen, along with millions of others, to such central items of the national culture as 'The Amateur Hour', John Dease's 'Quiz Kids', 'The Lux Radio Theatre'; or to dramatisations (on a commercial station, not the ABC) of such classic novels as *Emma* or Harrison Ainsworth's *Old St Paul's*, or to the long-running serials whose twists and turns of plot made up, next day, part of the nation's shared conversation in school playgrounds, at Smoko in work-places, and over morning-tea at McWhirter's or David Jones.

This was the nation's culture: low to middle-brow and very nearly universal.

The ABC orchestras were there, and the ABC broadcast its own symphony concerts and played a limited range of 'classical music', but what made up the bulk of what was to be heard on virtually every radio station – along with the Big Bands, Broadway

267

melodies and the latest hit tunes from the movies, some early country music and a whole range of popular ballads – was something called 'light classical', an odd mixture in which the enduring favourites, known to pretty well everyone, were Handel's 'Largo', Liszt's 'Liebestraum', Rachmaninoff's Prelude in C Sharp Minor, 'The Nun's Chorus' from *Casanova*, and half a dozen arias from opera or operetta. Virtually nothing in this almost universal mix was Australian save by adoption. It was what might have been heard at that time anywhere in the UK, and with a few local variations, in any other part of the English-speaking world, from Christchurch to Calgary.

Our tie to a particular world, to occasions and the memory of occasions, is intimately bound up with the emotions inspired in us by the songs we sing. Music, of all the arts, goes directly to the heart, catching us out sometimes when in another part of ourselves we have already moved on. There are a good many of us, I'd guess – committed republicans, rejecters of all things English, all things British – who still feel a shameful tug at the heart when we hear the first bars of 'Land of Hope and Glory' or any number of those folk-songs, and hymn tunes and ballads, that once made up the fabric, not simply of what we listened to and sang along with, but of our deepest feelings. It is impossible, in the end, to disentangle what was merely personal in what we felt back there from what tied us to a household and its rituals, and through a dense intermingling of cultural associations that grounded us deeply in both place and time to at least two countries, one of them always Australia.

My father, a Rugby League footballer and professional boxer in his youth, later the owner of a small trucking business, had little formal education, but was fond of music and played both the piano and the piano-accordion by ear. He had a high, sweet tenor voice, his model, of course, John McCormack, who had also been the idol, two decades earlier, of James Joyce. One of the strongest memories of my early childhood, in the late thirties and early forties, is of him singing in the car on the hour-long drive to Scarborough down the bay, or on Sunday nights round the piano – my mother playing while he sang 'Mother Machree' or 'Just a Song at Twilight' or, with one of my mother's friends, 'The Indian Love Call'.

The locally-born son of Syrian (Lebanese) migrants, he was passionately Australian, but that his patriotism included strong feelings for England, a place to which he had no connection and had never seen, went naturally, it seemed to me, with what he took up from the English and Irish ballads he liked to sing. He would have said, I think, that Britain represented all he most admired in the world he had grown up in: fair play, decency, concern for the weak and helpless, a belief that life, in the end, was serious.

Of course even a culture that is on the whole coherent and uniform has its elements of the exotic, and of dissatisfaction and dissent.

I did not think of us as exotic, we were too ordinary, too much like everyone else, for that; and despite the name and the 'background', my father was too Australian. But he did have mates who were different; disaffected in ways he was not – dissident even – and I remind myself that at the precise moment of which I am writing, though unknown to me, Clem Christesen's *Meanjin Papers* was getting under way, which had a very different notion of what our national life might be, and that on the other side of the river, across Victoria Bridge, at The Pink Elephant, a late-night café run by Frank Mitchell and financed in part by the painter Donald Friend, writers, artists, and young men in lipstick and high heels were preparing to shock us out of our suburban complacency with explosions of Modernist colour and Expressionist visions of our world that by interiorising it, by allowing imagination a part in how we might regard it, would break the mould of our thinking, and with it the old 'British' culture in which we had for so long been comfortably stuck.

One of my father's friends from the Markets was Max Julius, who was a big noise in the local Communist Party. Through him we went to a showing of the first part of *Ivan the Terrible* at a big fundraising affair at the Town Hall for the Russian war effort, and I had my first encounter with Russian cinema, which I would follow up, a decade later, at the monthly showing of the latest Soviet extravaganza, at the Lyric, West End.

What all this represented was a quite different line of interests and affections from the one my father followed. But it was an aspect of the 'coherence' of the time that he was in close contact with it, and while remaining fiercely loyal to Australia and to Empire, allowed it a place. I have no idea how he voted in the 1951 referendum to outlaw the Communist Party, but my guess is that for all his admiration for Mr Menzies he might have allowed even more to his misguided friend Max Julius.

This is a world so distant from our own, here at the beginning of the twenty-first century, that we are inclined to misread its cultural homogeneity as simpler than it was; to see it as unsophisticated and nationally unaware. In fact people were very aware of themselves as Australian, not English, when it came to such local symbols as Bradman, or the Light Horse, or Phar Lap or Gallipoli. But no distinction was made in other areas. In the case of food, for example, Yorkshire pudding was *Australian*. It was what we had always eaten, what else could it be? When my father declared it his favourite, it was because, like his other favourite, Worcestershire Sauce, which he poured even on his roast beef and peas, it was what, in growing up as an Australian, he had quite unselfconsciously taken as local, and adopted with all the rest.

To what extent all this was part of Australia's economic dependency on Britain, on the fact that we made very little of our own, and that most of what passed through our hands in daily use came from England – because we belonged to the British market, and because 'Made in England' was an indisputable guarantee of quality – is another question altogether. We were part of the Empire, what other market would we belong to? The American? – But we *did*. What about all those Buicks and Pontiacs and Chryslers on the road? What about Caltex? What about the movies? The Japanese? – That too. The place was flooded with cheap Japanese goods in exchange for the wool they bought from us and the pig-iron we sent them. Which is why, after Pearl Harbor in 1941, people smashed virtually every cup, saucer and dinner plate in the house. Japan is where the contents of whole kitchen cabinets had come from. Only the *best* tea-cups and dinner plates were English.

The feelings that were bound up for us in old songs like the 'Eriskay Love Lilt' or 'God Rest Ye Merry Gentlemen' were part of an emotional world that was deeply Australian because we could not have seen it as anything else; and the feelings of loyalty such emotions embodied – to England or Scotland certainly, but also to that Australia to which these things had always belonged, and since we shared them, to one another – were what held that world together and defined it, defined *us*. As Australians. And much else, too, that did not strictly belong: Max Julius' Communist Party, the sort of country music Tex Morton sang (American in origin like the rodeo world that went with it but since *he* was singing it Australian by adoption), even, at a pinch, The Pink Elephant. All these disparate elements could be gathered in and included, because providing a place for what was contrary – the non-conformist and dissenting – was a quality of the culture itself. If some of these fellers chose other affiliations and loyalties, people like my father simply shook their head, shrugged their shoulders and left them to it. What a man chose to believe and devote his life to was his own affair. Part of the ethos – and this was so deeply British as to be essentially Australian – was that you did not interfere.

Like Nothing But Itself

But this 'Britain' we evoke so glibly, as if we were all agreed on what is to be understood by it, is in fact a multiple phenomenon and one that is continually shifting shape; as how could it not be when for so long before the founding of Australia it had been made up of two separate states and kingdoms, not to mention Ireland, the principality of Wales and such distinct regional worlds within England itself as the West, the North of England, the North-West, each with its own history and dialect and culture, and all existing, at best, in an uneasy relationship with the centre and with one another. In the half-century before 1788, England had put down two rebellions in Scotland, one in 1715, the other in '45, and before the century was out would face another in Ireland.

This is significant because these divisions at home were also transported. Englishmen, Irishmen, Welshmen, Scots would carry over to the new place a history, passionately embodied in such names as Drogheda, The Boyne, Culloden, that would go on being remembered here. In so far as they were for a long time, most of them, Englishmen or Irishmen or Scots-in-Australia, this would continue to affect their relationship, as 'Australians', with England and with one another.

All this ought to make us wary of what we mean by 'British' or 'English', and more alive than we some- times are to the contradictory factors involved on both sides when we speak of the attitude, at any time, of 'Australians' to either.

I say 'at any time' because Britain, as well as being in itself diverse and divided, has also, over the two centuries of our relationship with it, been in a state of almost continuous transformation. A good many of what we think of as changes in our *own* history have been a repetition, or at least a reflection, of changes there.

*

The Britain of the mid-nineteenth century, for example, that in 1855, sixty-seven years after the arrival of the First Fleet in Botany Bay, granted New South Wales and other states their own legislative assemblies, was a very different nation from the one that had founded the colony in 1788; different in itself, but different as well in its attitude to its possessions and to the world at large.

As the supreme maritime and industrial power of the day, though already under challenge from Germany and the United States, it was moving rapidly, in the 1850s, to that period of high empire that would reach its peak between the 1880s and the First World War, when something like a quarter of the globe would be under its sway. The various Australian colonies – as independently governed English-speaking offshoots of the motherland, with their own economies and armies – had a privileged place in this patchwork ensemble, with a status quite different from that of, say, India or the West Indies, or the newly acquired territories in Africa.

But by 1926, less than a decade after the Great War, Britain had entered a new phase, and allowed the Empire to devolve. On the urging of the Canadians and South Africans, but with resistance from Australia and New Zealand, the four 'Dominions' were declared, under the Statute of Westminster in 1931, to be 'autonomous Communities within the British Empire, equal in status, in no way subordinate to one another in their domestic or external affairs, though united by a common allegiance to the Crown and fully associated as members of the British Commonwealth of Nations'.

This represented a different relationship again with Britain, and in fact a different Britain; one that, while retaining the benefits of empire (imperial preference for example), was eager to free itself from some of the obligations – such as the need for its fleet to operate across the whole globe in defence of its Pacific colonies, which had become a particular burden, and got harder and harder to bear with the arrival, early in the century, of a new power in the area, Japan.

Then, after the Second World War, there was a further change and more radical devolution. A Britain that had been severely debilitated by war granted India and Pakistan their independence in 1947, and the old Empire became a Commonwealth.

This post-war Britain was no longer the world's largest naval and industrial power, and no longer the place that older members of the 'white' empire had for so long looked to as the source of all things good and true. It was by now a power of the second order, and, following a path we too would follow, but a decade later, a multi-ethnic and multicultural place. By the mid-fifties, whole suburbs of London – Brixton and West Kensington, for example – had become West Indian or African enclaves, and towns like Leicester in the Midlands and Bradford in the North were largely Indian or Pakistani. A decade later, just as we were beginning to change our migration policy to something more open, the British, overwhelmed by Indians who had been expelled from Uganda, changed theirs to a more restrictive one that would catch us too in its net.

In the world Britain now saw itself in, the old dominions, even the white ones, could have no special place or privilege in its decision making. When, after nearly a decade of negotiations and passionate debate at home, and with great bitterness on the part of Australia, New Zealand and other members of the old Commonwealth, Britain at last became a full member of the European Common Market, Australia had to recognise that in its old form – one based, in the most cynical view, on the flow of wheat, butter, beef, hides in one direction and rolling-stock, machine tools, investment, capital, Mini-Minors and impoverished migrants in the other – the tie was broken. We needed to detach ourselves and discover new ties elsewhere. No wonder our relationship with this protean monster is so difficult to track.

*

Consider our extraordinary reluctance, in the thirties, to take up the independence that was offered us by the Statute of Westminster.

Canada ratified it at once; and so, in 1934, did South Africa – the delay there had to do with a belief, on the part of Malan's National Party, that it did not go far enough. We and the New Zealanders rejected it as 'unnecessary', and it was 1942 before we had an overseas representative of our own, even in Washington. Canada had representatives, first in Washington, then in Paris and Tokyo, in 1927.

This may have been timidity, an unwillingness to stand on our own two feet in the world; it may have been, as is often suggested, a misguided loyalty and affection for a mother who basically didn't care a damn for us. But the thirties were anxious years in Australia. The Depression had come earlier here than in other places – there is a good argument to be made that the economic slump of the 1890s, so clearly visible in Sydney in the kind of houses and public buildings that went up before the nineties and the meaner sort of buildings that followed, had never really gone away. Then there was the question of our security in a world of shifting alliances that was moving rapidly towards war.

But other possibilities also suggest themselves. We tend to assume that Federation was a union that was universally desired. It was not. The states deeply distrusted one another, they still do. The tie with Britain was sometimes seen not as a threat to independence but as a guarantee of it against what we would now call 'Canberra' and the other states. Britain could be relied on because it stood at a certain distance. It was the other states that were predatory and too close.

In a late Kipling story, 'A Friend of the Family', a group of Freemasons and First World War veterans is meeting at Lodge 'Faith and Works', 8537 E. C.

A thin, dark brother on my left, who had been attending to a cold pork pie . . . suddenly lifted his long head, in which a pale blue glass eye swivelled insanely.

'Well,' he said slowly. 'My motto is "Never again". Ne-ver again for me.'

'Same here – till next time,' said Pole, across the table. 'You're from Sydney, ain't you?'

'How'd you know?' was the short answer.

'You spoke.' The other smiled, so did Bevin who nodded. 'I know how your push talk, well enough. Have you started that Republic of yours down under yet?'

'No. But we're goin' to. *Then* you'll see.'

'Carry on. No one's hindering,' Bevin pursued.

The Australian scowled. 'No. We know they ain't. And – and – that's what makes us all so crazy angry with you.' He threw back his head and laughed the spleen out of him. 'What can you do with an Empire that – that don't care what you do?'

Perhaps the real truth, as Kipling's not so gentle irony suggests, is that it was the easiness of the tie that made it so difficult to break. After all, we had not had to fight for our independence, it was freely offered. We could make the *final* break whenever it suited us. Why hurry?

Of course not everyone felt like this, any more than every Australian feels now that there is no need to hurry on the republic because we are still free, eighty years later, to take it 'when we please'.

*

When we look at the long history of our relationship with 'the mother country', what we might chiefly be impressed by is the large privilege it has offered us, and how wary we have been of endangering the advantages it brought us.

In the mid-nineteenth century the white, Athenian-style colonies as we might call them, the ones that were largely transplanted offshoots of the mother country – the Australian states, New Zealand, Canada, South Africa – found it easy to think of themselves as overseas provinces of Great Britain rather than colonies, standing in much the same relationship to the centre as other provincial places, Yorkshire or Scotland or Wales; and this was especially true after 1872 when the telegraph was completed. A message sent overnight from London – travelling by submarine cable from Falmouth to Lisbon, Gibraltar and Alexandria, overland to Suez, by cable again to Aden and Bombay, overland to Madras, by cable to Penang, Singapore and Batavia, overland to Benjaewangi, by cable to Darwin and overland to Adelaide – could be in Sydney or Melbourne before morning. As *The Argus* put it: 'the deep sea cables have linked the whole British race together'. Sydney was now as close to London as Aberdeen.

'Too close' for Francis Adams, and dangerously so for Archibald Michie, who as early as 1859, when the line was still being laid, foresaw a time when at a single call from the Empire 'millions of British citizens may any morning be mustered by the wires for the defence of any part'.

But in feeling at least these places had always been close. Melbourne especially, but Sydney too in the 1860s, saw itself as related to London, and all it stood for, in the same way as any other large provincial city – Manchester, for example, or Leeds or Birmingham; places that had grown to be cities in the same period, and where much the same culture was to be found. The same grand buildings, the same plays and operas (Melbourne saw its first performance of Gounod's *Faust* just six months after the London opening), the same books in the public libraries and reading-rooms, the same serialisations of new novels by Dickens or Mrs Gaskell or George Eliot to be breathlessly awaited and passed from hand to hand.

It was only later, when the Empire itself became nationalistic, that a similar nationalism grew up in the various 'regions'; in the form of Scots and Welsh nationalism, and, as the centenary of settlement approached in the eighties, and increasingly in the nineties, in Australia. In the pages of *The Bulletin* for example, and as we see it in Joseph Furphy's defiant reference to his 'bias', in *Such is Life*, as 'offensively Australian'. In all of these places nationalism was a passionate movement, and a noisy one. Whether, except in Ireland, it was very widespread is another matter.

The move towards nationhood in Australia was to say the least leisurely. The strongest argument was geographic – to make the borders of the nation and the continent one. Outside *The Bulletin* and its supporters, and some Irishmen and Scots who remained more anti-English than pro-Australian, very little of the push towards union was fed by the wish to assert a local identity over a British one.

What did exist among Australians in the late nineteenth century, and for a good deal of the twentieth as well, was the uneasy feeling that in being 'provincial' they were also, in all those aspects of Australian life that had to do with education and culture, second-rate – though it's worth pointing out that people would have felt pretty much the same in Cardiff or Belfast.

The best Australian families sent their sons to get a 'real' education at boarding schools in England, then to Oxford and Cambridge. Our most ambitious artists and intellectuals, like their provincial counterparts elsewhere, went to London, and in most cases never came back.

We get a good idea of the bitterness this provoked in those who stayed from Victor Daley's 'When London Calls', where the great metropolis at the heart of the Empire appears as a bedizened harridan, ancient and malign, a heartless Lorelei calling her victims to what looks like a festival but is really a cannibal feast:

> They leave us – artists, singers, all
>   When London calls aloud
> Commanding to her Festival
>   The gifted crowd.

She sits beside the ship-choked Thames,
    Sad, weary, cruel, grand;
Her crown imperial gleams with gems
    From many a land . . .

She sits beside the ship-choked Thames
    With sphinx-like lips apart –
Mistress of many diadems –
    Death in her heart!

If there was a disease at the heart of colonial life, it was the haunting suspicion that it was only *outside* Australia, in that source of all value and meaning, and of all objects too, since virtually everything we used was imported from there, that experience was authentic and real. Only in England were real lives to be lived, real books to be written, real conversations had and real loves discovered. It was also, as Joanie Golson in *The Twyborn Affair* knows, where an Australian had to go to get to the 'real shops'.

All this points to the deepest imbalance of all between Australia and the 'motherland': a sense that life here was somehow thin and insubstantial. After all, what happened in the books one read happened *there,* and Australians were inveterately bookish. Not only in that they read a great deal, but in the belief that what happened in books was the way life really was – and since there were no books, no *real* books, that were Australian, what that meant was, *not here*.

If one thinks of the average Australian reader of the late nineteenth century as a middle-class or lower-middle-class woman living in the suburbs, say, of Melbourne or Adelaide, it is difficult to see what appeal she might have found, either to thought or feeling, in the kind of *Bulletin* writing that presented itself in the nineties as the only form of writing in Australia that spoke for true national spirit. Only life in the Australian bush, and bush values as embodied in the lives of bush workers – all male of course – are authentically 'Australian'. Any form of suburban existence, and the whole world of women, is rejected. Half a dozen of Lawson's later stories, admittedly not his best, are devoted to the spectacle of a once independent male, a mate of the narrator, who has fallen victim to marriage, a regular job in town, temperance and religion – the last two especially being the sphere of baleful female influence. (What a bold and intelligent woman thought of all this we know from the stories of Lawson's contemporary, Barbara Baynton, where the bush male of *Bulletin* fiction appears in a different light altogether.)

There *is* another mode of Australian writing in the 1890s, but it has barely survived. We see it in Tasma's *Uncle Piper of Piper's Hill* and in Rosa Praed's novels of political life in Brisbane (or Leichhardt Town as she calls it) in the years after the declaration of the new state.

Praed's novels have a good dash of melodrama, but can be emotionally complex and are very convincing in their observation of provincial – that is, colonial – snobbery and pretension. She is good on landscape, the lush mountain ranges and rainforests of south-east Queensland, and on Aboriginal life and conditions (not much of *that* in *The Bulletin* writers), but was dismissed out of hand by Australian critics, as if no form of middle-class life in Australia was worth writing about because the thing itself was derivative and 'English'.

In fact that was not at all how the English themselves saw it. Life as it was lived in Melbourne and Sydney was, from an English point of view, a very poor and degraded imitation. Altogether too 'free'. Too lacking in nuance and refinement. Too strenuous and pushing – or to use Darwin's word, 'ambitious'. Which is another way of saying that Australians had already, in British eyes, begun to create their own version of 'Englishness', which would in time move further and further from the original.

To the extent that the imitation was a 'bad' one, it had already, even if it had not been recognised as such, and most of all by those who were living it, gone its own way and become a variant. Something new and like nothing but itself.

Homeland

Because we find it so difficult to imagine any history but the one we have actually experienced, and because what we know and find ordinary seems less attractive than what might have been, we tend to undervalue what was handed to us – by accident as it were, but fatefully – when we were founded in 1788 by the British rather than one of the other European powers of the time that might have done so. I say 'might have' as if this were a real possibility, but it is doubtful in fact whether anyone but the British, at that point in the eighteenth century, possessed the administrative capacity, or the naval capacity either, to organise a colonising venture on so large a scale and to a place whose conditions of climate and soil were so completely unknown. What is pretty well certain is that no other European power possessed the capacity to maintain and service such a colony.

The First Fleet was a sizeable small armada, as we see from the models of the eleven vessels at the Museum of Sydney. Any suggestion that it was carelessly got up is a myth, and a foolish one, created by historians for whom nothing the British did in the case of Australia could ever be good. As Alan Frost shows very convincingly in his *Botany Bay Mirages*, this was the most ambitious, but also, in the event, the most successful colonising venture ever undertaken by a European power.

European nations in the eighteenth century were obsessed with trade, and with that natural outcome of trade, empire. What was needed to ensure both was almost continuous warfare. If we include the role played by the French navy in the American War of Independence, Great Britain and France fought five wars between 1701 and 1815, in continental Europe, India, North America and at sea, till Britain realised that it was at sea that she must finally prevail.

But the eighteenth century was also interested in other forms of conquest: the conquest of time and the conquest of space; and Australia, while it was founded on the needs of trade, really grew out of this second interest. It was a product of *mind*, in its active form as discovery, rather than a by-product simply of empire. John Harrison, the inventor of the chronometer, Cook and a whole line of French and English geographers and cartographers, intellectual rivals rather than enemies – these were our true founding fathers. It was the mystery of how time and space might be linked and made one that drew Wallis and Carteret, and Cook and Bougainville and La Pérouse and d'Entrecasteaux, to venture so boldly across space and then so meticulously, day after day, to chart and place their discoveries at this or that 'minute' of distance from the great dome at Greenwich.

The French first laid claim to the western part of New Holland in 1772, and by one of those quirks of fate, La Pérouse, with his ships *La Boussole* and *L'Astrolabe* (wonderfully eighteenth-century and appropriate, those names), appeared at the entrance to Botany Bay just as the First Fleet was preparing to move on to Port Jackson.

Fifteen years later, Nicolas Baudin, in the *Geographe* and the *Naturaliste*, was mapping the south coast of South Australia in one direction while Flinders was mapping it from the other; their point of meeting, in April 1802, is commemorated in 'Encounter' Bay. In the account of Baudin's voyage by François Péron, what we know now as South Australia is called Terre de Napoléon.

As late as 1819 a French Council of Ministers appointed a committee to investigate the possibility of establishing a penal colony near what is now Albany in Western Australia. When, in December 1826, the British sent a party of convicts, under Major Edmund Lockyer, to found their own settlement at King George's Sound, it was a move hastily made to counter a suspected French move in the same direction; as earlier it had been French interest after d'Entrecasteaux's charting of the Derwent that had led to the founding of Hobart. The French have had this much of a part in our early history that they were indirectly responsible for the settlement of two out of the seven states.

But the French, for all the size and experience of their navy, had trouble with supply; and we can imagine, from what very nearly happened in the case of Botany Bay, how quickly a small and isolated French settlement in the place might have gone under. And its history, of course, if it had not, would have been that of metropolitan France: a revolution in 1789, with the sort of internal divisions and violence that plagued d'Entrecasteaux's expedition in 1793; two major coups in '94 and '99; a fifteen-year dictatorship under Napoleon, a restoration of the Bourbons in 1815, two more revolutions in 1830 and 1848, then another dictatorship under yet another Napoleon from 1852, then another bloody rising in the Paris Commune of 1870.

Compare this with the quiet evolution of New South Wales from penal settlement in 1788 to a colony with its own Legislative Assembly in 1855.

As for other possibilities, Darwin's comparison of New South Wales with the colonies in South America in 1836, together with what we know of their subsequent history, gives us a good notion of where we might be after the sort of administrative disorder and military coups we would have imported from Portugal or Spain.

Aboriginal people have no reason to rejoice that it was a British invasion and displacement that destroyed their way of life and savagely reduced their numbers, but when we look at what happened to the Caribs, or in Guatemala and Brazil, one wonders if they would have had less to endure under an occupation by the Spanish or Portuguese.

*

Britain at the end of the eighteenth century was a mercantile power, its lifeblood trade – a nation of shopkeepers Napoleon would call it; interested only in markets, the sea-routes that served them, and the ports of supply that kept those sea-routes open. Overseas territories, great tracts of land that needed to be maintained and serviced, and with populations that had to be controlled, were more trouble than they were worth.

Of course the loss of the American colonies was a blow to British pride, and the war, especially when the French joined it, had been expensive and very nearly fatal. But the revolution itself was inevitable – wasn't it only to be expected that the same spirit of dissent and love of liberty that had led men to escape the tyranny of Church and Crown on one occasion would make them want to escape again? From the British Government's point of view, the loss of the American colonies could be tolerated, and might even be welcome, so long as the French could be kept from Canada. What mattered was that the American *market* should be retained.

So why a new settlement, and so far off? Why the Pacific?

In the 1770s, Cook had put the continent we call Australia on the world map, and in two ways: once, as we all know, in his first voyage in 1770, by charting its east coast and claiming possession of it in the name of the King; more importantly, in his second voyage in 1772, by establishing a passage to the Pacific – a westerly passage through the Southern Ocean, and in the zone of the Roaring Forties – that was faster than any other and, from the British point of view, safer: it could still operate if Britain's enemies, especially France, threatened the other routes; by drawing Holland, for example, which held both Trincomalee (Ceylon) and the Cape, into a hostile alliance. What was needed to make this new route viable was a safe harbour in the south, a station that could provide port facilities but also fresh fruit and vegetables against scurvy on the long haul to India. A place too that would in time offer as many as possible of the civilised amenities to those who would be stationed there.

The strongest reason for the establishment of a settlement on the east coast of Australia was to protect the East India Company. The convicts are a separate story. Sydney was first and foremost to be a port, like Penang; and that perhaps was *all* it was to be, though Phillip, because he was large-minded and saw more, had ambitions. This is why so little attempt was made in the first twenty years to penetrate the hinterland or to open up the surrounding country, and none at first to occupy the rest of the continent. The whole life of the place had to do with the sea, not the land. All its early governors were naval officers.

Our beginnings are sometimes spoken of as 'accidental'. The old jibe continues to be repeated that Botany Bay was founded in a fit of absent-mindedness by the Pitt Administration. But this surely is denied by the size of the First Fleet, the trouble that was taken in getting it up, and, as Alan Frost has shown, the cost per convict involved in that first act of transportation, which for a responsible Administration would hardly have been economical if all they had in hand was the getting out of the country of a few hundred 'undesirables'. These convicts must have had something more to contribute than mouths to be fed and bodies to be housed, and they did of course. They had their labour.

The fact is that the colony in New South Wales was *founded*, not simply acquired – even Canada was acquired – and it is one of the *first* colonies; one of the earliest and oldest, not at all late. Perhaps this is why, for all its geographical distance from Britain, or perhaps in defiance of that distance, it has always been keen to present itself as the closest in affection, and was till recently, along with New Zealand, the most enduring in its reluctance to break away. And of course it was no disadvantage to the fledgling colony of the 1780s that Britain was the richest power of the day.

Economically vibrant, technologically advanced to a degree almost unimaginable in other parts of Europe, Britain also had a political system whose efficiency and stability was the guarantee of the rest.

A century earlier, the Civil War of 1641–49 had settled the conflict between King and Parliament on the parliamentary side, and what that bloody conflict had left unresolved was finished at last, in 1688, in a Bloodless Revolution that barred the Crown to any but Protestants, forbade a standing army in peacetime, and guaranteed yearly Parliaments, free elections, and (on paper at least, though in practice one or another of them was sometimes compromised or withdrawn) freedom of religion, opinion and conscience. By the end of the seventeenth century a set of political institutions had been established that continues to this day, and is the one, with some changes, that has granted political stability – the non-violent transfer of power from one administration to the next – for 300 years in the United Kingdom, more than 200 in the United States, and 150 here.

The system we inherited in 1788, and which became officially our own with the institution of representative government in 1855, was the British two-party system of oppositional government, the Westminster system with its guarantee of a separation of powers between the executive and the judiciary, and an independent and responsible Civil Service with its own culture of dedication to the public good. All this, together with the long and varied discourse that had argued and sustained it, was transported to New South Wales along with the rest: British Low Church puritanism and fear of the body and its pleasures – but also British drunkenness; British pragmatism and distrust of theory; British philistinism and dislike of anything showy, theatrical, arty or 'too serious'; British good sense and the British sense of humour – all there for us to deal with and develop in our own way, or after due consideration to reject.

The extent to which the early colony was maintained, even in wartime, and grew, can be seen in the astonishment with which Nicolas Baudin, who spent three months in Sydney in 1802, writes of 'the immense work that the English have done during the twelve years they have been at Port Jackson. It is . . . difficult to conceive how they have so speedily attained to the state of splendour and comfort in which they now find themselves.'

This 'splendour and comfort', as Baudin calls it, had been achieved at a cost – the sweat and blood of the men, the convicts of the First and later fleets, who made the roads and built the barracks and warehouses and wharves he so much admired.

What is not so often recalled is that there was an alternative to this; and the British Government's decision that the colony should be established on the labour of convicts rather than the labour of slaves is one of the great determining factors of our world and of its moral and spiritual tone even today.

*

When the possibility of a new settlement in the Pacific was mooted in the 1780s, the slavery question had been at issue in Britain for almost a century. The list of public figures who had spoken out against it is both long and prestigious: Baxter, Richard Steele, Pope, Sterne, Dr Johnson, Cowper among the writers, but also Paley, Wakefield, Josiah Wedgwood, Adam Smith.

In 1772, Lord Mansfield had brought down the watershed judgement that a slave, as soon as he set foot on British soil, was free. From that moment slavery within the British Isles was illegal, though not in such British territories as the West Indies, where, to Jamaica alone, over 600,000 Africans were brought between 1700 and 1775. It was not until 1807 that a bill was finally enacted in the British Parliament that no vessel 'should clear out for slaves from any port within the British dominions after May 1807' and that no slave be landed in the colonies after March 1808. But the first motion on the subject, that 'the slave trade is contrary to the laws of God and the rights of man' was moved as early as 1776 (by David

Hartley, son of the philosopher, Coleridge's friend), and by 1788 a committee of the Privy Council had been set up to consider the trade in all its respects. There was no possibility, when the establishment of the new settlement was being debated in the early eighties, that it could be founded on slave labour, and since the chance of attracting *free* labour to such a remote area of the globe was minimal, that left only convicts, and as we know, a good many convicts, held in overcrowded jails and in the hulks, were readily available.

In being spared the institution of slavery we were saved many things; most of all the enduring social and moral stigma of being descendants of a world in which some of us had suffered the injustice and physical degradation of being chattel slaves and others the spiritual degradation of having been their owners and keepers. The 'convict stain' as we came to call it, and which was for a long time deeply felt, was one that was bound to fade – the child of a convict is born free. It might even, in time, be redefined as a mark of distinction. The stain of slavery is ineradicable, and on both sides.

In rejecting 'the institution' we were saved from having our world *shaped* by slavery: by laws made first to establish and then to abolish it, and by a whole apparatus of equivocations and bad faith that would have made a mockery of all those aspirations to egalitarianism that we regard as the best of what we are. We have never had to equivocate in the use of the word 'liberty', in such phrases as 'liberty of opinion' or 'liberty of conscience', to justify the official existence among us of those who do not have the most essential liberty of all, the ownership of their own bodies.

Americans enshrined the word in their Constitution, and earlier still in the Declaration, both noble documents – we have nothing to equal them; but as Thoreau points out in *On the Duty of Civil Disobedience*, 'one sixth of the population of the nation that has undertaken to be the refuge of liberty are slaves'. At the time when he was writing this, in 1848, the most valuable single item of the United States economy was not agriculture, or minerals or manufactured goods, but chattel slaves.

*

Our history here has been, by most standards, unviolent, and there are no doubt many reasons for this. One is that prohibition of 1688 against a standing army in peacetime, which has offered no opportunity here to an elite officer corps with a five-star general at its head to intervene in the political life of the country and save us from 'democratic chatter' and the divisiveness of parliaments. No military coups, no tanks in the street. Another is the formalisation of the sort of violent factionalism that characterised English political life in the seventeenth century as 'Her Majesty's Government' and 'Her Majesty's Loyal Opposition'. But another, surely, was that early avoidance of institutionalised slavery.

Violence is essential to the maintenance of slavery, and, where slavery has become entrenched in the economic and social structure of a state, is essential also to its removal, as we see in the case of the Civil War in America and the long history of bloody rebellions and massacres in the West Indies and Brazil. States where slavery once existed continue to have a higher level of violence than places where it did not.

One Australian state, Queensland, did attempt to create a plantation society here, on the model of the American South. A bill of the Queensland Parliament in 1862, just three years after Separation and at the very mid-point of the American Civil War, licensed the importation into the state of 'Kanakas' as three-year indentured labourers, and over the next forty years some 60,000 were brought in from the Pacific Islands, many of them kidnapped or 'black-birded'.

The other Australian states, where opposition to cheap 'coolie' labour had become a plank of the labour movement, were passionately hostile, and until the Kanaka question was settled no move towards Federation could be made. In the end Queensland gave in. Most of the Pacific Islanders were repatriated. The rest became Australian citizens.

Shameful as this episode is, one point needs stressing. These were indentured labourers, not chattel slaves. The most enduring effect of all this came after Federation, in the move against any but European (and for a time any but *northern* European) migration, the White Australia policy; which began as a protection of Australian workers and ended, farcically, as a search of the displaced persons camps in Europe, after World War Two, for blond, blue-eyed Balts and others who might pass in time for British.

*

All these ways of experiencing the world, of thinking about it and creating institutions for dealing with it and with the affairs of women and men, were for better or worse passed on to us at the moment of our founding. And along with them – inherent in them we might say – another quality, less easy to define and talk about than institutions or the ideas on which they are based.

This is that 'habit of mind' we think of as being essentially and uniquely Anglo-Saxon: one that prefers to argue from example and practice rather than principle; that is happy, in a pragmatic way, to be in doubt as to *why* something works so long as it does work; is flexible, experimental, adaptive, and scornful of all those traps it sees in theory and principles. It is the habit of mind that created the Common Law, devised the British parliamentary system, gave Britain its head-start in the new Scientific Age and the Industrial Revolution that grew out of it, and was vital, here in Australia, to the capacity of the early settlers to abandon whatever expectations they had arrived with, and adapt, quickly and with the success that is noted by so many early commentators, to new and unknown conditions – and this at every level. On the part of ordinary men and women as well as governors and administrators.

Like all forms of strength it has its weak side: anti-intellectualism and complacent philistinism; a preference for moderation that can all too easily become mediocrity – deficiencies that Charles Darwin identified in the new colony as far back as 1836, along with material progress and the energy that produced it, and which, as they dismayed him then, would dismay him even more perhaps today. But the strengths are real ones.

Most of all, it is a habit of mind that is inherent in the very shape and tone of the language we speak. As how could it not be, when the language is its most complete and perfect creation?

*

I referred to the language earlier as what we all, as English speakers, come home to; that other country of which we are by nature citizens. But what do we mean when we think of ourselves, and of the Americans, Canadians, New Zealanders, Jamaicans, Pakistanis, and the very diverse inhabitants these days of the British Isles, as 'English speakers'? Don't we need to ask ourselves, in each case, in what sense 'speakers', and 'which English'?

It is all very well to regard language as simply 'a means of communication'. It may be that for those to whom it is new and unfamiliar, who use it only for the most basic exchanges. But for most of us it is also a machine for thinking, for feeling; and what can be felt and thought in one language – the sensibility it embodies, the range of phenomena it can take in, the activities of mind as well as the objects and sensations it can deal with – is different, both in quality and kind, from one language to the next. The world of Chinese or Arabic is different from the world of German or French or English, as the worlds those European languages embody and refer to differ from one another. A language is the history and experience of the men and women who, in their complex dealings with the world, made it; but it is itself one of the makers of that history, and the history it makes is determined – limited – by its having developed in one direction rather than another; in one direction to the *exclusion* of others. It is also shaped and changed by what is said in it.

The English, for example, that contains the works of Shakespeare, the English we know and use, is a very different language from the one that existed before he took hold of it and showed that the real motive force of thinking in English is the creative leap that occurs in metaphor.

Other languages move by logic, English, as we see from even the most common idioms – a 'tower of strength', 'a dog's breakfast' – by association. Whether or not Shakespeare actually invented this use of language, he demonstrated how it could be put to use, and in using it, taught us to do so. He changed the way men and women think in English, and feel through it, wherever the language is spoken, and this over and above what is there in the works themselves: in characters, in metaphysical or psychological insights, political arguments, in vividly dramatised situations, or in quotations and idioms that have become part of daily usage.

But a language, as a living organism, is always changing. New objects or new technologies come tumbling in and require new terms and new formulas to express them. New technologies and the ideologies that come with them change people's relationships with one another, in factories and other workplaces, in families, on the land. New poems, songs, books and other cultural artefacts introduce new modes of feeling and new passwords in the exchange of feeling. Shifts, large or small, in the relationship between the governors and the governed bring changes to the tone and rhetoric of public discourse, that language of explanation or persuasion or negotiation through which power speaks to its constituency and the constituency speaks back.

We can track such changes very easily through written texts, and when it comes to daily speech from the language of plays, and later, novels. By the way characters in the fast-moving 'journalistic' comedies of Thomas Middleton for example – the card-sharps, pickpockets, confidence tricksters and whores of *Your Five Gallants* (1607) or the Puritan shopkeepers and householders of *The Familie of Love* (1602) – address one another, within families and across classes, in shops, taverns, chapels, eating-houses, and the very different language through which characters interact in, say, Jane Austen or Mrs Gaskell, or later again in *Ulysses*, or in a novel by Jonathan Franzen or a play by Harold Pinter or Edward Albee.

Or we might compare the throwaway style of the editorial in yesterday's *Herald* with the formal tone and sentence structure of a similar editorial of a hundred years ago, or the language of Triple J with the language of a commercial station of the fifties, or John Howard or Kevin Rudd's answers to a caller on talk-back radio, or in an interview on TV, with the sort of rhetoric that would regularly have been heard from a Menzies or Doc Evatt.

The tone that is acceptable from any politician

now has been changed utterly by the reduction in 'distance' over the past forty years between audience and speaker. The public figure is no longer sixty feet off on a platform, or a mere voice on the air-waves, but right there in our living-room. Different perceptions of sincerity and trust must be taken account of, different conditions of intimacy apply.

*

Australia was founded at a particular turning-point in the evolution of English, and the form of English we inherited has been a strong shaping influence on what happened here, and on the way it happened.

The American colonies, founded in the first decade of the previous century, inherited a different English altogether. Passionately evangelical and utopian, deeply imbued with the religious fanaticism and radical violence of the time, this was the language of the Diggers, Levellers, English Separatists and other religious dissenters of the early seventeenth century, who left England to found a society that would be free, as they saw it, of authoritarian government by Church or Crown. It was far removed from the cool, dispassionate English in which, 180 years later, in the 1780s, a parliamentary committee argued the pros and cons of a new colony in the Pacific. This was the language of the English and Scottish Enlightenment:

sober, unemphatic, good-humoured; a very sociable and moderate language, modern in a way that even we would recognise, and supremely rational and down to earth.

What had happened to change the language so radically in that 180 years?

Elizabethan and Jacobean language, like the society it expressed, had been violent, and violently abusive. That was a large part of its liveliness. We see this in the plays of the period in the so-called 'Wars between the Theatres', and in satirical poems, pamphlets – like those that were tossed back and forth in the scurrilous 'Marprelate' controversy – and in the 'cony-catching' novels of such muck-raking adventurers as Thomas Nashe and Robert Greene. All these writings, right down to the pamphlets of a figure as austerely fastidious as Milton, are marked by an extraordinary level of public vituperation.

Englishmen abroad, as contemporary observers present them, are swaggering bully-boys, drunken loud-mouths, forever on the lookout for a quarrel and constantly provoking brawls. Ben Jonson, who knew something of all this from his tour of the Continent with the young Wat Raleigh, Sir Walter's loutish and ungovernable son, gives us a good picture of such a figure in Sir Politic Would-be in *Volpone*.

When the scion of a good county family came up to London, as young Kastril does in *The Alchemist*, it was to learn to 'quarrel', to be a 'roaring boy'. Quarrelling and the language of quarrelling were at the heart of the sectarian and political violence that led to the Civil War, which had from the beginning been as much a war of words, of the way opposing ideas found violent language to clothe and arm them, as a war with muskets and pikes.

What had to be reformed in the aftermath of the war was not simply factional politics and a tradition of angry dissension and dissent, but the language through which these were encouraged and spread. English had to be purged of all those forms of violent expression that had led men to violent action. By limiting the one, you would limit the other. The language itself was to be disarmed. Irony would replace invective; good-humour, a middle tone, balance of syntactical structure, would ensure the proper weighing of pros and cons that would make extremist views so crass and undisciplined, so ungentlemanly, as to have no place in polite society. Moderate language would produce moderation.

And it worked. By the early years of the eighteenth century the English 'roaring boy' had become, in the description of Continental commentators, the phlegmatic English gentleman. Young men who had previously gone up to London to learn how to quarrel now learned to be 'polite'. The business of politics became negotiation, and of conflict compromise.

This was the 'reasonable' language of the English and Scottish Enlightenment that became the language in which social institutions in Australia argued and resolved their difficulties, and in which, when the time came, our plain, uninspired Constitution would be written – nothing there of those utopian aspirations and emotional appeals to the great abstractions that we get in the American version.

It was, very largely, the language we inherited – late-Enlightenment English – that created that peculiar mildness of social interaction here that has for more than two centuries kept all kinds of extremism beyond the possibilities of acceptable public discourse and the worst forms of social violence at bay. And this despite the many dissidents, rebels, Chartists and agitators, some of them violent, from the Scottish Martyrs of 1793 to the Tolpuddle Martyrs of 1834, who were brought here to make things 'quieter' at home.

One might have thought that in a place that had already set out to become a working man's paradise, the presence of all these radical imports would produce movements here that were revolutionary at least, if not violently rebellious. But with some exceptions, notably the great Shearers' Strike of the nineties, it was negotiation and arbitration, not violent confrontation, that secured workers' rights in Australia. And Patrick O'Farrell has this to say of another group that is sometimes seen, in potential anyway, as violently disruptive, the Irish rebels who were first transported to Australia after the Rebellion of 1798: 'Thus was established a duality vital to the practicalities of Irish behaviour in the colony. Rebels conformed in peace, setting up a marvellous tension between myth and reality which gave the Australian Irish the best of both worlds – the proud and fearsome reputation for rebellion, heroism and devotion to principles of freedom, and a quite profitable stake in the new colony . . . the heroes had taken the quiet path.' This is all the more remarkable because the history of Ireland itself in the later nineteenth and early twentieth centuries was very violent.

No-one I think would accuse Australian English of lacking boldness or colour, but these arise for the most part from a strong sense of humour and a larrikin sense of play, qualities we might trace back to the cockney and criminal world of the convicts. (We owe a good deal as well to Irish eloquence and fantasy.)

What the local language found no place for was that mixture of libertarian individualism and hostility to 'government' that in the United States goes right back to the founding of the various states and commonwealths in the seventeenth century, and to a contemporary (that is, Jacobean) rhetoric of violent dissent; no place either for the language of utopian optimism and a later and related language of the transcendental. And this, for all our similarities and the fellow feeling we share as New World places, marks a difference between us.

We appreciate American eloquence, we are even impressed by it, as when Bill Clinton addressed the two houses of our Parliament to universal applause. But we also distrust it. It is, in the last resort, simply not our style.

*

This introduction of the USA into what is primarily a discussion of Australia's relationship with Britain is, as I suggested earlier, neither accidental nor wilful. It is integral to the relationship itself. Invocations of the older New World seem almost from the beginning to have been obligatory in assessing the prospects of a new world here. Peter Cunningham's engaging and richly observant account of the new colony, *Two Years in New South Wales*, which appeared in two volumes in 1826–27, consistently uses America, as he calls it, as a reference point for his descriptions of the landscape and resources, the trade, population and manners of New South Wales, and he makes a special distinction in favour of Americans as members of an extended 'family' in what is already, clearly, a more multi-ethnic and multicultural place than the purely British one we sometimes imagine. 'Gentlemen foreigners,' he writes, 'of all nations may be met with now in our

Sydney streets, tempted by the fineness of our country and climate to take up permanent residence among us. French, Spaniards, Italians, Germans (Americans I had almost added, but kindred feelings proclaim the impossibility of classing them as such) all add to the variety of language current among us.'

These 'kindred' ties and feelings begin of course with the language we share, and our common derivation, though at different periods, from the same mother source, but they were inherent as well in the British notion of the colony in Australia as a new and improved version of the former colonies in America.

The American colonies had simply emerged, in an unplanned way, haphazardly; New South Wales was planned from the start. It was to be an Enlightenment experiment, a controlled one, in which the Administration's mistakes in the earlier case would not be repeated. Which is to say that from the beginning of our life here, what had happened in America was always in the background, shaping, in a shadowy way, what was to be done here; an example of what might be emulated, but also, in the use of slave labour for example and the raising of taxes, of what should be avoided.

The new colony was a creature at first of the East India Company, which until 1819 had a monopoly over its trade and in the early years controlled all ships that entered its port. The only exception to this in the early days was Americans, who were not subject to British trade rules, and after 1802 the ships of the Southern Whale Fisheries, both of whom played a key role in the early productive life of the colony. This was focused on the sea and its resources – not the land: on the whales that crowded the waters off the east coast and the Southern Ocean, and on the seal-rookeries of Bass Strait, and since whaling and sealing, as we might know from our reading of *Moby Dick*, were industries that were largely in American hands, this was one early link that kept American know-how and ambition clearly in mind in the new colony, and Americans in relatively large numbers coming and going from our shores, where no doubt their example as independent, non-English English-speakers was strongly felt.

Thirty years later, when gold was discovered, thousands of men, neither American citizens nor Australians but with a stake in both places, moved back and forth between California and the east coast of Australia, mixing the population and sharing jargons, slang, folklore and folk music, but also touring opera and theatre troupes and celebrity entertainers. When, in the years leading up to Federation, a model was sought for the new nation-state and its constitutional arrangements, the United States had a strong shaping influence on the discourse and eventually on the form of the two houses, and this was made easier because the American model was itself a variation of the Westminster system, whose principles and practice both we and the Americans shared.

But a triangular relationship is not always a comfortable one.

Britain and the US had, in the earlier part of the nineteenth century, been enemies, and for the rest of the century they remained watchful of one another culturally and bitter rivals in trade.

Two of the areas in which Britain and the US had increasingly different interests were China and Japan – and in so far as this involved the Pacific, it was of crucial importance to Australia as well. And Australia, as a rapidly growing market, was increasingly the scene of Anglo-American competition. Australian loyalty and Australian sentiment were divided by 'kindred feelings' for powers that did not always, themselves, recognise ties of kin.

In 1902, in an attempt to contain Russia, Britain entered into an alliance with Japan, an act that must have rung alarm-bells in the new Federation, which had always seen Japan as a possible threat. Then, in May 1905, the Japanese destroyed the Russian navy in a decisive battle in the Tsushima Strait, and the whole balance of power in the Pacific shifted. Japan became a threat to Britain's Asian and Pacific interests; especially if, as seemed likely, the United States thwarted Japanese ambitions in China and drove them south.

But the arrival on the scene of Japan as the dominant

sea-power in the Pacific alarmed the Americans as well. From 1907 to 1909, thirty-one ships of the United States Pacific Fleet made a grand tour of the region, and the visit to Australia, in August 1908, of what came to be called the Great White Fleet, is one of the shining moments of our national memory. What began to be clear, in the huge outpouring of emotion for America and Americans, was that it was not only Britain whose kindred ties might be appealed to if we needed protection, or the British navy that might protect us, and this precisely at a moment when Britain had begun to worry about the change in the pattern of Australian imports – away from Britain towards 'others'; chiefly, as a Board of Trade enquiry of that year made plain, the United States.

The trend increased. By the end of the next decade the American film industry had a virtual monopoly over film distribution in Australia, the big boys of the American automobile industry, Ford, General Motors and Chrysler, were displacing British cars from our streets, and American petroleum (Standard Oil) had made such inroads into the Australian market that in 1920 the Commonwealth Government, in collaboration with the Anglo-Persian Oil Company (later BP), formed the Commonwealth Oil Refinery to protect British interests. By the end of the twenties, British anger over America's refusal to write off Britain's debt for war materials in the 1914–18 War, American anger at Britain's refusal to let United States oil-companies into the Middle-Eastern territories it had occupied (Iraq and Persia) after the collapse of the Turkish Empire (Britain now controlled 50 per cent of the world's oil-resources) led American military leaders, in 1929 – extraordinary as this may now seem – to draw up contingency plans for a possible war with Great Britain.

It is within the context of these tensions, in some of which Australia was intensely involved, that we need to think of the triangular relationship in the difficult years that led up to December 1941 and the Pacific War.

In September 1939 Britain, and as a natural consequence Australia, went to war with Nazi Germany. In September 1940, with Britain fighting alone in Europe and hard-pressed in North Africa, and three Australian divisions involved there and in the Middle East, Japan signed a Tripartite Pact with Germany and Italy, occupied air and military bases in Vichy French Indo-China, and demanded further bases on the Malayan border in southern Thailand.

At that point, in a moment that looked back more than three decades to the apparition in our world of the Great White Fleet, the American navy made another ceremonial visit to Australian waters. What Australians saw in the occasion, though the Americans had offered no commitment, was a guarantee against what now presented itself as an alarming future. I remember being taken by my father to Newstead Park one morning in March 1941, just before my seventh birthday, to see two ships of the United States Pacific Fleet sail grandly into the Hamilton Reach of the Brisbane River, with hundreds of white-capped and white-uniformed sailors – the ones we knew already from the 'Shanghai Lil' sequence of *Footlight Parade* – lined up in dazzling rows along the decks.

Events moved rapidly after that. On 8 December the Japanese bombed Pearl Harbor. On the 10th the *Prince of Wales* and the *Repulse*, which constituted Britain's major naval force in the Pacific, were torpedoed and sunk off the coast of Malaya. On the 25th Hong Kong surrendered. On the 27th, with Japanese armies sweeping south, the Japanese navy poised to invade, and Australia virtually defenceless, Prime Minister Curtin made the announcement that had in many ways been coming for nearly half a century: 'Without inhibitions of any kind,' he told us, 'I make it quite clear that Australia looks to America, free of any pangs as to our traditional links or kinship with the United Kingdom.'

One might have assumed that this was it, the turning point. That from here on there could be no way back. That the place of Britain as the predominant power in our consciousness, the predominant influence on our lives, was done with forever. But that is not the way things went.

For all that it had been the Yanks who saved us, Australian loyalty to Britain, and Australian affection for the little island that had gone it alone and triumphed, for the people who had fought the Battle of Britain, endured the Blitz, and come through, was stronger than ever in the years immediately after the war and in the Menzies years that followed.

The big P & O and Orient liners once again carried Australian tourists to London on the old 'colonial' route via Singapore, Colombo, Bombay, Aden, Suez, and on the return journey brought us British migrants on assisted passages – they paid ten pounds for the one-way trip. Postgraduates still went off to Oxford and Cambridge, or to London University, rather than to Harvard or Johns Hopkins or Stanford, and we could still read American authors – including thinkers who, from their new base in America, were creating sciences and disciplines that would reshape the age – only if they came to us through English publishers. Outside the obvious area of popular entertainment, it is astonishing how little influence America had on us in its great high period in the two decades after the war. A prejudice still prevailed among our 'best minds' – poets, academics, editors, intellectuals of every kind – in favour of all things European or English over the cheapness and commercialism of what came from 'across the Atlantic': American movies, American jazz and pop music and musicals, American plays and novels, the barbarisms of the New York school of painting, all splash and dribble.

But 1941 *had* been a turning point, and Vance Palmer recognised and found words for it in a piece he published in the March 1942 issue of *Meanjin Papers,* as it was then called, just three months after Curtin's December address:

The next few months may decide not only whether we are to survive, but whether we deserve to survive. As yet none of our achievements prove it, at any rate in the sight of the outer world. We have no monuments to speak of, no dreams in stone, no Guernica, no sacred places. We could vanish and leave singularly few signs that, for some generations, there had lived a people who had made a homeland of this Australian earth. A homeland? To how many people was it primarily that? How many penetrated the soil with their love and imagination? . . . If Australia had no more charter than could be seen on its surface, it would be annihilated as surely and swiftly as those colonial outposts white men built for their commercial profit in the East – pretentious facades of stucco that looked imposing as long as the wind kept from blowing. But there is an Australia of the spirit, submerged and not very articulate, that is quite different from these baubles of old-world imperialism . . .

What had changed under the threat of imminent invasion was the willingness in the early part of that paragraph to take a hard look at what Australia actually was, free of the usual swagger and whistling in the dark, and to accept the challenge to get below the surface. To penetrate the soil of Australia, as Palmer puts it, 'with love and imagination'; to give that submerged and inarticulate spirit voice.

The threat of invasion, and the arrival of the Americans to save us, did not break our tie with Britain, or make it inevitable that we would one day become a minor constellation among the Stars and Stripes. What it did was bring Australia – the land itself – fully alive at last in our consciousness. As a part of the earth of which we were now the custodians. As soil to be defended and preserved because we were deeply connected to it. As the one place where we were properly at home, the one place to which we were related in an interior way by daily experience and, as Vance Palmer put it, through love and imagination, and which related us, in a way we were just beginning to grasp, to those for whom the land of Australia had always been this: the people we thought we had dispossessed but who had always 'owned' the place in a way we were just beginning to appreciate. The possibility of our own dispossession had woken in us a preliminary understanding both of what we had and might lose, and what those people might feel who had already, in one sense, lost it. But also that there is another sense in which, in love and imagination, it never can be lost.

If there is a break here, it has nothing to do with our having 'seen through' the British at last or with our replacing one dependency with another, but with a new way of seeing Australia itself, and ourselves and one another. Not through the eyes, now, of newcomers, unsettled settlers, but through eyes that had experienced the business of seeing only *here*, in the light as it falls in this place only; through what life had revealed to us, and would continue to reveal to us, only here. The freedom this offered was that we could now, without losing ourselves, make whatever relationships we pleased with the rest of the world; they would always be conditional: on events, on opportunistic political or economic factors, on passing modes of thought, on who was in or out of power. The one relationship that was unconditional, that mattered and would define us, was with Australia itself.

Made in England

We sometimes speak as if the question of what we refer to as 'identity', and the need to negotiate where we stand in the world – with neighbours in our immediate vicinity but also with those elsewhere who share our language and history – was somehow unique, a condition of our colonial past and the fact that we are a settler nation with a population, largely, of long-standing and recent migrants. As if there were countries elsewhere whose identity existed on an *un*conditional basis, and whose place in the world was fixed. Which countries, one wonders. Italy? Poland? Turkey? Great Britain?

One of the first facts we learn about English history is that Britain was invaded and settled in the fifth century by the Angles, Saxons and Jutes, and in the eleventh by the Norman French. Britain too is a settler state, though of long duration; a composite nation with a population, largely, of long-standing and recent migrants. And the fact of that original invasion and settlement, which the English keep strongly alive as part of the narrative, is not only a fact of history but a condition of identity (it is worth noting that the Romans too presented themselves in this way, not as natives of Latium but as invaders and settlers, immigrants from Troy). Such a notion of identity is unusual, and unusually liberating. Independent of the tie between blood and soil, between race and *Heimat*, it is not limited by it either. Identity is portable. It can be transported, and with no risk to its particular virtues and strengths, reconstructed on another shore. It is ideally suited, that is, to the creating of empire.

John of Gaunt may speak of 'this England', and

Rupert Brooke, as late as 1914, write of a foreign field that will be 'forever England'. People who work on the land – and some too who do not – may feel a tie of closeness to particular tracts of land and to the land itself. Poets may write passionately about particular landscapes. But the identity argument in Britain is not made in terms of blood and soil. It is made in terms of the social and emotional ties between individuals based on shared experience; shared occasions, ceremonies, symbols, and the emotions they give rise to: Agincourt, Shakespeare, John Hampden and John Milton as the upholders of English liberty; Nelson and Trafalgar, 'Rule Britannia', 'Land of Hope and Glory', Dunkirk. The advantage of this form of identity, and especially for an immigrant society, is that in being experiential rather than essentialist it is also, as the old Roman version was, transferable. It can be acquired.

Loose and provisional as it may be, the British have from the beginning found this a very practical way of binding a divided and sometimes divisive population, for as long at least as a sense of national unity is *required*; it being part of this kind of thinking that the need for such unity is mostly short-lived and intermittent.

We too have found it useful, and our view too is that the need for it should be no more than occasional and intermittent. Centred around a few symbolic events and objects that evoke shared feelings or affinities – the Eureka Stockade, Gallipoli, the Burma Railway, the Kokoda Track, 'Waltzing Matilda' – it is recognised in flashes, when the playing of the Last Post or the passing of the Olympic Torch (such moments may be unplanned and ephemeral) allows us a sudden revelatory glimpse of ourselves – all of us who are present – so that we look around and say, 'Ah, so that's who we are!'

If anything in all this is *unique* it is the relative peace in which we have been left to deal with such questions; the good fortune of having undisputable borders, a stable political system, and for most of our history a protector that just happened to be the major power of the day.

We have tended to take these advantages for granted, for the simple reason that they were there, but I suspect our politicians did not. They knew only too well what they had got hold of. Men like Deakin or Sir George Reid or Billy Hughes may have used the language of imperial sentiment when they saw a use for it, and the public may have swallowed it, but sentiment is not what really moved them. They had a very canny appreciation of what was to be got out of being a member of such a powerful confederacy as the Empire, and went very cleverly about securing us a special place in it. However much they and others might have complained at times about trade restrictions, bank debts, our lack of a free hand in the Pacific, and, more keenly, about being condescended to or ignored, they were very reluctant to lose those advantages by breaking away. It might be a good question, in the long view, which of the two, Britain or Australia, was the more exploited in our long relationship.

And some of those advantages we are still exploiting, though from a more independent position these days, and as it suits us; in our continuing close relationship with Britain and the US, in trading ties with North Asia, in the responsibilities we assume, now that we do have a free hand, as a rich and stable nation though a small one, and a good neighbour, in East Timor, in Papua New Guinea, in the Solomons. The relationship with Britain is just one of several now through which our presence is established and our interests served.

All that belongs to politics. But there are other ways in which we fit into the world that are closer to the interests of ordinary men and women, and give us a different but no less significant place in the order of things. Sport, for instance.

Sport as we now understand it was an Anglo-Saxon invention of the late eighteenth and early nineteenth century. The English made it central, both as a physical activity and as moral training, to their whole system of education. Wellington's famous dictum, that the battle of Waterloo was won on the playing fields of Eton, must have been as incomprehensible to his

Prussian and Russian allies as it was to the French, but has endured as a kind of shorthand for a culture in which the playing field, like the Greek palestra, is seen as a training ground for life; for the development of Athenian minds in Spartan bodies, and for an ethos in which terms like 'fair play', 'sportsmanship', 'team spirit' are meant to be translated out of the narrow world of schoolboy rivalry and endeavour into the world of action and affairs; not as metaphors but as practical forms of behaviour. The supply of dedicated civil servants and subalterns who ran the Empire, especially India, depended on this ethos and on the education system that sustained it. Nowhere but in the Anglo-Saxon world, and in places like India, Pakistan, and parts of Asia, Africa and the Pacific where English forms of education have been 'naturalised' – along with school uniforms, the prefect system, sports halfs, houses – has organised sport become an integral part of the school curriculum, the central place where that discipline of the spirit as well as the body is developed that is at the very centre of the culture.

Can we imagine how much thinner our involvement with the rest of the world might be if this peculiar Anglo-Saxon passion had not worked on us, and on the Pakistanis and Indians, and the West Indians, New Zealanders, South Africans and others, who come together to play one-day and Test cricket and Rugby Union and League football? It has made alliances for us with peoples with whom we have a special relationship in which we are trusted to 'play fair', and to speak fair too, that has been extended, at times, into other areas where we are also trusted – as in our stand on Apartheid in the seventies and eighties, in Fiji during the crisis of the nineties.

It was the teams we sent to England in the 1880s that first established us, in British eyes, as a single nation, long before we had made the move to official nationhood, and it was through rivalry on the field, in which we often turned out to be superior, that a kind of equality grew up between us. The symbol of the Ashes, playful as it was, gave Australia a place in British popular mythology that none of the other colonies enjoyed, and in an area that mattered, had weight, in a way that, outside the magic circle of Anglo-Saxon thinking, would have been inconceivable.

It is small things that make up the real fabric of a relationship; things that 'history' may not know about or miss. But then sport is just the sort of area where to make too much of a thing would be to miss the real thing altogether.

The accident of empire has delivered us a network of relationships right across the globe, pairing us with Trinidad and St Kitts, but not with Guadaloupe or Martinique, with Guiana but not its neighbour Surinam, with Sierra Leone and Tanzania but not with Guinea-Bissau or Eritrea. On occasions when we come briefly together, as at the annual judging of the Commonwealth Literary Prize for Fiction, an Australian or Canadian may be astonished to discover a fellow writer from some small African or Caribbean state he has barely heard of whose experience almost exactly mirrors his own, down to the sort of poems and stories that made up his childhood reading and all those myths and popular allusions one takes for granted as universal, but which turn out to be specific to the Anglophone world.

There was a time when we came to such gatherings like poor relations to a table where the British played host, bringing with us, each one, a wariness of the rest that came from the reluctance of one poor relation to see his lowly status reflected in another's. Australians and Canadians, Australians and Scots, tended to ignore one another.

Those days are gone. Britain no longer sits at the head of the table. The rest of us no longer use the British, or need them, in our dealings with one another. As often as not it is the British representatives at such gatherings now who feel marginalised and out of place.

The fact is, there is no longer a 'centre' around which we circulate and dance. We have all shifted place. In terms of where Australia and Britain now stand in relation to one another, the world has turned upside down.

In the nineteenth century Australia was an under-world place, literally at the bottom of the world; exactly opposite where Britain stood. It was as far off as you could go, people told one another, before you started coming back again. A place where it was glaring sunlight while you slept, and when you were awake was wrapped in a darkness swarming with unlikely blacks and even more unlikely animals; a place at the antipodes – not just of the globe but of consciousness; of everything that belonged to normality and light.

And now?

Almost the reverse has become the case. Australia, just twenty-two hours from London, is the place of perpetual light – of perpetual *lightness* – where it is always sunshiny and warm; a place that is different but familiar; where people make good, and which has itself made good; and where, if you are lucky, your own freer self might suddenly break loose. We have slipped out of the shadows and out of Britain's own shadow. What they see in us is a lighter version of *themselves*, which had always been there, at least in potential, on the other side of consciousness, and has now at last revealed itself, and for just a few hundred pounds can be *had*.

This is a romantic view, of course, and we can't live up to it, as in the old days our view of England, London, 'home', was also romantic and almost always let us down; as those volunteer Diggers of

328

1914 discovered, the 'six bob a day' tourists who set off expecting to see Piccadilly at last, and Leicester Square, and instead saw Passchendaele, and the many artists and writers and others who were drawn to one of the great flesh-pots and glories of the planet. We smile at such things today.

Our being British took us into the world the first time round by providing us with a network of English-speaking relations, some closer than others, all over the globe. Later, when Britain joined the Common Market in the early seventies, it took us out into the world in a different way, forcing us to find new markets for our wheat and wool, our meat, hides, minerals, in China, Korea, Russia, the Middle East; forcing us – and this was the real challenge – to reconsider our attitudes to these new trading partners as people; to take account, as we might put it now, of their 'sensitivities', both cultural and political, but also to reconsider our migration policies with regard to them, to see them not only as neighbours but as fellow citizens.

A whole complex of changes in the sixties determined our move away from the White Australia policy. Some of them were local – like the Yes vote in the '67 referendum that was the culmination of twenty years of slow change in our thinking about the place of Aboriginal people in our society but also in our history. Others were part of a general move, in nations like our own, to a rethinking of racial attitudes under the influence of the United Nations Declaration of Human Rights. Others again were determined by our need to be more open-minded in our dealings with the world, with thinking again about the kind of country we wanted to be and the way we wanted others, now, to see us. Britain's selling us down the river (as some saw it) in the early seventies may turn out, in the long view, to be more significant than that other and more obvious 'betrayal', Singapore, in that it pushed us out at last into a complex and demanding world where we were forced to discover in ourselves the qualities we would need to meet it: qualities of alertness, competence, improvisation, openness that would make us a more complex and inventive people. The captive market in Britain that we had for so long relied on had kept *us* captive – to a lazy belief that all we had to do was go on producing the same old goods at the same price. Being tumbled out of the nest was the making of us. It set us free at last to be something more than we had been and more than we might otherwise have imagined.

*

At the stroke of midnight on 15 August 1947, India ceased to be a British colony. After more than 300 years of occupation and rule by a foreign power it reverted to a culture and civilisation that had already been in existence for nearly three millennia when the British arrived and, in all its variety and richness, had gone on interruptedly while they were there. Very sensibly, they retained the laws and institutions the British had brought that would allow them to become a unified modern nation rather than a collection of rival princedoms.

For us the end of colonialism can never be 'declared' as it was for the Indians at a single stroke, because we were never a colony as India was. Made in England and exported like so much else, we were a bit of the motherland set down in a new place and left to develop as the new conditions demanded, as climate, a different mixture of people, changes in the world around us, and our reaction to them, determined: an overseas province of Great Britain, but allowed, in an experimental fashion, to govern itself and go its own way and to its own ends. We have, most of us, no previous history in the place that we can, like the Indians, 'revert to', and those who do cannot give us one. Our culture is the one we brought with us and adapted, in an experimental and improvisatory way, according to what we found here and to immediate need. We laid it down over the existing native culture, which slowly, over the years, has seeped through and begun to colour what we are, and to modify any conviction we might have had, as Westerners, that our way of seeing the world, and our way of dealing with it, is the one *right* way; but it is not a culture we can revert to because it was never ours. Unlike the Indians, it is not only Britain we have to deal with, it is our own Britishness – a very different thing, and much more difficult to track down and confront.

We may treat Britain itself in any way we please. We may remove the Union Jack from our flag if it seems useful to do so, and the Queen from our political life. What we cannot remove is the language we speak, and all that is inherent in it: a way of laying out experience, of seeing, that comes with the syntax; the body of half-forgotten customs, and events, fables, insights, jokes, that are at the root of its idioms; a literature that belongs, since there is nothing that ties it mystically to one patch of soil, as much to the English-speaking reader in Perth, WA as in Perth, Scotland.

We may modify and 'naturalise' the institutions we brought here, the Westminster system, the Common Law, so that they make a better fit with what we now are, but they have provided so much of the context of what we have created here, and value and would want to preserve, that to abandon them, or allow them to be diluted or to decay, would be an act of national suicide. And there, for the moment, we stand.

This venture we call 'Australia' was always an experiment. It has taken us a long time to see it in this light, and even longer to accept the lightness, the freedom, the possibility that offers as a way of being. It keeps us on our toes, as curious observers of ourself. It has made us value quick reflexes and improvisation – lightness in that sense too. It ought to make us sceptical of conclusions, of any belief that where we are now is more than a moment along the way.

An experiment is open, all conclusions provisional. Even the conclusiveness of a full stop is no more – so long as there is breath – than a conventional gesture towards pause in an open and continuing argument.

First published as 'Made in England', Quarterly Essay, *by Black Inc.*

THE STATES OF THE NATION

BACK IN 2001 WHEN THE centenary of Federation was looming, I was inclined to joke that we had to make a song and dance about it because the thing itself had never really happened.

It had of course; in history and in the history books, and we had a constitution to prove it, but not in the many places where Australians actually live; in Cunnamulla or Queenstown or Port Hedland, and in those even more numerous places, the hearts of those of us who, without hesitation or doubt, call ourselves Australians, and have a vivid sense of what the country itself is, but in our daily lives, and in the place where our feelings are most touched, have little interest in the idea of nation.

The day of the centenary came and went like any other. Flags were raised, medals struck and distributed, speeches made, but there was little excitement. The country returned next day to life as usual. Boat people arrived and asked to be taken in, life support systems were turned on or off, a new generation of five-year-olds posed and were photographed, smiling or not, in their school uniforms.

Federation may have established the nation and bonded the people of the various states into one, but nations and peoples, unless they arise naturally the one out of the other, rather than by referendum or edict, are likely to be doubtful entities, and the relationship between them will be open to almost continuous question. Of course when they arise *too* naturally – that is when they claim to belong to nature rather than to human choice – they are dangerous.

Our Federation is on the whole an easy one. We take it lightly as suits our cast of mind, which is pragmatic (anti-theoretical), wryly off-hand, and sceptical of big ideas and their accompanying rhetoric. The union works and we can be proud of the society it has created, but we don't care to talk about it, and unless the country is under threat as it was in 1941, or involved in conflict overseas, we take it as given – and even then, as with Vietnam, the Gulf War, Iraq and Afghanistan, there are some who will remain doubtful, or embarrassed, or openly hostile. We are easiest with 'Australia' when what we are referring to is a national team.

To quote the authors of *The Oxford Companion to Australian History* (2001 edition), the states remain 'set in their ways and as suspicious of one another as they were before the union was declared' – though we should be as wary of making too much of the suspicion as of the union.

These days the suspicions between the states are as low-key – except when it comes to water management – and as intermittent, as our sense of nationhood. A lot of the rivalries are joking ones, and when they are formalised in such institutions as the State of Origin matches between Queensland and NSW, might just as easily be read as bonding. Most people, like men and women everywhere, are concerned with local questions and local affairs. Their lives take place within a few square kilometres and are determined by local conditions: local needs and customs and habits, local opportunities for schooling and shopping and entertainment, local forms of speech. They turn to community rather than nation when they ask themselves where they belong, and think of those they share their days with as neighbours rather than fellow Australians. 'Fellow Australians' carries with it an air of fake familiarity that belongs to the political platform, the political speech. Fellow Queenslanders, on the other hand, or fellow Tasmanians, is another matter.

*

Federation, as we might expect, came to us in a very Australian way, one that is consistent with the rather off-hand manner in which it has been received and is still considered. Not the flowering of a great utopian ideal, or the coming together, after a long period of yearning, of a people that had known the anguish of division, or the achievement, through national unity, of a 'manifest destiny' – though there were some, especially in the latter case, who felt that way.

After thirty-five years of intermittent lobbying and resistance, and a lot of bickering over such non-idealistic questions as Preference versus Free Trade, the opposition lapsed and the federationists took advantage of a moment of unexpected agreement to pop the question. The popular election that voted for union was not based on universal suffrage, was not uniform throughout the states, and the turnout itself was low: 30 per cent of eligible voters in 1898, 43 per cent in 1899. The areas of control granted to the new federal government were limited – chiefly defence and trade; the rest remained reassuringly with the states. Of course the central government was expected to evolve over time and has done so. In the 100 years since 1901, the Commonwealth government has replaced or duplicated state powers to the point that it can be argued that in our present three-tiered system, state governments are not only redundant and wasteful but also obstructive, and should go. The federal government alone would be left to govern, with below it a system of regional bodies. The states, with no effective powers, and no visible reason to exist, would wither away.

Given our preference for practical solutions, and the tendency these days for all problems to be presented and resolved in terms of economy and good management, it is inevitable, I suppose, that this question too will be reduced to what is the best value for money and the most efficient way of bringing uniform practice to what is now a set of multiple authorities: roads, railways, social welfare and health systems, and seven different police forces and courts of law. As if the real goal of Federation had all along been uniformity, and the only criterion needed for justifying it was efficiency and cost.

But if uniformity from ocean to ocean is what we are to have, then that represents a radical change from what the fathers of Federation intended and what the people of the various states, with their strong histories and their 'set ways', believed they were getting. And what about us? Is this really our preferred choice?

If the argument is couched solely in economic and management terms, then clearly there is no argument at all. But perhaps we need other terms altogether, that have to do not with efficiency and cost but with the sometimes untidy and diverse and contradictory needs of those who are to be managed.

So what does it mean to be a nation, and how is that large concept related to place and land, or as we experience it personally – on the ground as it were – as *locality*, a particular tract of land: a town or a few streets in a town; a church hall, a local pub, schools, a football ground, a shopping precinct? And how is nation related to that other large and emotionally charged concept, a people?

*

In most places, the transition from people to nation is clear, or is at least presented as clear. A single people, inhabiting a particular homeland, is at last politically united and becomes a nation.

It is never quite clear of course: the borders of the land may be open to dispute, and no people is entirely pure. But this is how it happened over three or four centuries among the ancient Greeks, when a scatter of independent city-states became an empire, and among the Romans, the French, the Russians, and in the mid-nineteenth century the Germans and Italians. Australia, like other settler nations, did it in reverse. Having declared that we were a nation, we had still to attract the people to fill it and decide who those people might be.

What defined our nation was not people but geography. The various states – all settled at different times by different groups and classes, and, within the British political system, under different conditions and with different aims – happened to occupy a continent whose borders were fixed because it was an island. Once the British, eastern half of the continent and the Dutch west were declared a single possession under an undisputed (British) claim, political unity became first a possibility and then an imperative, though a mild one. For all the talk in some quarters in the late nineteenth century of a New Britannia that would carry forward the torch of British civilisation when the old country had fallen into decay, there was little of the fervour here, or the passion for political theory, that characterised the great constitutional conventions of the 1760s in America. We produced no political thinkers of the quality of Madison or Jefferson or Alexander Hamilton or Benjamin Franklin. Our local fathers of Federation, practical men of the late nineteenth century, level-headed traders and politicians and lobbyists, good Christian gentlemen but of a secular bent, *did* want to create a free and fair society, but unlike their counterparts in a more radical and utopian age had no feeling for rhetoric of the French or American variety. A 'fair go' is a very down-to-earth version of Liberty, Equality, Fraternity, and no-one here expected, or wanted, the tree of Liberty (or the wattle) to be watered even occasionally with blood.

This down-to-earthness extends to the land itself.

In other places, and to other peoples, the land has presented itself as sacred or holy. This, as we know from Russian novels, is the way Russians have seen it, how indigenous people, including our own indigenous people, see it and how the Nazis saw it when they articulated the philosophy of *Blut und Boden*: as a deep ancestral tie between a people and the soil they inhabit.

A settler population can hardly make such a claim. The Roman and British imperial cultures, with their founding myths of an arrival from 'elsewhere', offered a different model: one in which nation was transportable and national identity or citizenship transferable. If Australians see in the land something they might feel as transcendent or mystical, it is land in its form as space rather than soil, an almost infinite openness; and that is a very useful notion if you are a settler. It suggests that there is always room. That just as the land made room for you, so, with no threat or pressure, it will find room for others.

*

The idea of nationhood was embodied, in 1901, in a constitution, but the question of who the nation's people were to be remained open. White and British in the first draft, no more Chinese, the Queensland

Kanakas to be sent back to the islands. No black Africans of any kind. No Muslims. A language test (European) to be applied against the rest. Then increasingly after the wave of European – including southern European – migrants after World War II, it was to be a mix; then, after the lapse of the White Australia policy in the late sixties, a *multi-ethnic* mix, then a mix that would be both multi-ethnic and multicultural – an interesting experiment, but not so easy to make work. Just as well that the idea of nation was a light one, and that lightness in the approach to difficult questions, an anti-theoretical stance, easy-going and humorous, should be the temperament of the people who had to live with it.

I called the imperative to nationhood geographic, as if the continent itself, once it found a single name ('Australia' in 1804), made the emergence of a single nation the obvious next step. But this is about as far as our notion of the 'gift outright', as Robert Frost called it in the case of the United States, would ever get. Very few of us here have ever fallen for the notion of 'manifest destiny', it's not our style.

The odd thing in our case – but odd things are apt to be the most revealing – is that our earliest appearance as a single people was on the sporting field, as a team rather than a nation.

'Australia' first presented itself to the world (that is, to the British) in the form of the combined cricket teams that toured Britain in the 1880s (the earlier Aboriginal team was too exotic to be representative) and created the myth of the Ashes. What they brought news of was a new tribe, a new 'type', a new society. The qualities they represented were ones the British could recognise and respect because they were looser versions of their own, the product of a later and different history in a new place, and it helped that sport, and especially cricket, was already seen as the proper sphere for the creation of a moral and social elite – the challenge in this case being that these 'colonials' were *not* an elite. The other sphere of course was war.

Following on what the cricket teams had created in the national consciousness – the image of Australians as a single tribe and a new and original 'type' – it might be best to ignore the usual evocation of our national coming of age, in 1915–16, as a baptism of sacrificial fire, and consider the Diggers at Gallipoli and in France as a team rather than an army.

Once again, what was being demonstrated, this time on the larger stage of history, was a national character and style: courage certainly, endurance – the extended campaign at Gallipoli, the fifty-three continuous days in the front-line trenches at Villers-Bretonneux – but also a licensed indiscipline that was not quite anarchy, the 'civilian' triumph, among the professional army generals, of John Monash, and at home the refusal, in two referenda, of conscription.

The observers of all this may have been the world at large, but when we speak of it as the moment when nationhood itself was confirmed, what we are really registering is the reflection back from outsiders to the players themselves, and even more importantly to their people back home, of what, against all the usual class and colonial prejudices, Australians were now seen to have achieved.

That is the original Anzac story, but it is only half the story. The other half has to do with something else altogether: the understanding that war is *not* sport. That it involves injury, trauma, death, and to wives and parents and children and fiancées, in hamlets and towns and working places all up and down the country, a sense of irreparable loss that was made actual, in the years after the war, in thousands of war memorials, small and large, from one side to the other of the continent.

These are mourning places that mark a national tragedy: a recognition of loss and grief as being central both to the community, the nation – 62,000 men, mostly young men, lost from a population of fewer than four million – and to individual families and lives. That, a binding of the people at every level in a shared grief, is what 'coming of age' might be about, and explains the power of Anzac Day, and how it has come to be chosen, by the people themselves, as our day of national unity.

When young people these days are drawn to Anzac, it is partly, I think, because they are moved by the drama of youthful death, and partly because, in a nation that makes so little of public ceremony, this day offers a larger, and more solemn view of what life may be, than is general in a culture whose norm is chatter, noise, almost continuous sensation.

What Anzac Day offers is quietness, contemplation. It appeals, in the young, to what is serious in them. Asks them to attend. Invites them to take part in an occasion that speaks, at both a personal and communal level, for continuity. And this may be what attracts another group that might otherwise see this day as an occasion from which they are culturally excluded: recent migrants. What Anzac Day offers them is the possibility, which may be rare, of seeing what it is that these people they have attached themselves to are moved by. As an occasion whose commemoration of loss is something they too feel for, it becomes, for recent migrants, a way of entering emotionally into the life of the community at large. As Auden puts it in the very last of his poems: 'only in rites / can we renounce our oddities / and be truly entired.'

These are delicate matters. At an individual level, difficult questions of identity or belonging, of what it is that might bind us as fellow citizens, may be resolved more simply than we believe.

Where argument, however open and enlightened,

may get nowhere, or lead only to further complications that cannot be resolved, a moment of 'drama', of empathy and understanding, will simply annul the question at a stroke. And one might add here – and by no means as a mere footnote – that a wounding sense of loss, and a perception, deeply felt, of the place of the tragic in our lives, does not strike a community only in one place or on one occasion. Perhaps if we were to institute a Sorry Day to mark the sufferings inflicted on indigenous people in the establishing of a nation whose existence we take lightly, but which has been a heavy fact in indigenous lives, some shared understanding of that grief too might be possible, a second occasion, shaped over time as Anzac Day has been, in which we would discover yet another point of national unity.

It is the fragility of such moments of cohesion, of shared emotion and presence, that alert us to equally fragile but no less significant moments of difference. It is not only unity that characterises a nation or a people.

For most of the time what distinguishes a nation, like any other community, is the variety provided by difference; variety of need and interest, of response to such local factors as climate and land and water use; forms of domestic architecture and language, local custom and lore – even local forms of suspicion and potential conflict; all those conditions, that is, that will have grown up over time among people who live in a particular place and have created their own version of the nation's history.

Nations, as I suggested earlier, grow out of the desire of a single people to be one. It is an historical imperative driven by ties of language and culture but also of shared experience. Federation on the other hand is a political union made on practical grounds, though the hope is that state loyalties and affiliations will in time be supplemented at least by national ones, and may even grow to replace them.

In a Federation where separate tribes and people come together, as in most African states, and as has happened in ex-Yugoslavia, ex-Czechoslovakia and Belgium, the two loyalties will often pull against one another and the tension between them may not be capable of resolution.

Our case is unusual, because for all the difference in class and style of their founders, the different environmental conditions they faced and the economies they created in response, the Australian colonies had for the most part the same demographic make-up, spoke the same language, inherited the same culture and legal and political system, and were accountable, in the matter of aspiration and restraints, to the same authority, the British Colonial Office. There is little danger here of the Federation's collapsing. We have none of the deep-seated cultural and religious divisions that broke the old Yugoslavia and, in a less violent way, threaten Belgium. Our threat is the more insidious one of a tidy uniformity.

Is it only, I wonder, because I grew up in what I hear referred to as one of the 'outlying states' – outlying from where, I ask – that I am so keenly aware of the different styles of our state capitals? The subtle or not-so-subtle difference in the way people deal with one another in Brisbane and Melbourne for example, or Brisbane and Adelaide, and what this represents of different ways of thinking and feeling. The variation from place to place of building materials and domestic habits that have created the houses people live in, the way they move about and dress. The turn of mind that has created our various education systems. The demographic mix that has shaped not only the forms of speech we use but our different ways, from state to state, of addressing one another and establishing intimacy and ease or the opposite. It isn't sentiment alone that might make us want to preserve these distinctions, but a belief that variousness is also richness, and that different ways of solving a problem or meeting a difficulty may make possible a new, or more original or creative way that would otherwise fail to emerge.

We need to be discriminating here. It is entirely proper that control of all cross-border issues – inter-state highways, railway links between the capitals, water management of our river systems, workplace conditions, banking – should be in the hands of a single authority, and that decisions in these areas should be made on a national basis and in the national interest, overruling if necessary the interests of individual states. But I wonder if those parts of our lives that involve individual needs and are shaped very largely by local conditions – distance from a major town or city, availability of transport, weather (seasonal floods for instance) – or by local ways of doing things and word-of-mouth contacts that are socially or culturally based, are really best managed from a centre that may be thousands of kilometres off, and by decision-makers who, however well-intentioned, may have little grasp of how differently people see things in inner Melbourne, or Kalgoorlie, or Far North Queensland.

Cost and efficiency cannot be the only consideration here, or even fairness. These are bureaucratic criteria that speak only for one side of the contract. The other, the human side, is about how close people feel to those who are dealing with them; how comfortable they feel with the style and language of the transaction. People act in ways that suit their needs, and follow the unpredictable and sometimes irrational lines of their own nature and habits. They live in places within themselves that know nothing of jurisdictions or borders. This is not necessarily a perversity. It is a fact, and a society of the kind we mostly support, and would hope to achieve, should remain open and flexible enough to make provision for this, so long as it is not obstructive to others. The last thing we want, however gratifying a vision it might be to a federal minister for education, is an entire generation of six-year-olds singing sweetly from the same page.

First published in The Monthly,
June 2010

David Malouf is the internationally acclaimed author of novels and stories including *The Great World*, *Remembering Babylon*, *An Imaginary Life*, *Conversations at Curlow Creek*, *Harland's Half Acre*, *Dream Stuff*, *Every Move You Make*, *Collected Stories*, *Ransom* and the autobiographical classic *12 Edmondstone Street*. His most recent books are *A First Place*, *The Writing Life* and *Being There*. He was born in Brisbane in 1934 and lives in Sydney.